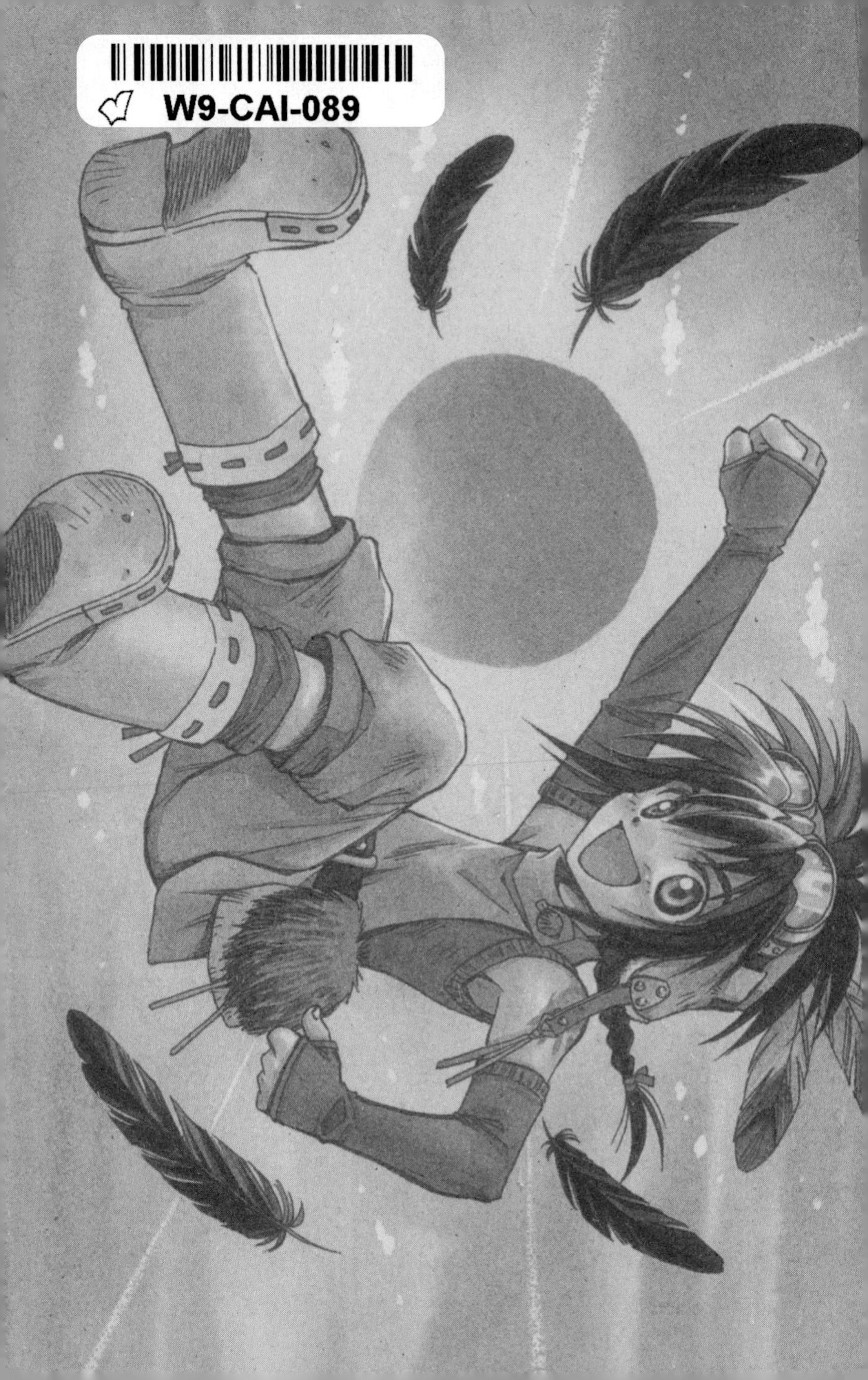

+Anima Vol. 2
Created by Natsumi Mukai

Translation - Alethea Nibley
English Adaptation - Karen S. Ahlstrom
Copy Editor - Peter Ahlstrom
Retouch and Lettering - Camellia Cox
Production Artist - Jennifer Carbajal and Jose Macasocol, Jr.
Cover Design - James Lee

Editor - Troy Lewter
Digital Imaging Manager - Chris Buford
Managing Editor - Vy Nguyen
Production Manager - Elisabeth Brizzi
Editor-in-Chief - Rob Tokar
VP of Production - Ron Klamert
Publisher - Mike Kiley
President and C.O.O. - John Parker
C.E.O. and Chief Creative Officer - Stuart Levy

A ⊙ TOKYOPOP Manga

TOKYOPOP Inc.
5900 Wilshire Blvd. Suite 2000
Los Angeles, CA 90036

E-mail: info@TOKYOPOP.com
Come visit us online at www.TOKYOPOP.com

ISBN: 1-59816-348-5

First TOKYOPOP printing: September 2006
10 9 8 7 6 5 4 3 2
Printed in the USA

Volume 2
by Natsumi Mukai

HAMBURG // LONDON // LOS ANGELES // TOKYO

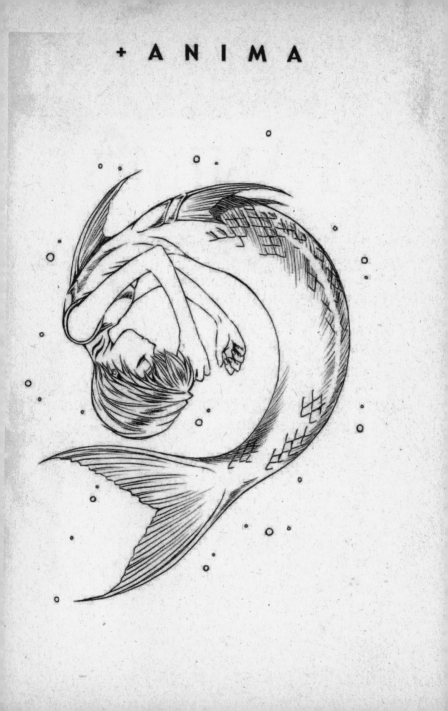

+ANIMA

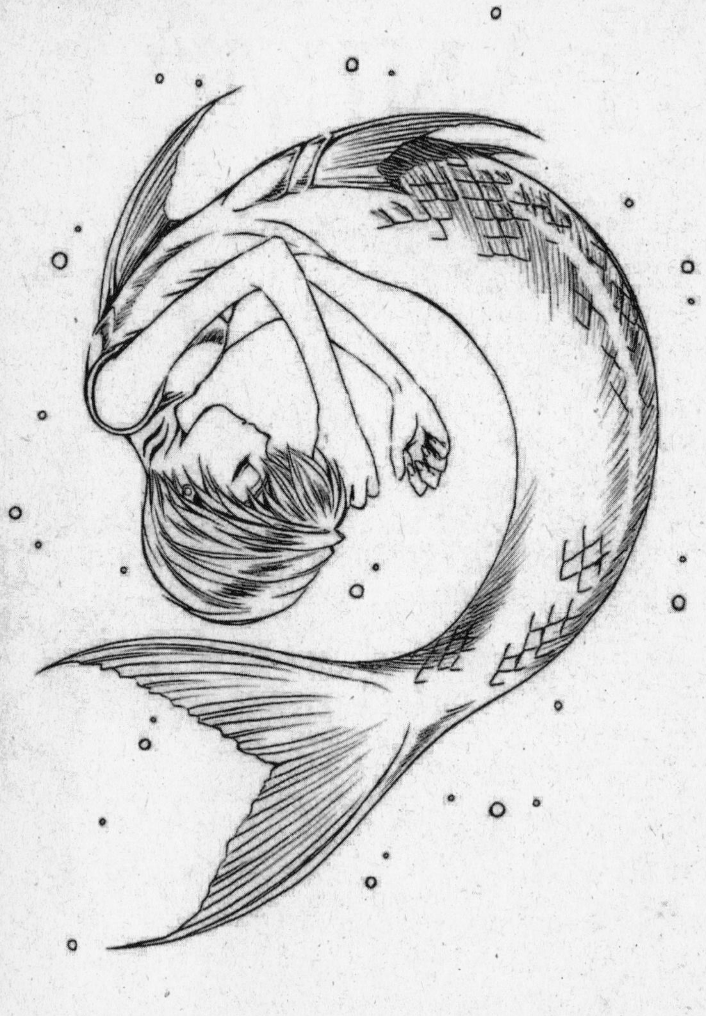

+ANIMA

プラスアニマ

迎夏生
NATSUMI MUKAI

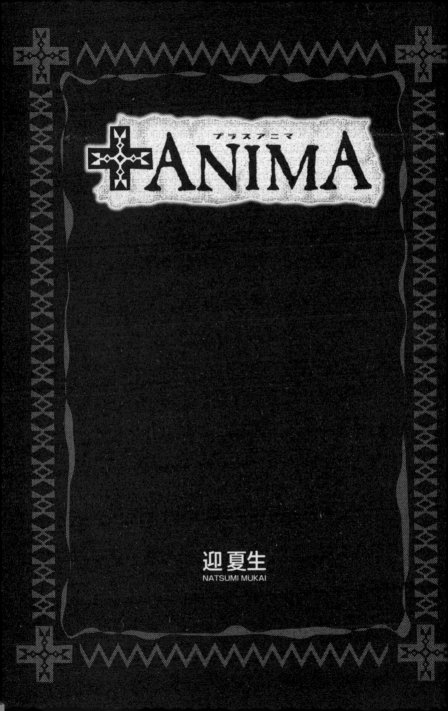

STORY & CHARACTERS

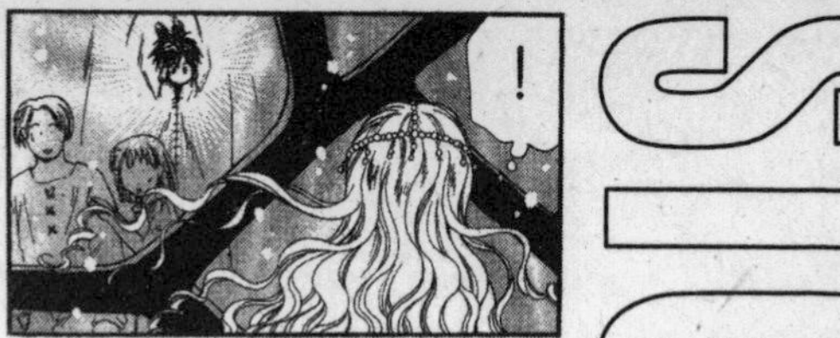
!

At the village of Abon, Cooro and Husky meet Senri, the bear +Anima, who is protecting the village from the Garrison Gang's scheme to dig a gold mine there. After Cooro and the others save the town and their famous plants, Senri joins them as they continue their travels...

In this world, there are those known as +Anima: humans who have within them the powers of animals. When Cooro (a crow +Anima) stops at a circus during his travels, he meets Husky, a fish +Anima who is performing there. Cooro and Husky escape from the circus and end up traveling together.

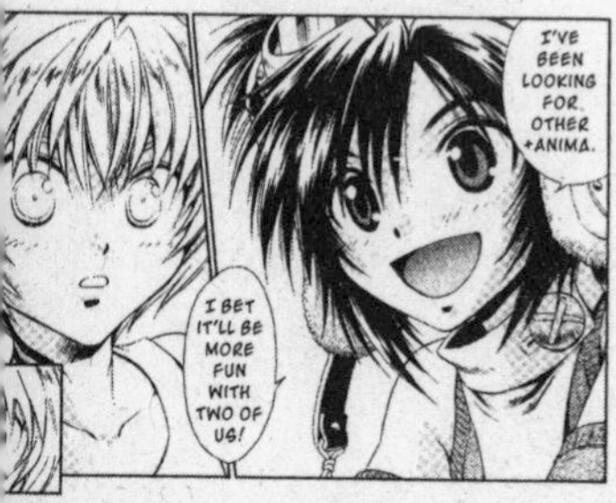
I'VE BEEN LOOKING FOR OTHER +ANIMA.
I BET IT'LL BE MORE FUN WITH TWO OF US!

クーロ [Cooro]

Crow +Anima. He spreads his pitch-black wings and soars to the sky...He's always on the lookout for something to eat.

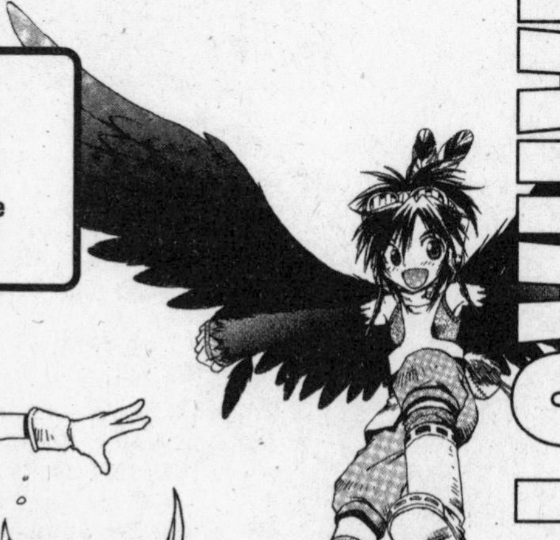

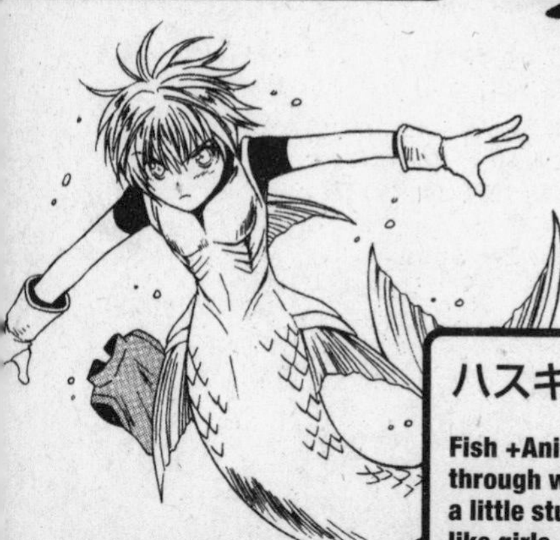

ハスキー [Husky]

Fish +Anima. He can swim freely through water like a merman. He's a little stubborn, and doesn't like girls.

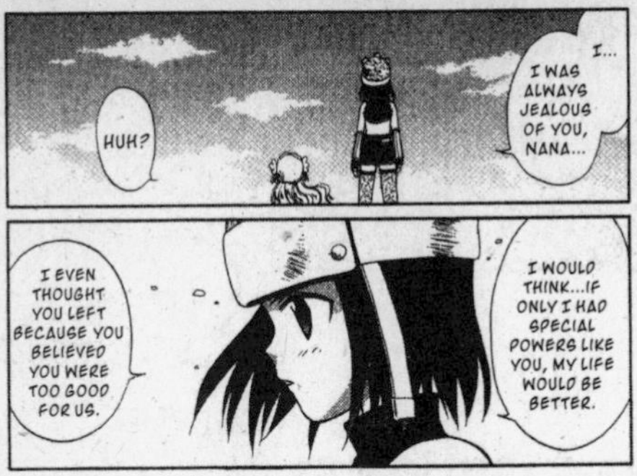
I... I WAS ALWAYS JEALOUS OF YOU, NANA...
HUH?
I WOULD THINK...IF ONLY I HAD SPECIAL POWERS LIKE YOU, MY LIFE WOULD BE BETTER.
I EVEN THOUGHT YOU LEFT BECAUSE YOU BELIEVED YOU WERE TOO GOOD FOR US.

In the city of Octopus, a group of orphaned children live and support each other in the underground ruins. Among them is a girl named Nana who lives alone because she's a bat +Anima. When Husky's pearls are stolen, we see a glimpse of the problems caused by being different from other humans.

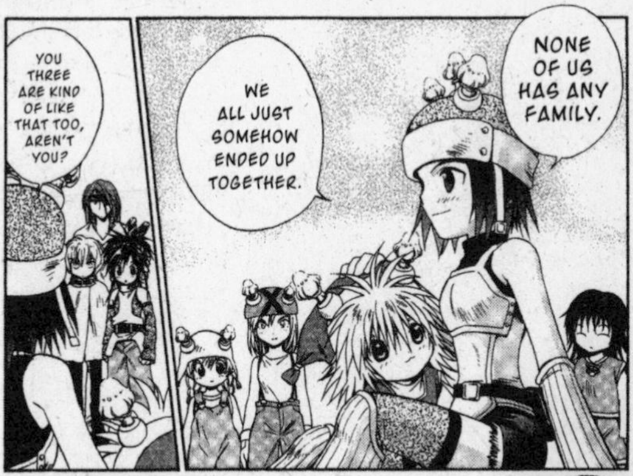
NONE OF US HAS ANY FAMILY.
WE ALL JUST SOMEHOW ENDED UP TOGETHER.
YOU THREE ARE KIND OF LIKE THAT TOO, AREN'T YOU?

Nana wants to travel with Cooro and the others, but Husky, who for some reason hates girls, is against the idea and takes off by himself. After hearing the details of how Nana discovered she was a +Anima, Husky accepts her as a member of the group.

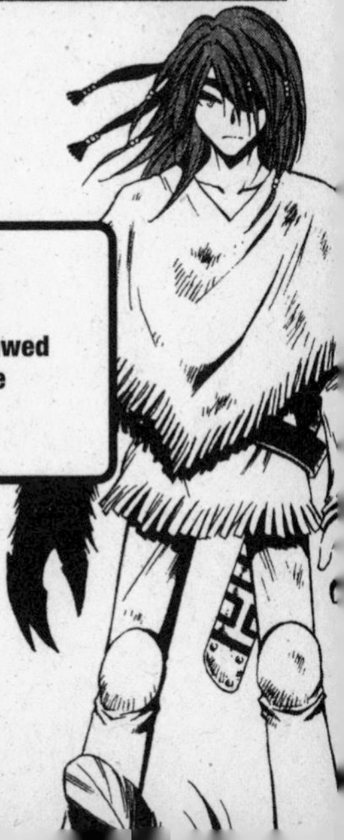

センリ [Senri]

Bear +Anima. His sharp-clawed arm is amazingly strong. He doesn't talk very much.

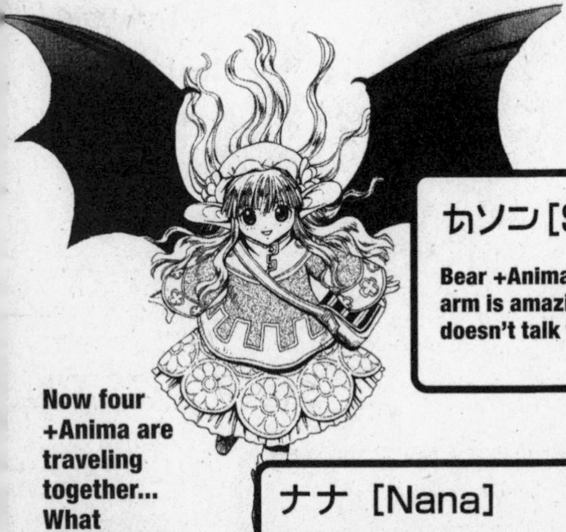

ナナ [Nana]

Bat +Anima. She can fly and has an ultrasonic screech. She loves pretty clothes and is scared of forests at night.

Now four +Anima are traveling together... What adventures await them on their journey?

C O N T E N T S

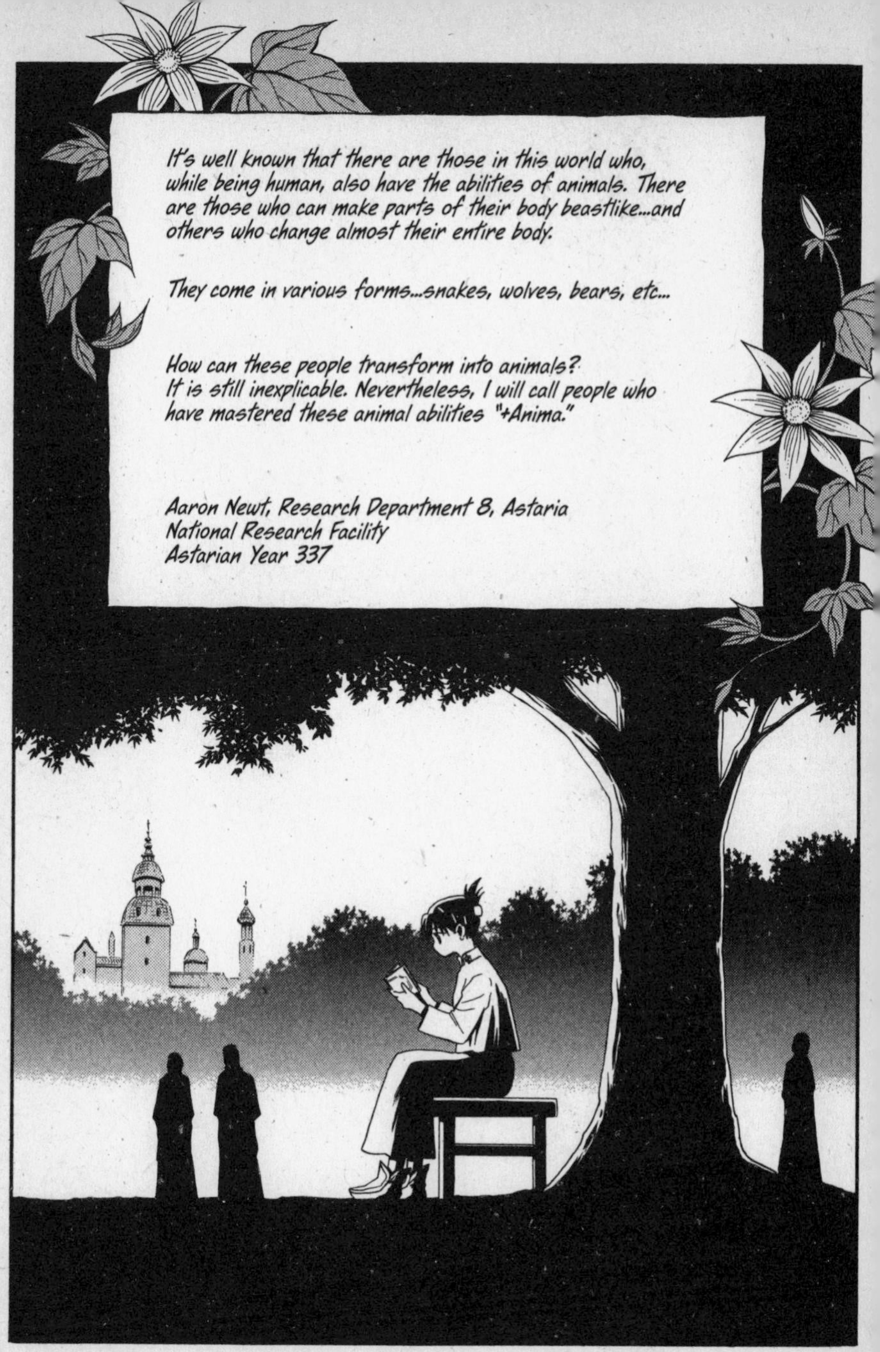
It's well known that there are those in this world who, while being human, also have the abilities of animals. There are those who can make parts of their body beastlike...and others who change almost their entire body.
They come in various forms...snakes, wolves, bears, etc...
How can these people transform into animals? It is still inexplicable. Nevertheless, I will call people who have mastered these animal abilities "+Anima."
Aaron Newt, Research Department 8, Astaria National Research Facility
Astarian Year 337

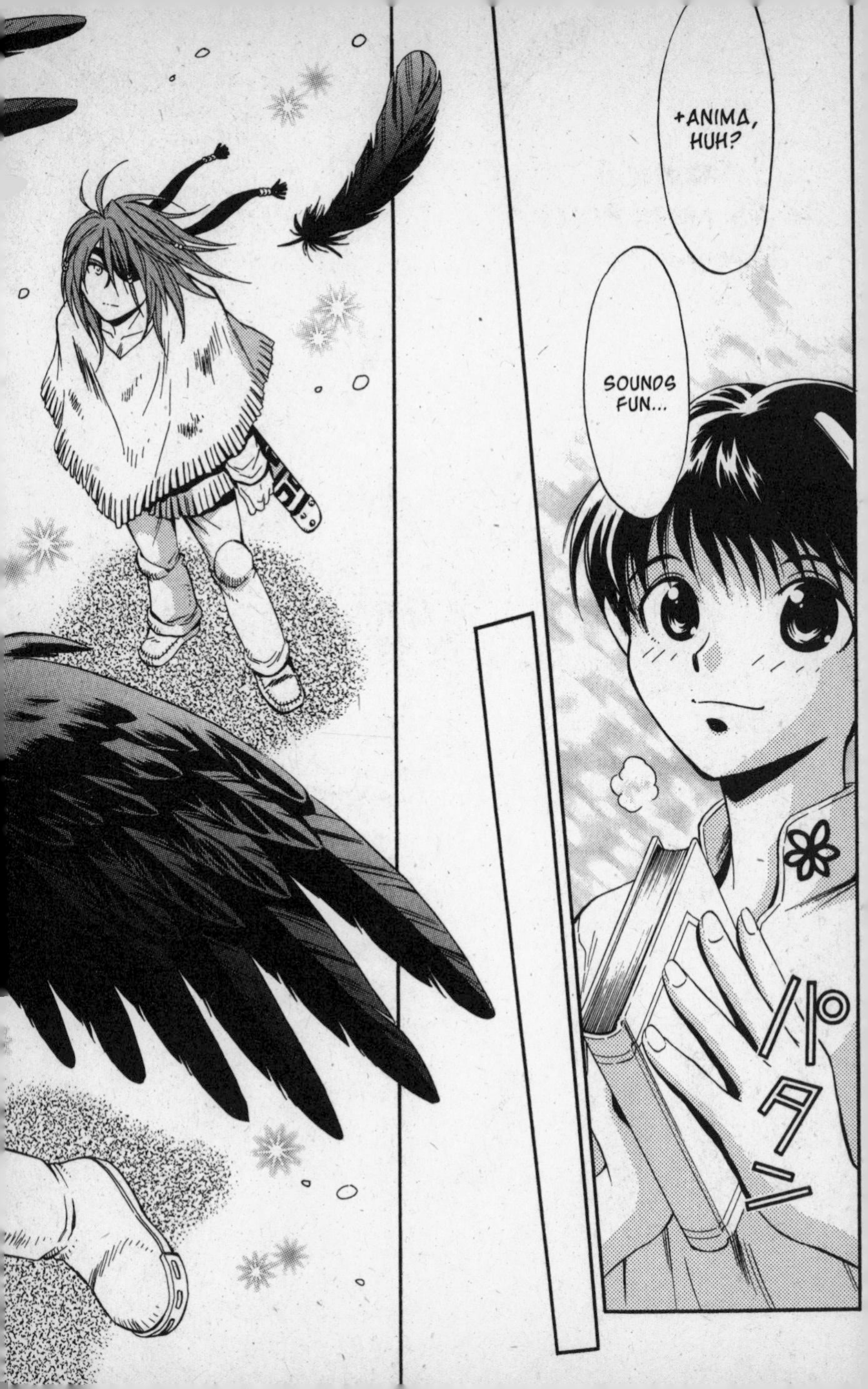
+ANIMA, HUH?
SOUNDS FUN...
パタン

Chapter 6
The Secret of Beehive Manor—Part 1

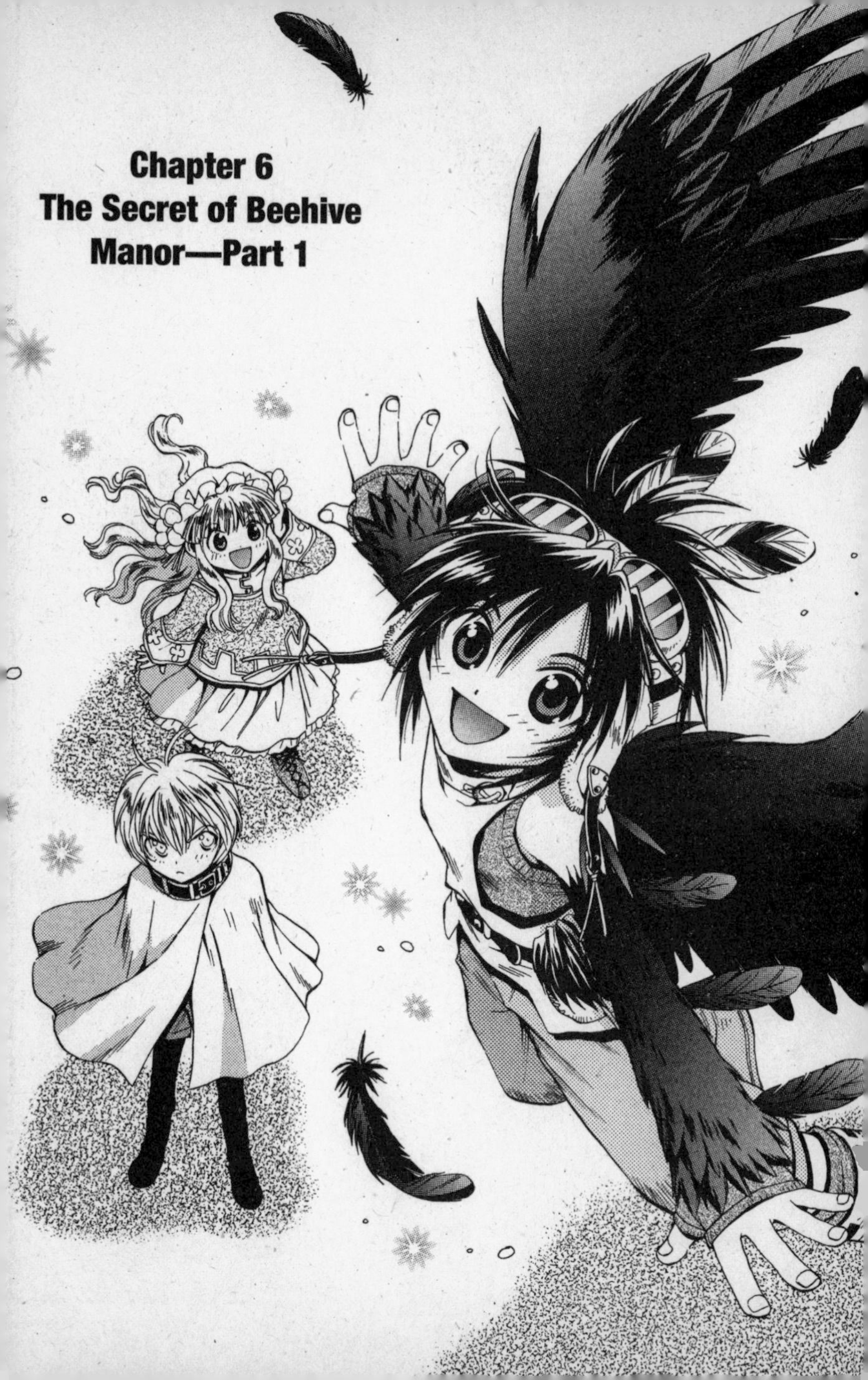

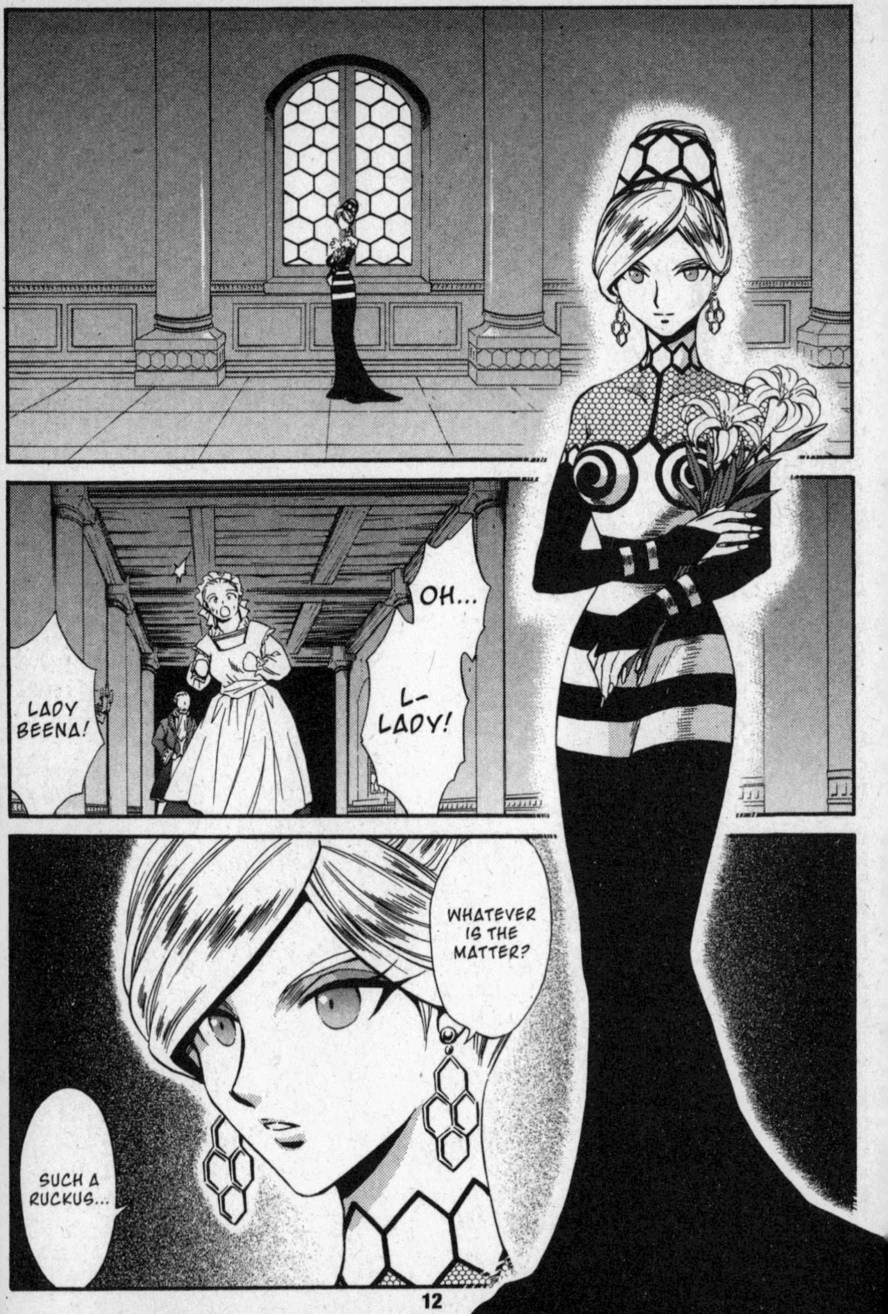
OH...
L-
LADY!
LADY BEENA!
WHATEVER IS THE MATTER?
SUCH A RUCKUS...

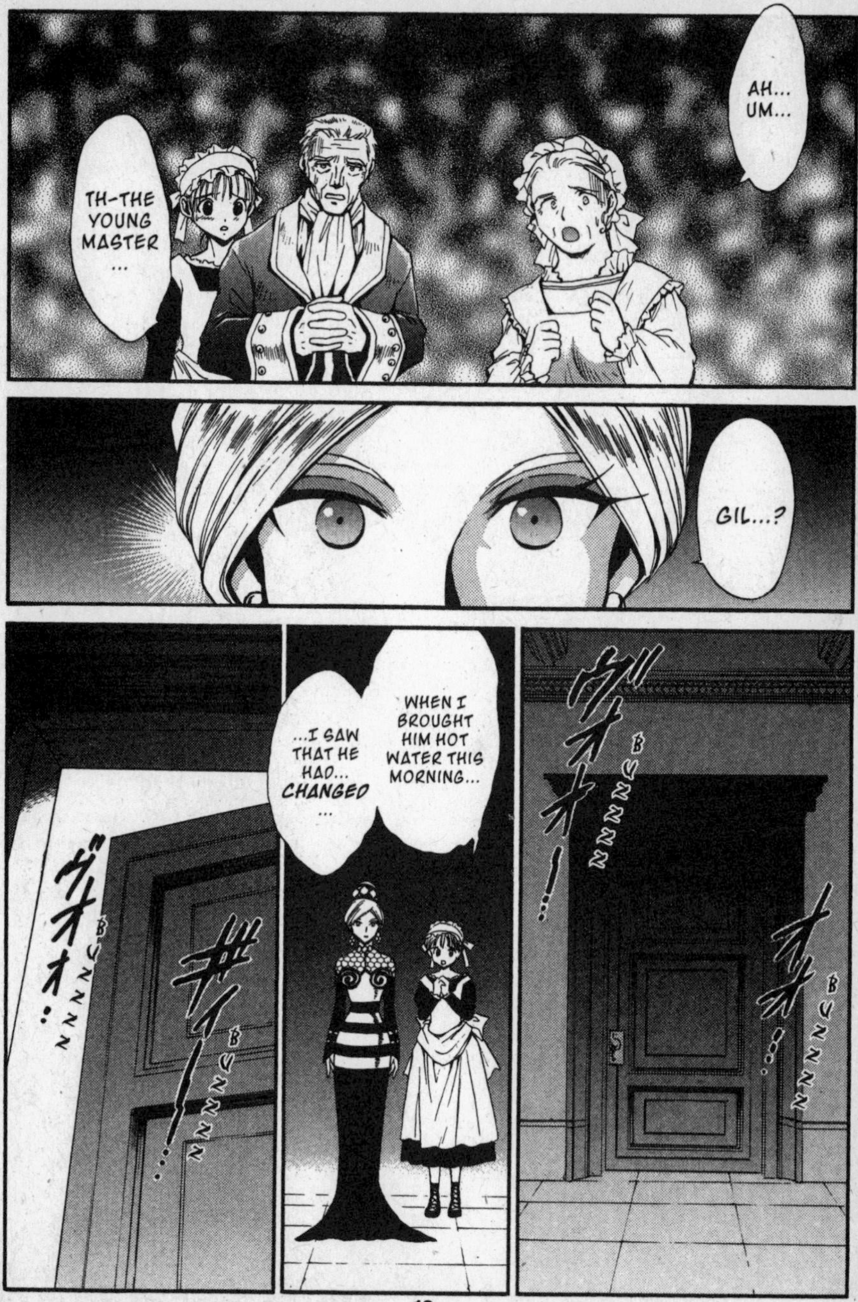
AH... UM...
TH-THE YOUNG MASTER ...
GIL...?
BUZZZZZ
BUZZZZZ
WHEN I BROUGHT HIM HOT WATER THIS MORNING...
...I SAW THAT HE HAD... CHANGED ...
BUZZZZZ
BUZZZZZ

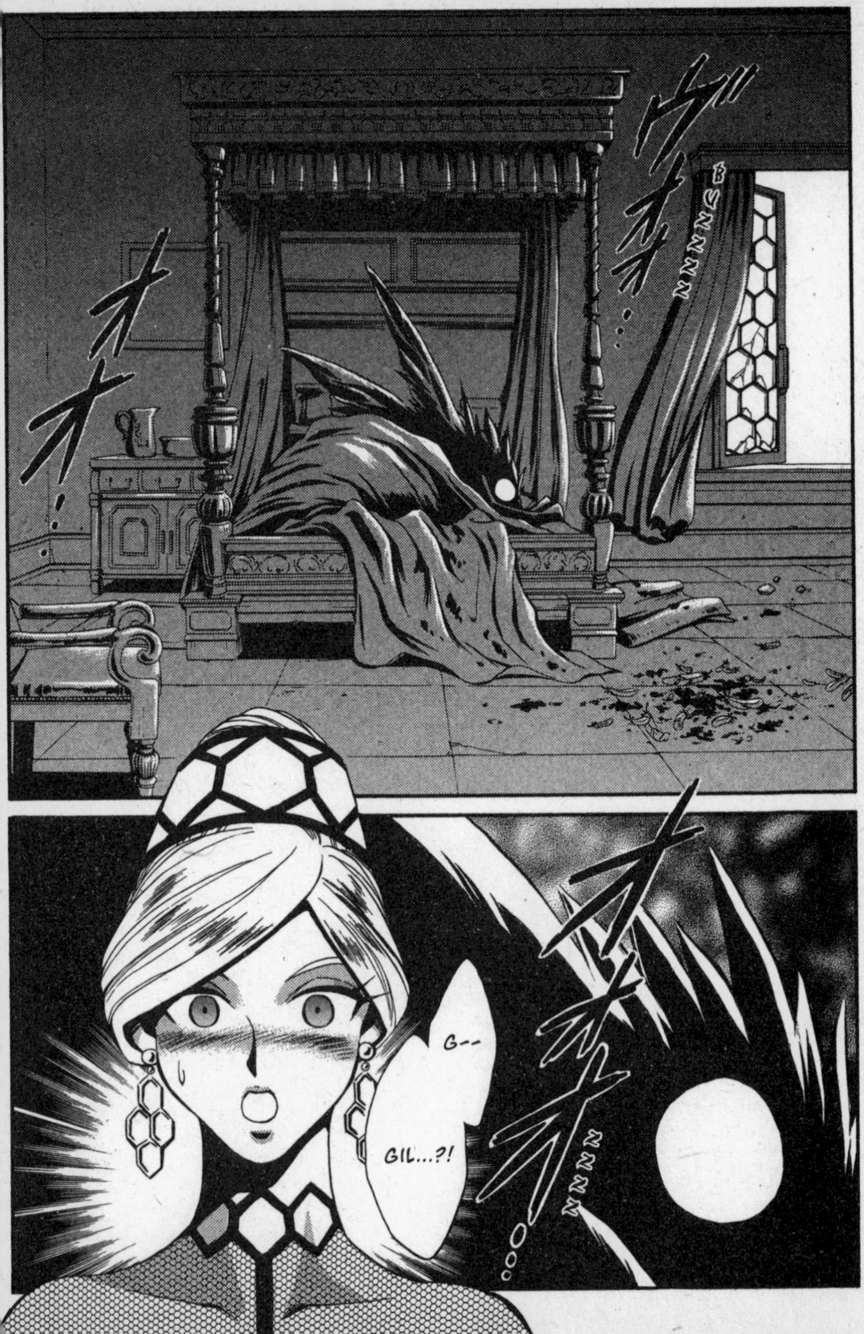
BUNNNNN
G--
GIL...?!
NNNN

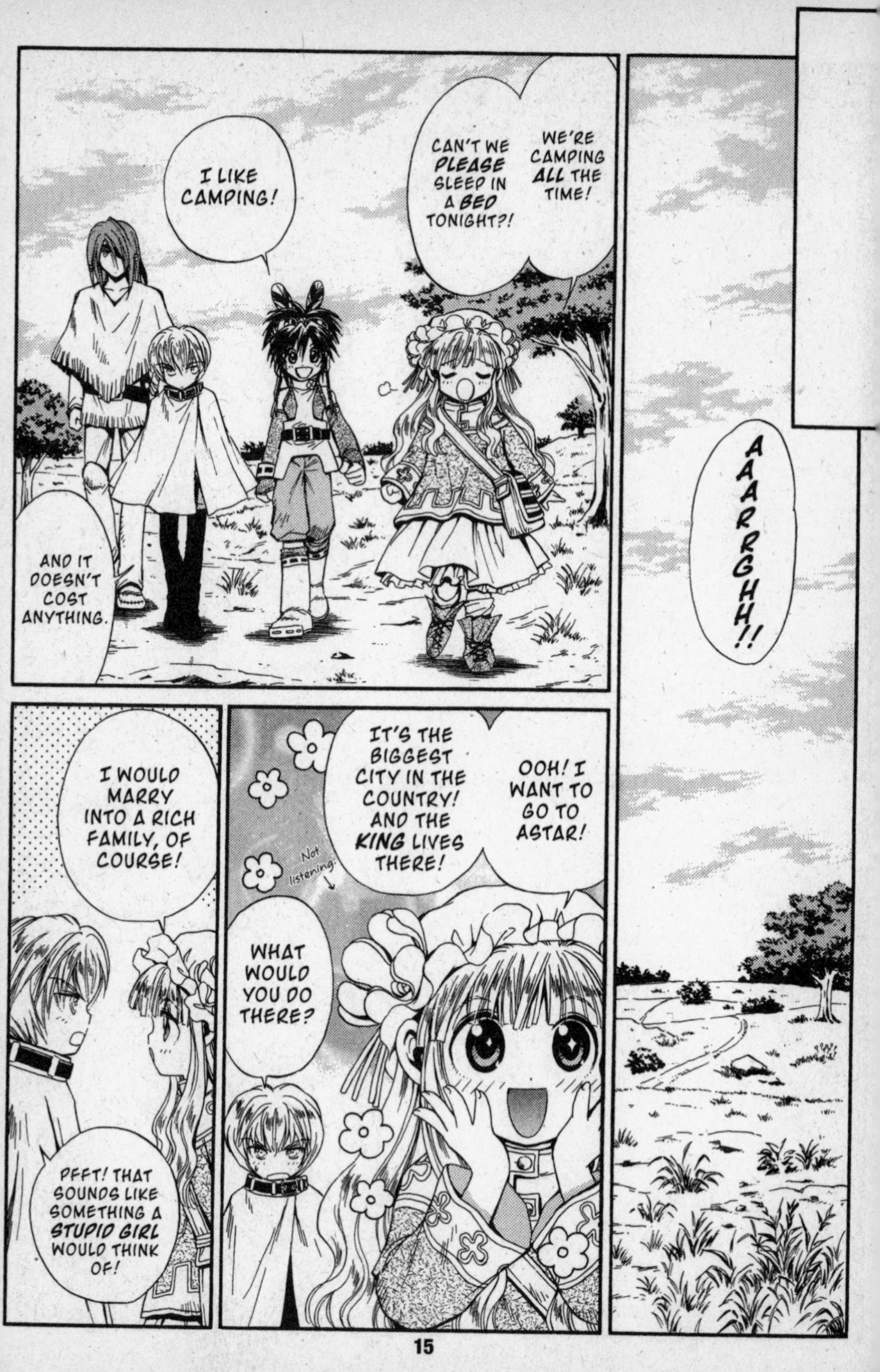
AAARRGHH!!
WE'RE CAMPING ALL THE TIME!
CAN'T WE PLEASE SLEEP IN A BED TONIGHT?!
I LIKE CAMPING!
AND IT DOESN'T COST ANYTHING.
OOH! I WANT TO GO TO ASTAR!
IT'S THE BIGGEST CITY IN THE COUNTRY! AND THE KING LIVES THERE!
Not listening.
WHAT WOULD YOU DO THERE?
I WOULD MARRY INTO A RICH FAMILY, OF COURSE!
PFFT! THAT SOUNDS LIKE SOMETHING A STUPID GIRL WOULD THINK OF!

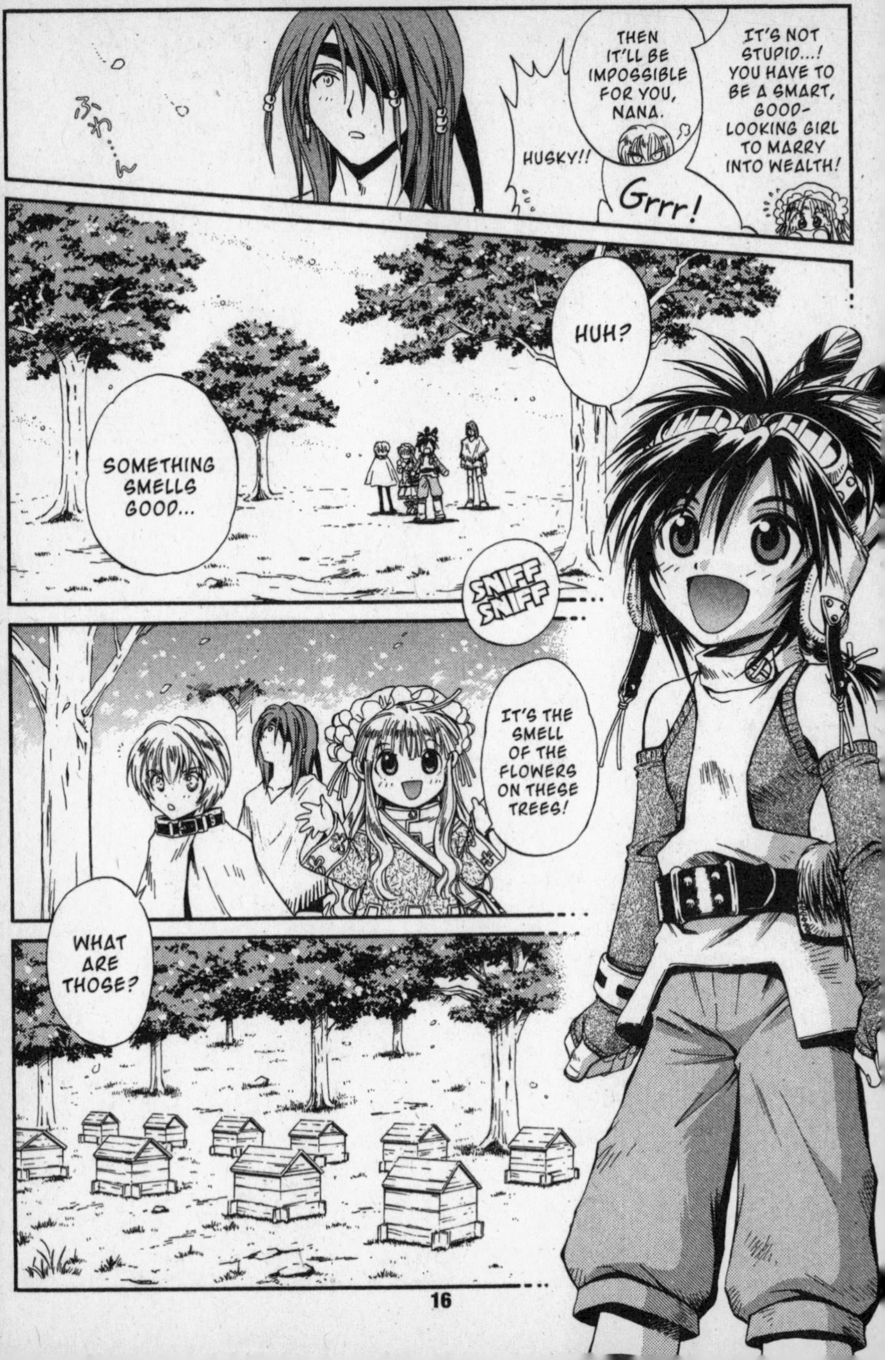
IT'S NOT STUPID...! YOU HAVE TO BE A SMART, GOOD-LOOKING GIRL TO MARRY INTO WEALTH!
THEN IT'LL BE IMPOSSIBLE FOR YOU, NANA.
HUSKY!!
Grrr!
ふわ…ん
HUH?
SOMETHING SMELLS GOOD...
SNIFF SNIFF
IT'S THE SMELL OF THE FLOWERS ON THESE TREES!
WHAT ARE THOSE?

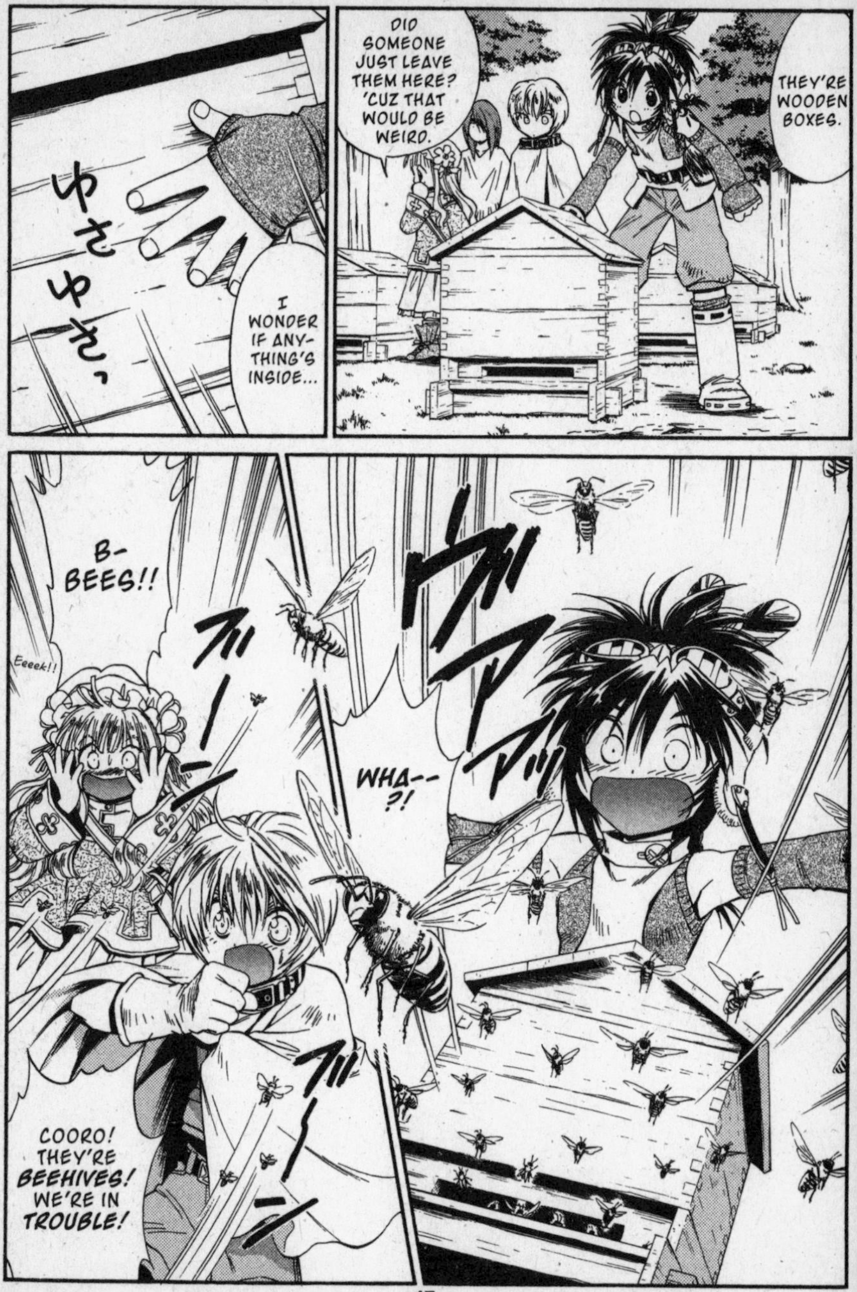
THEY'RE WOODEN BOXES.
DID SOMEONE JUST LEAVE THEM HERE? 'CUZ THAT WOULD BE WEIRD.
ゆさゆさ
I WONDER IF ANYTHING'S INSIDE...
ヴァアッ
WHA--?!
ブーーン
B-BEES!!
Eeeek!!
ブーーン
COORO! THEY'RE **BEEHIVES!** WE'RE IN **TROUBLE!**

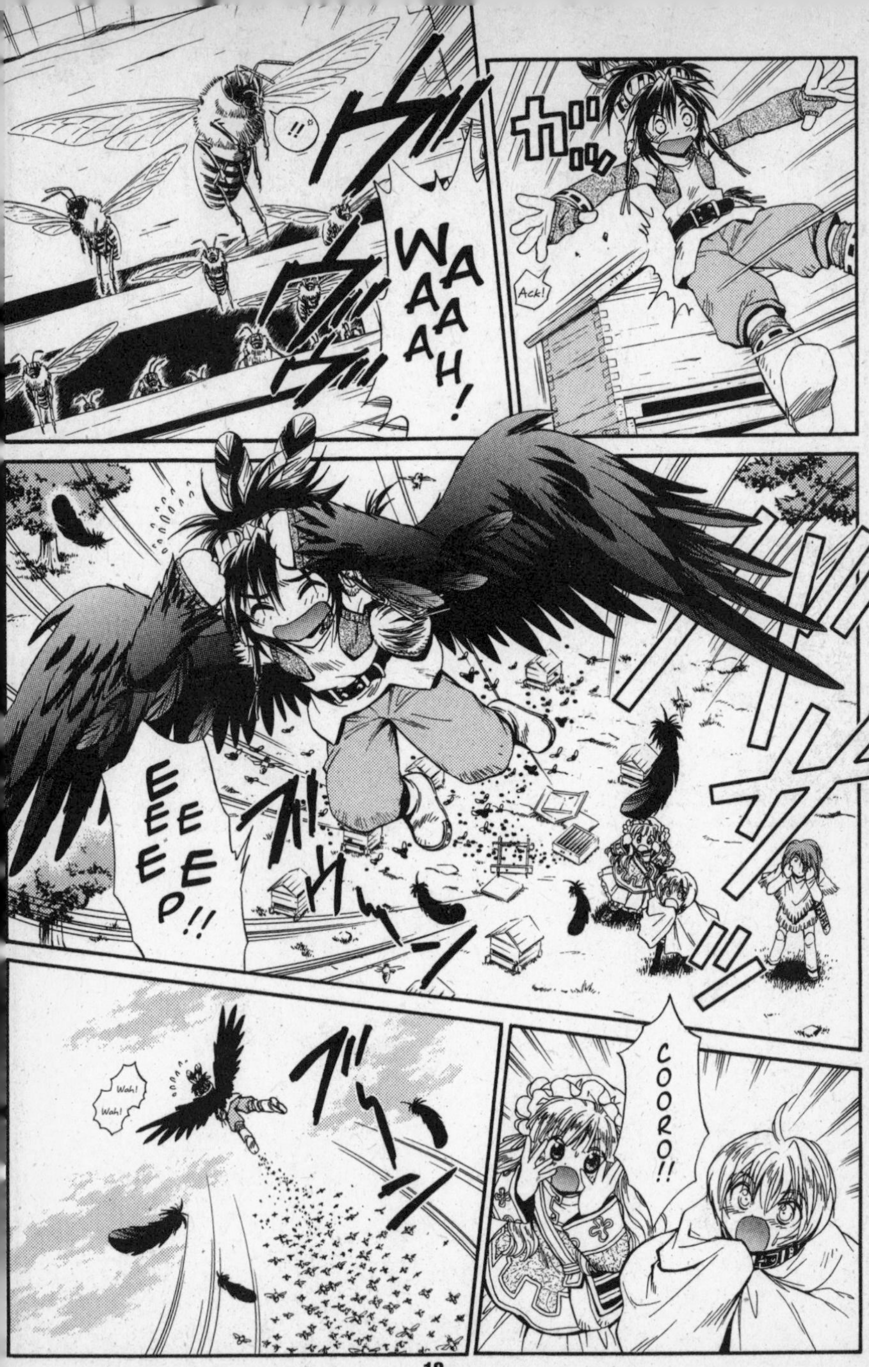
Ack!
!!
WAAAAH!
EEEEEP!!
COORO!!
Wah!
Wah!

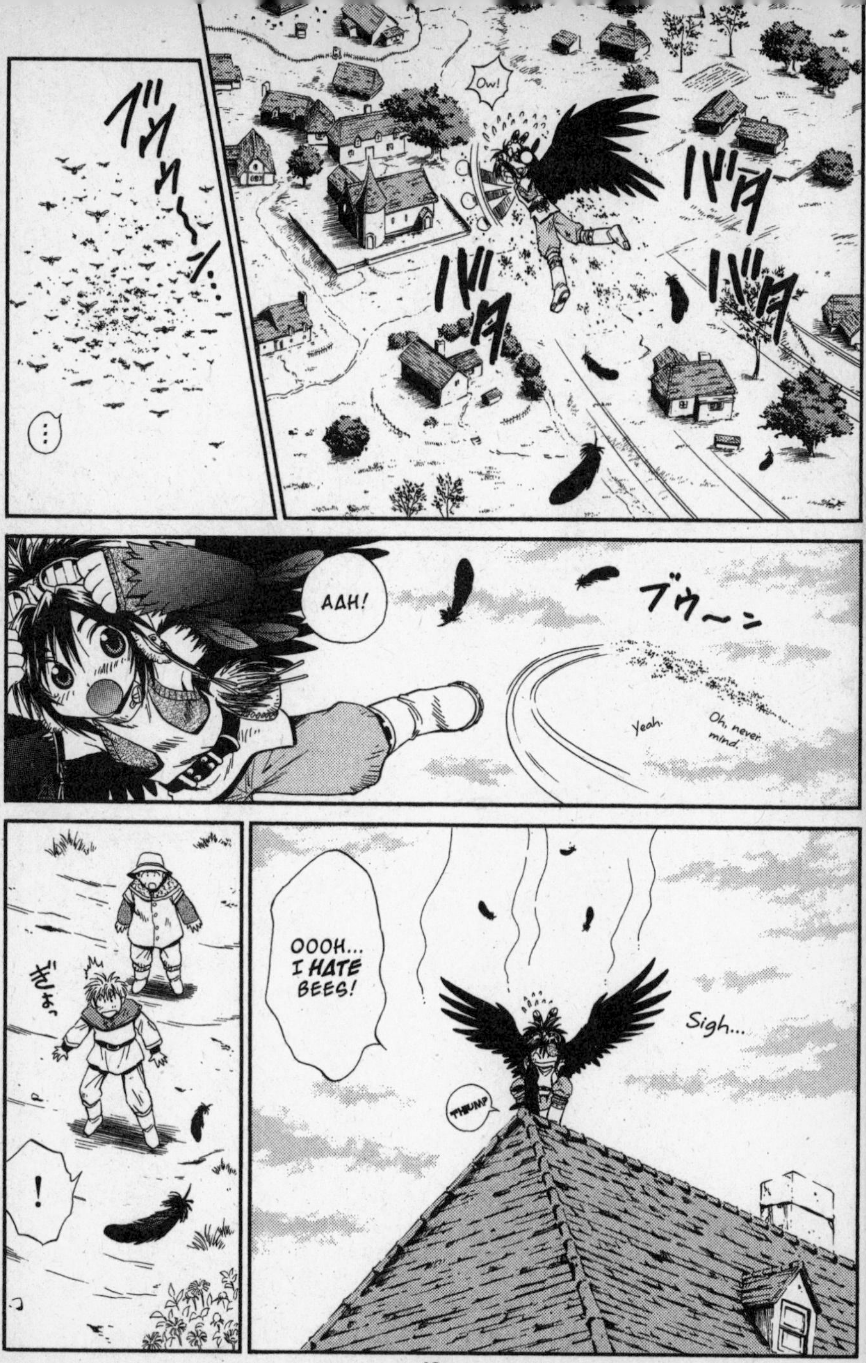
Ow!
バタ
バタ
バタ
ブゥ〜〜ン…
…
ブウ〜ン
AAH!
Oh, never mind.
Yeah.
Sigh...
OOOH... I HATE BEES!
THUMP
ぎょっ
!

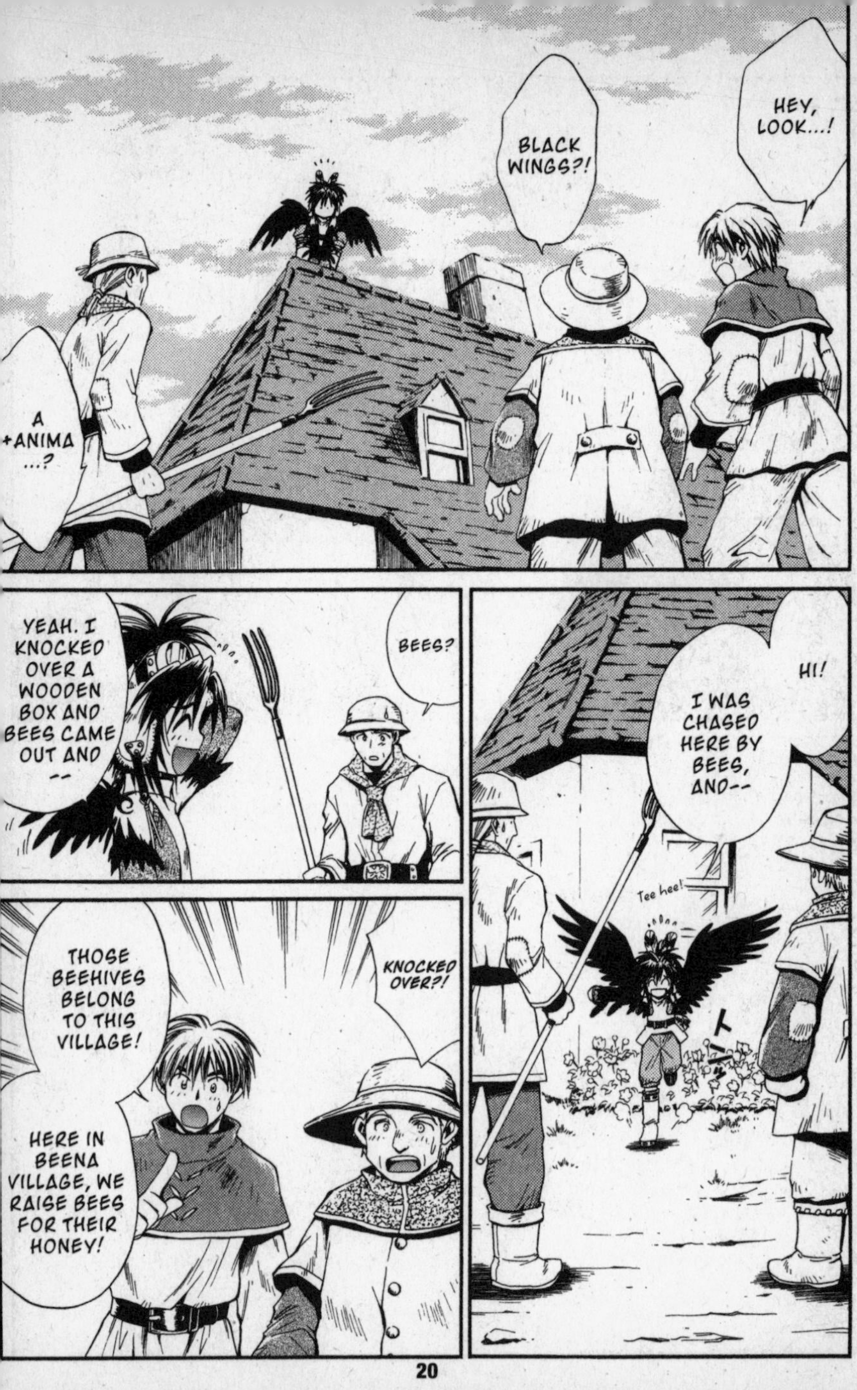
HEY, LOOK...!
BLACK WINGS?!
A +ANIMA ...?
HI!
I WAS CHASED HERE BY BEES, AND--
Tee hee!
BEES?
YEAH. I KNOCKED OVER A WOODEN BOX AND BEES CAME OUT AND --
KNOCKED OVER?!
THOSE BEEHIVES BELONG TO THIS VILLAGE!
HERE IN BEENA VILLAGE, WE RAISE BEES FOR THEIR HONEY!

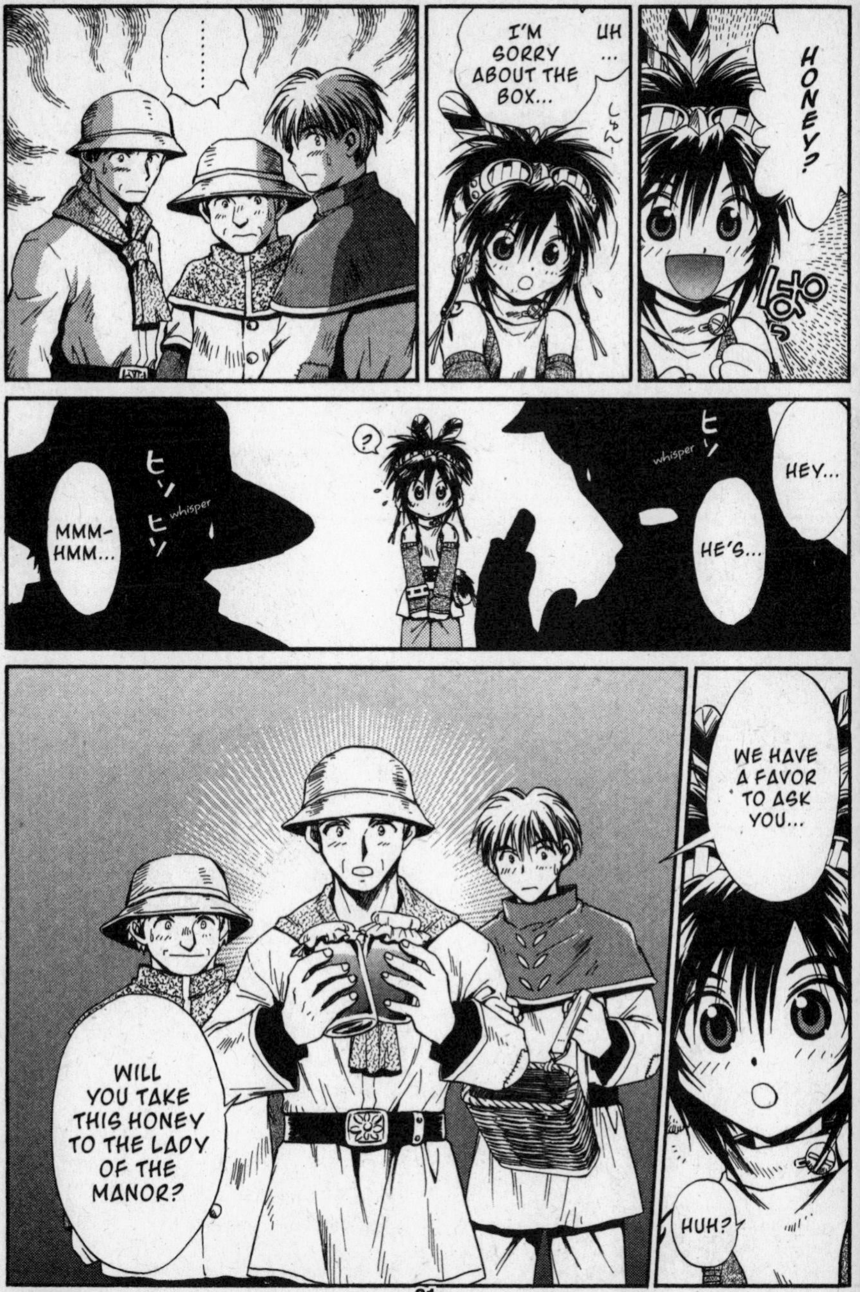
HONEY?
UH ...
I'M SORRY ABOUT THE BOX...
しゅん
......
HEY...
HE'S...
ヒソ
whisper
?
ヒソヒソ
whisper
MMM-HMM...
WE HAVE A FAVOR TO ASK YOU...
HUH?
WILL YOU TAKE THIS HONEY TO THE LADY OF THE MANOR?

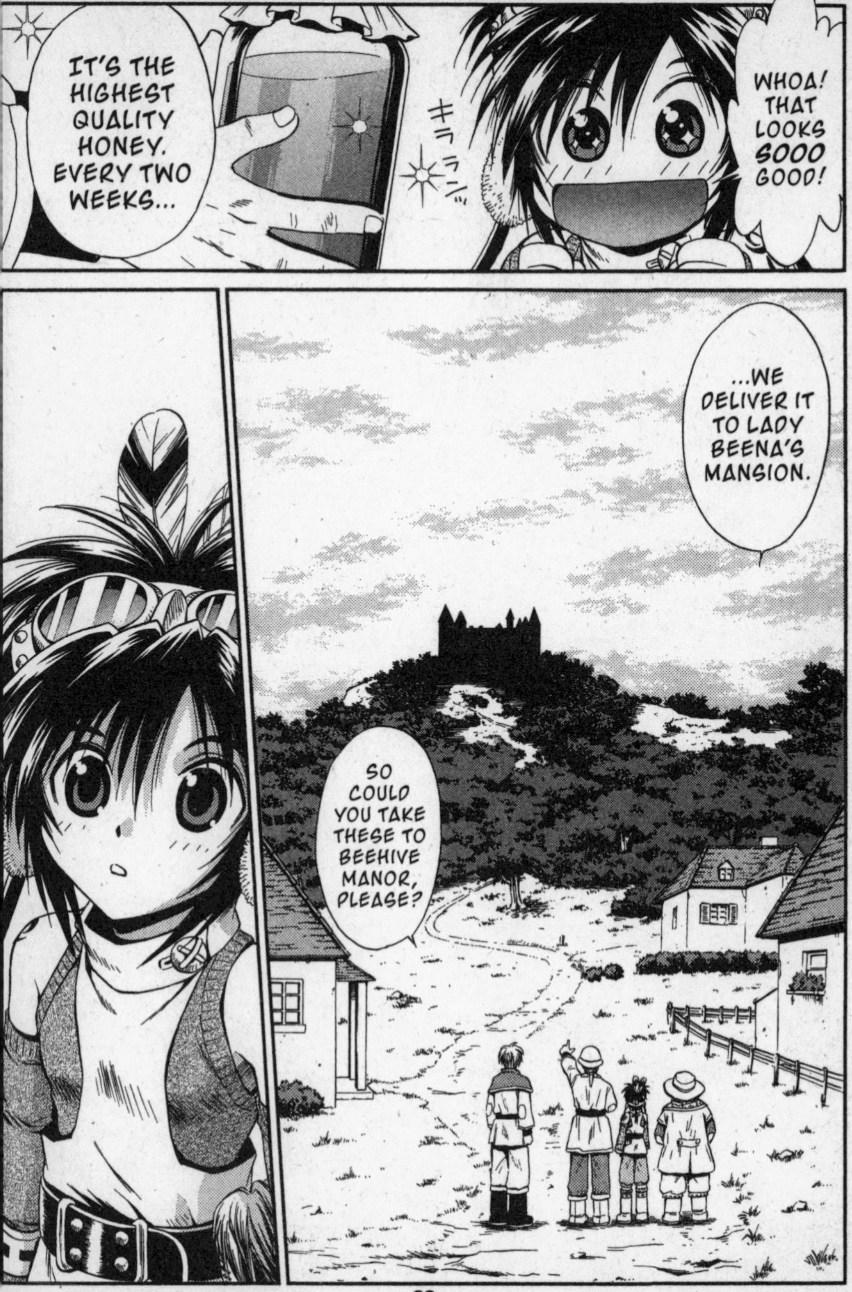
WHOA! THAT LOOKS SOOO GOOD!
IT'S THE HIGHEST QUALITY HONEY. EVERY TWO WEEKS...
...WE DELIVER IT TO LADY BEENA'S MANSION.
SO COULD YOU TAKE THESE TO BEEHIVE MANOR, PLEASE?

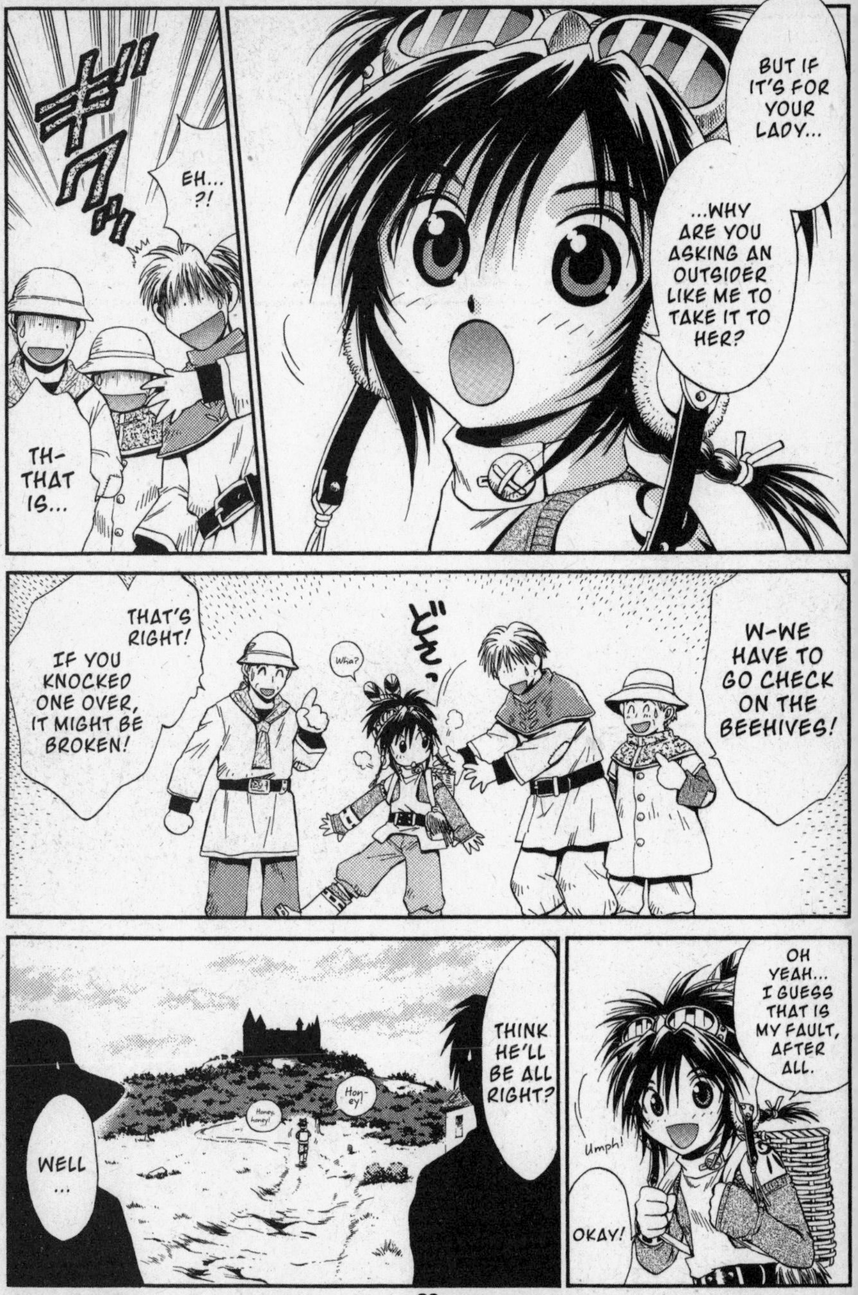
BUT IF IT'S FOR YOUR LADY...
...WHY ARE YOU ASKING AN OUTSIDER LIKE ME TO TAKE IT TO HER?
ギクッ
EH... ?!
TH-THAT IS...
W-WE HAVE TO GO CHECK ON THE BEEHIVES!
どさ
Wha?
THAT'S RIGHT!
IF YOU KNOCKED ONE OVER, IT MIGHT BE BROKEN!
OH YEAH... I GUESS THAT IS MY FAULT, AFTER ALL.
Umph!
OKAY!
THINK HE'LL BE ALL RIGHT?
Hon-ey!
Honey, honey!
WELL ...

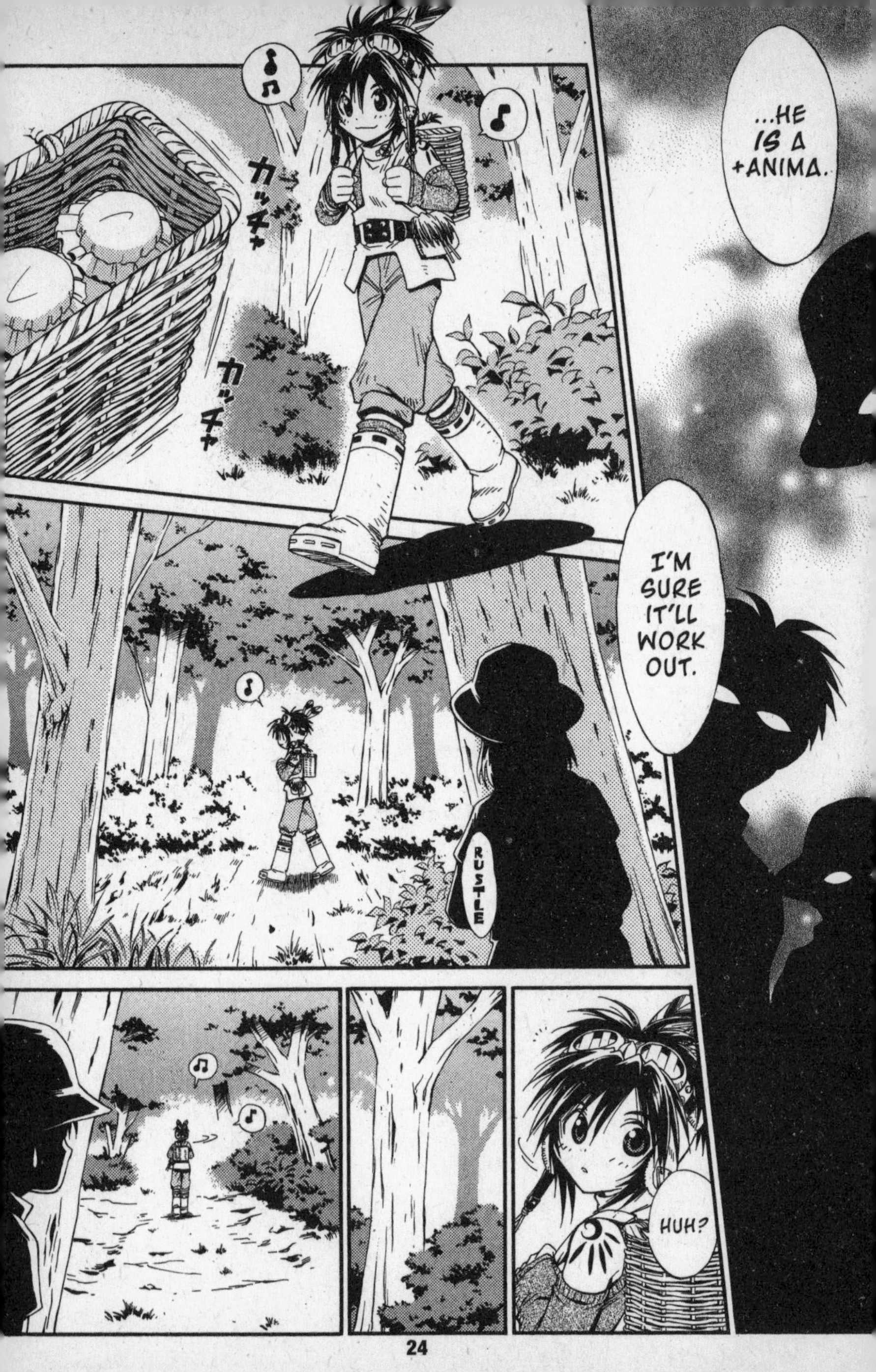

...HE IS A +ANIMA..
I'M SURE IT'LL WORK OUT.
♪ ♫
♪
カッチャ
カッチャ
♪
RUSTLE
HUH?
♫
♪

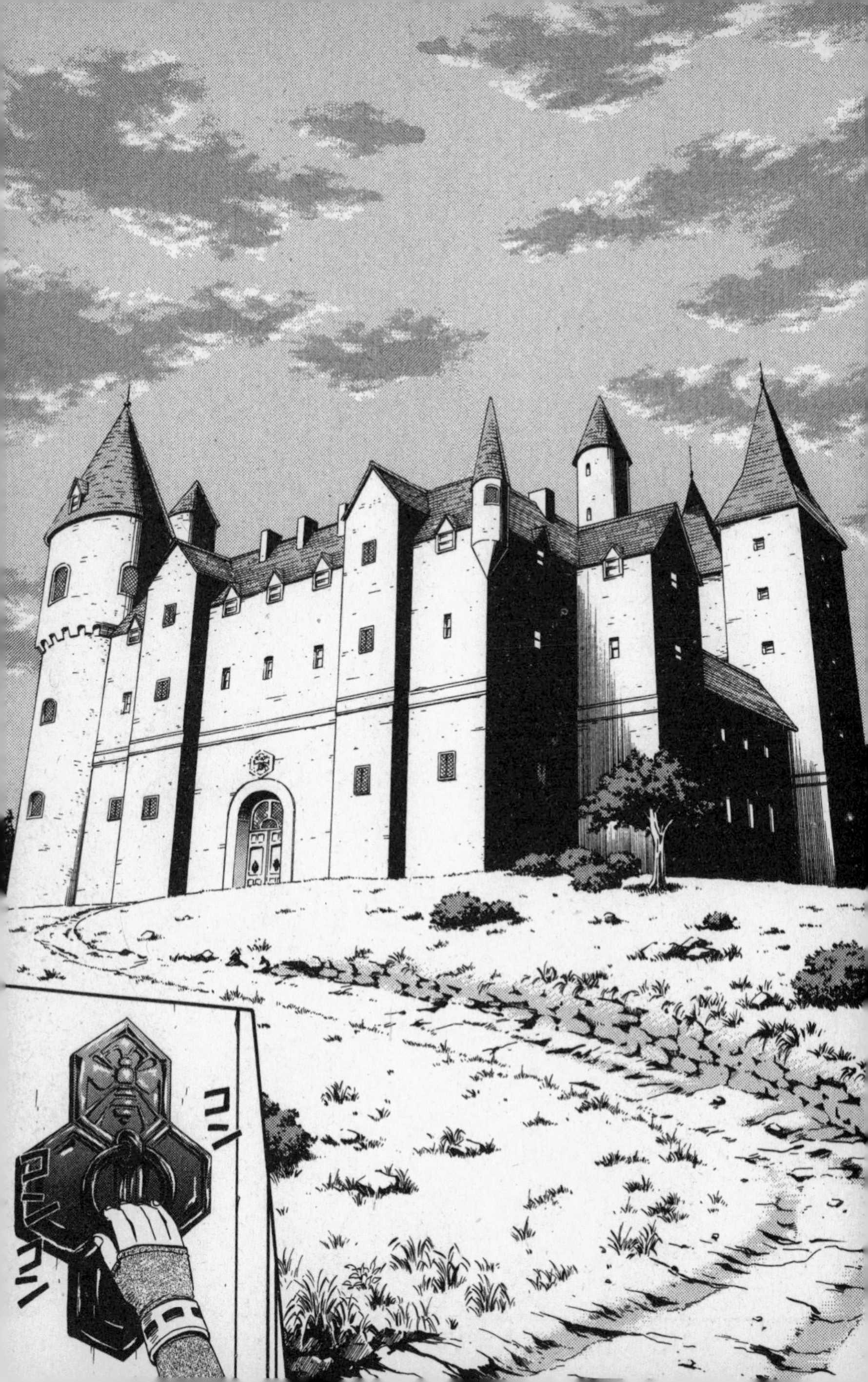
コン
コン
コン

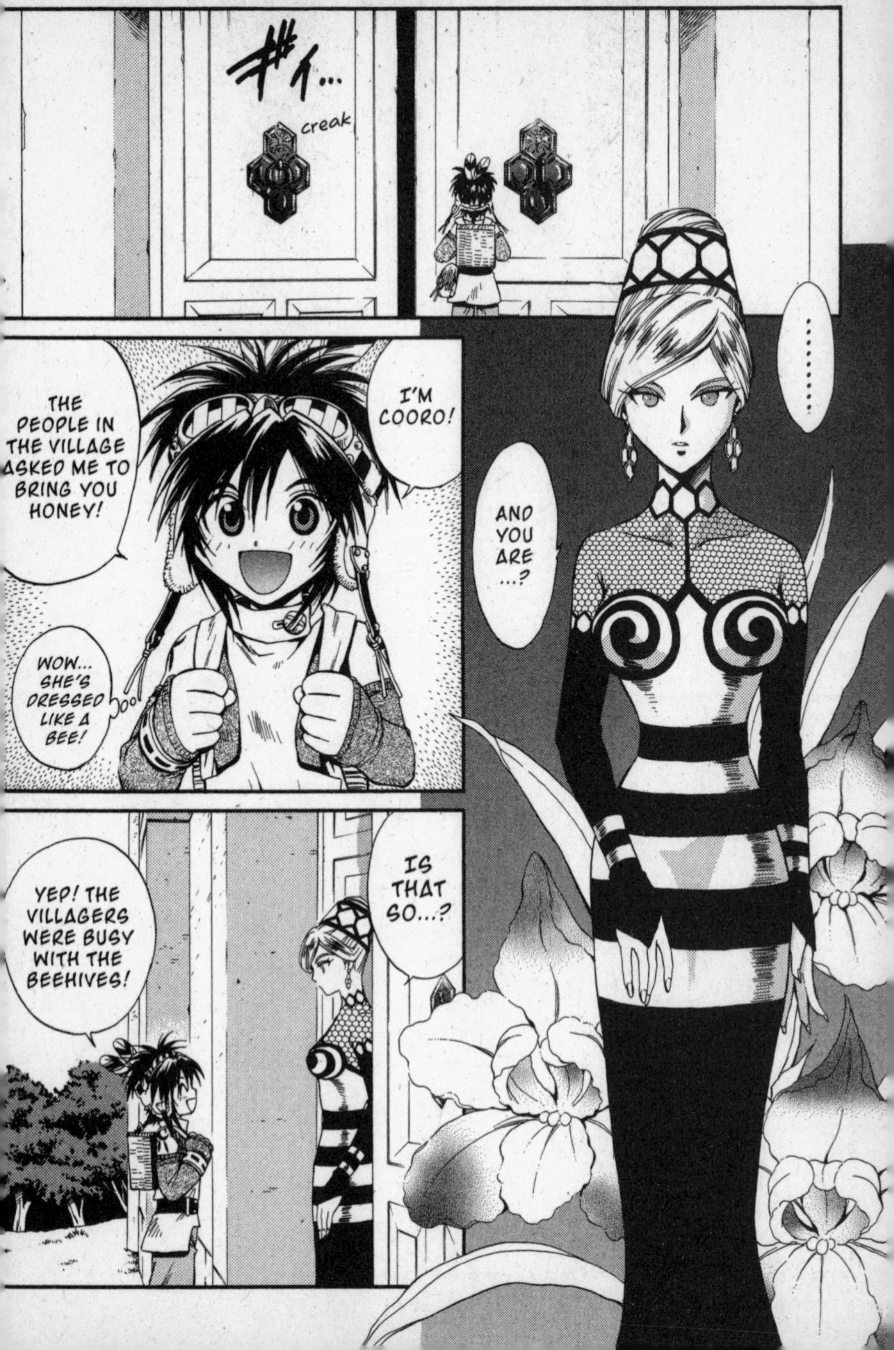
ギイ...
creak
......
AND YOU ARE ...?
I'M COORO!
THE PEOPLE IN THE VILLAGE ASKED ME TO BRING YOU HONEY!
WOW... SHE'S DRESSED LIKE A BEE!
IS THAT SO...?
YEP! THE VILLAGERS WERE BUSY WITH THE BEEHIVES!

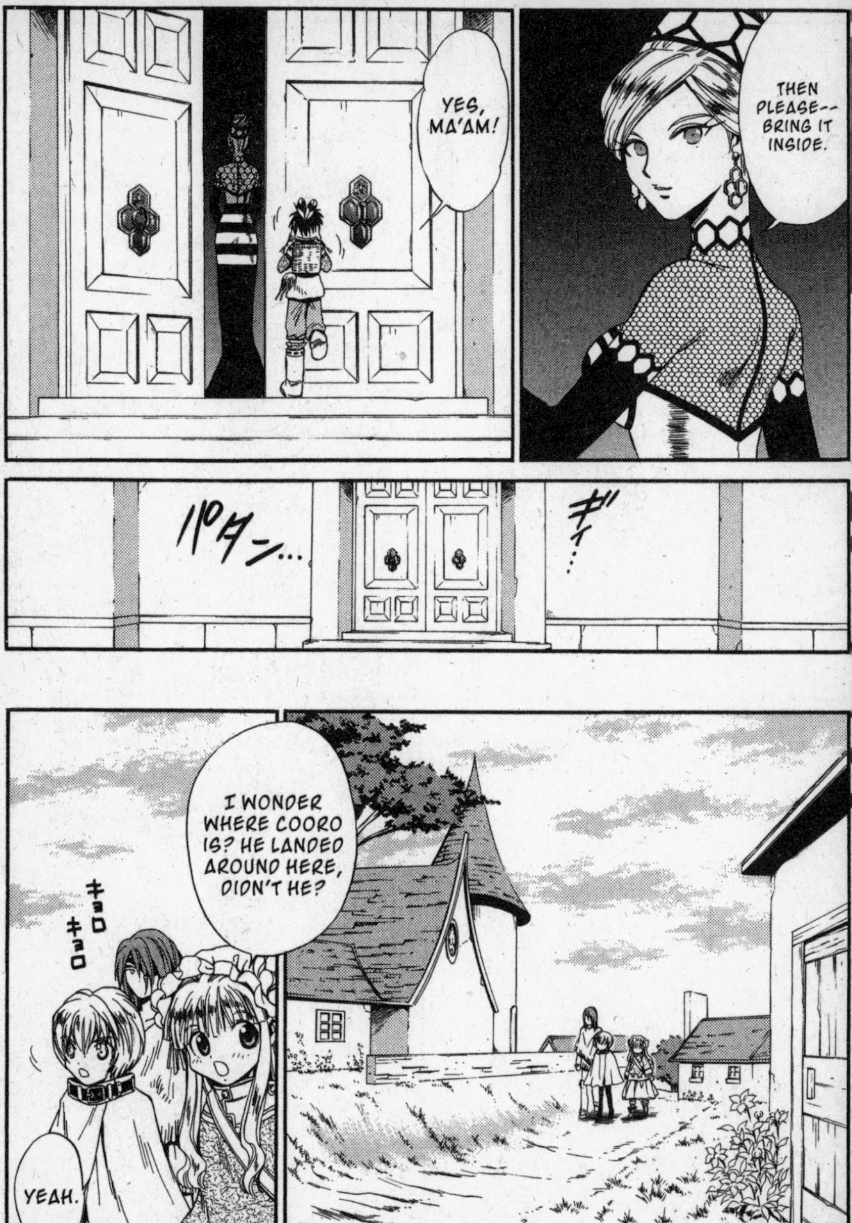
THEN PLEASE--BRING IT INSIDE.
YES, MA'AM!
ギィ…
パタン…
I WONDER WHERE COORO IS? HE LANDED AROUND HERE, DIDN'T HE?
キョロキョロ
YEAH.

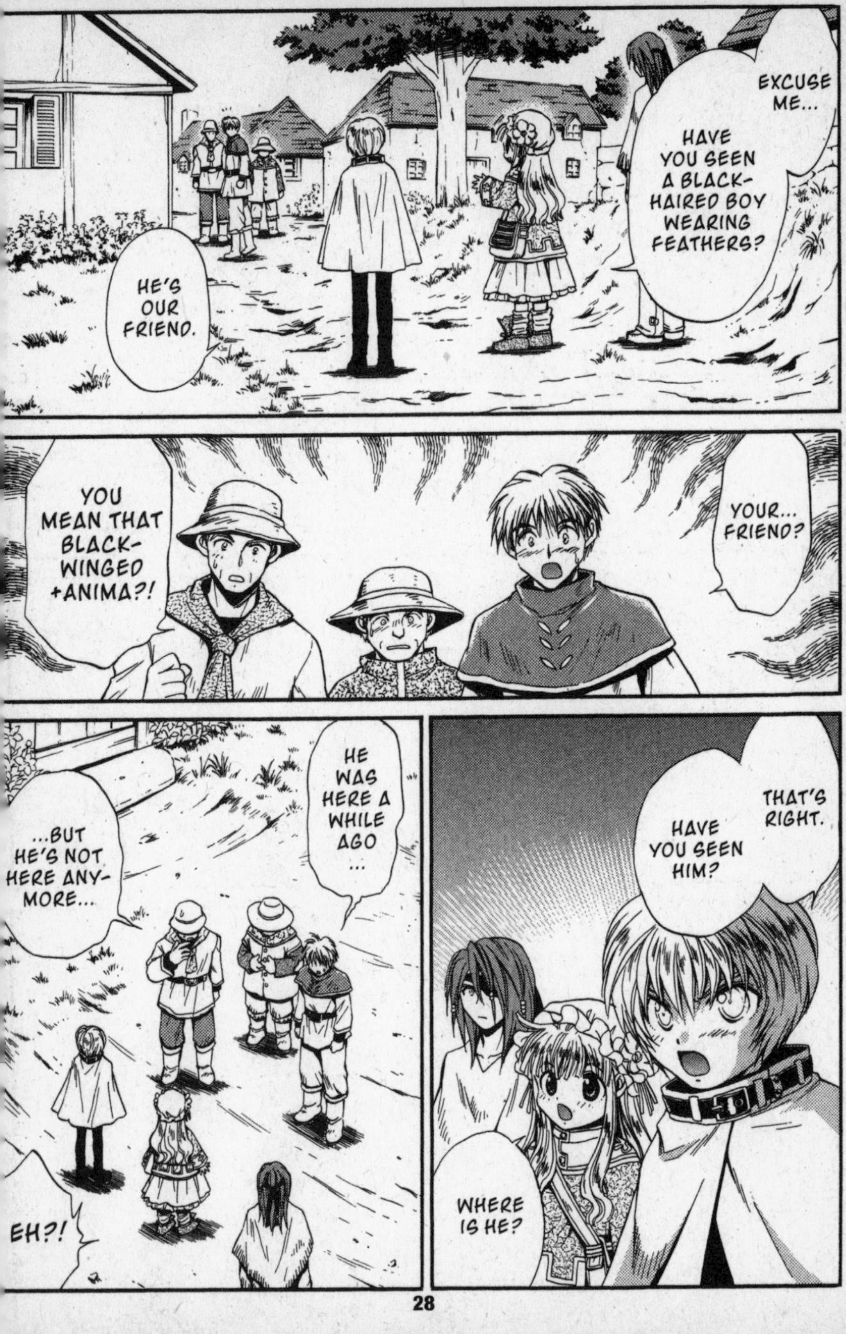
EXCUSE ME...
HAVE YOU SEEN A BLACK-HAIRED BOY WEARING FEATHERS?
HE'S OUR FRIEND.
YOUR... FRIEND?
YOU MEAN THAT BLACK-WINGED +ANIMA?!
THAT'S RIGHT.
HAVE YOU SEEN HIM?
WHERE IS HE?
HE WAS HERE A WHILE AGO ...
...BUT HE'S NOT HERE ANY-MORE...
EH?!

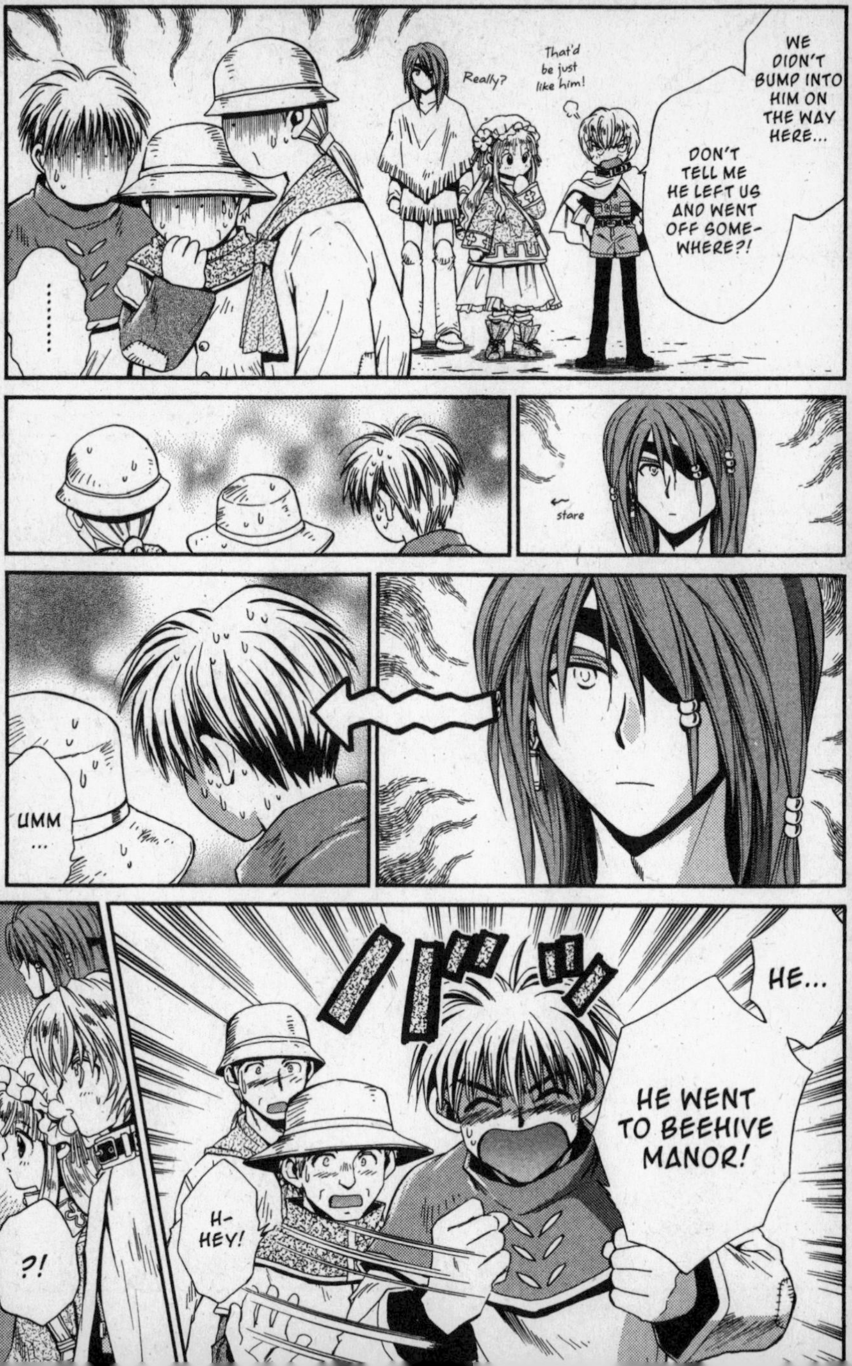
WE DIDN'T BUMP INTO HIM ON THE WAY HERE...
DON'T TELL ME HE LEFT US AND WENT OFF SOME-WHERE?!
That'd be just like him!
Really?
......
stare
UMM ...
HE...
HE WENT TO BEEHIVE MANOR!
H- HEY!
?!

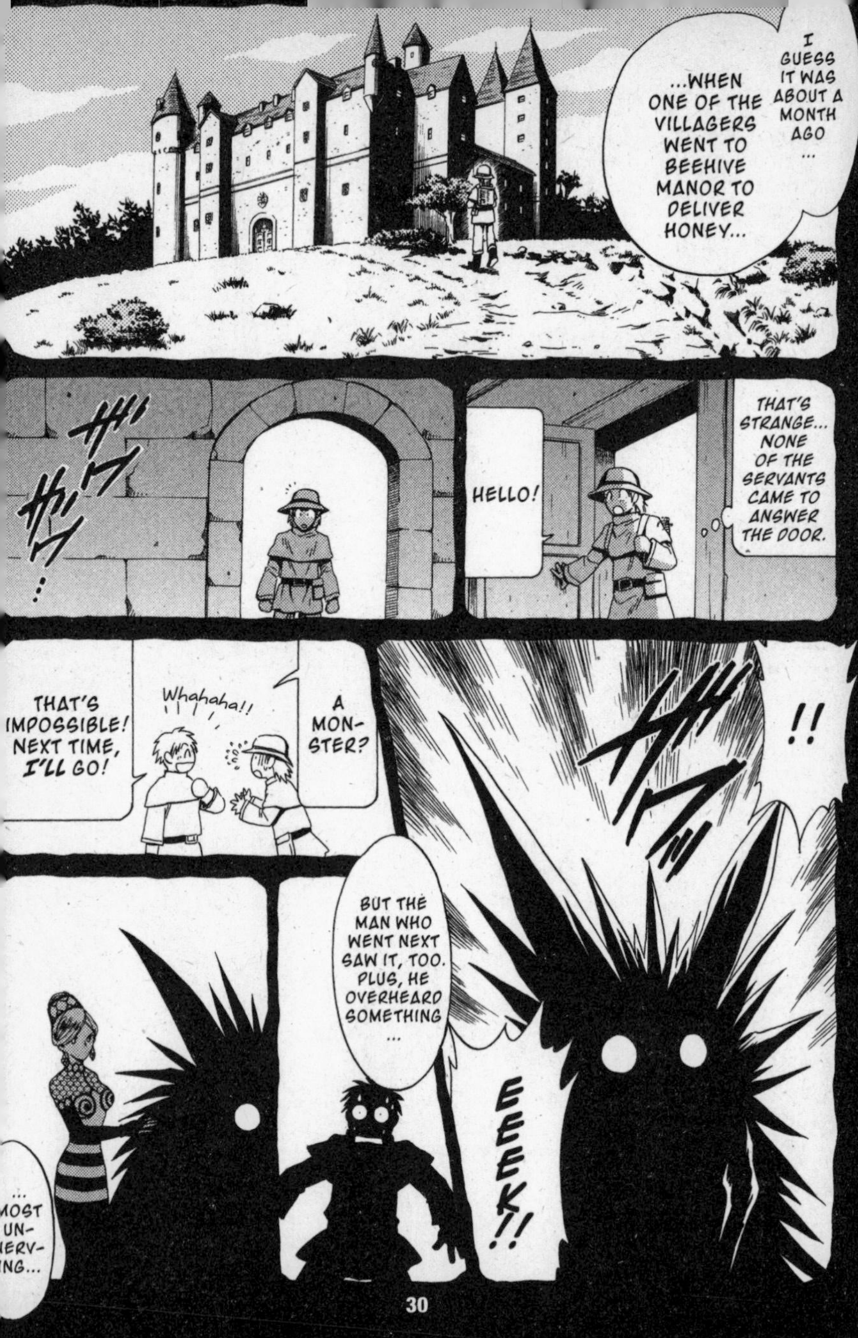
I GUESS IT WAS ABOUT A MONTH AGO...
...WHEN ONE OF THE VILLAGERS WENT TO BEEHIVE MANOR TO DELIVER HONEY...
THAT'S STRANGE... NONE OF THE SERVANTS CAME TO ANSWER THE DOOR.
HELLO!
...
!!
BUT THE MAN WHO WENT NEXT SAW IT, TOO. PLUS, HE OVERHEARD SOMETHING...
EEEEK!!
A MON-STER?
Whahaha!!
THAT'S IMPOSSIBLE! NEXT TIME, I'LL GO!
...MOST UN-NERV-ING...

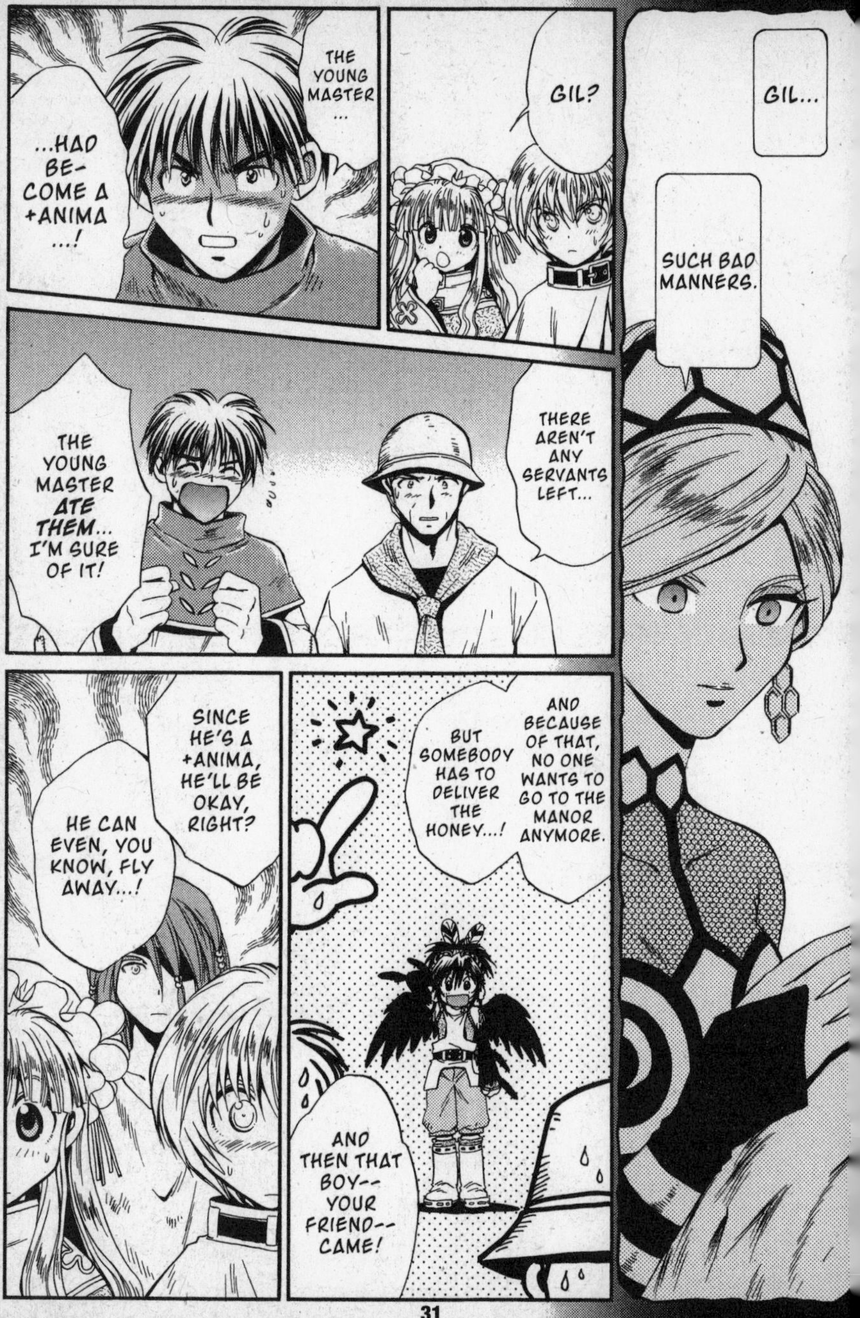
GIL...
SUCH BAD MANNERS.
GIL?
THE YOUNG MASTER...
...HAD BECOME A +ANIMA...!
THERE AREN'T ANY SERVANTS LEFT...
THE YOUNG MASTER ATE THEM... I'M SURE OF IT!
AND BECAUSE OF THAT, NO ONE WANTS TO GO TO THE MANOR ANYMORE.
BUT SOMEBODY HAS TO DELIVER THE HONEY...!
AND THEN THAT BOY--YOUR FRIEND--CAME!
SINCE HE'S A +ANIMA, HE'LL BE OKAY, RIGHT?
HE CAN EVEN, YOU KNOW, FLY AWAY...!

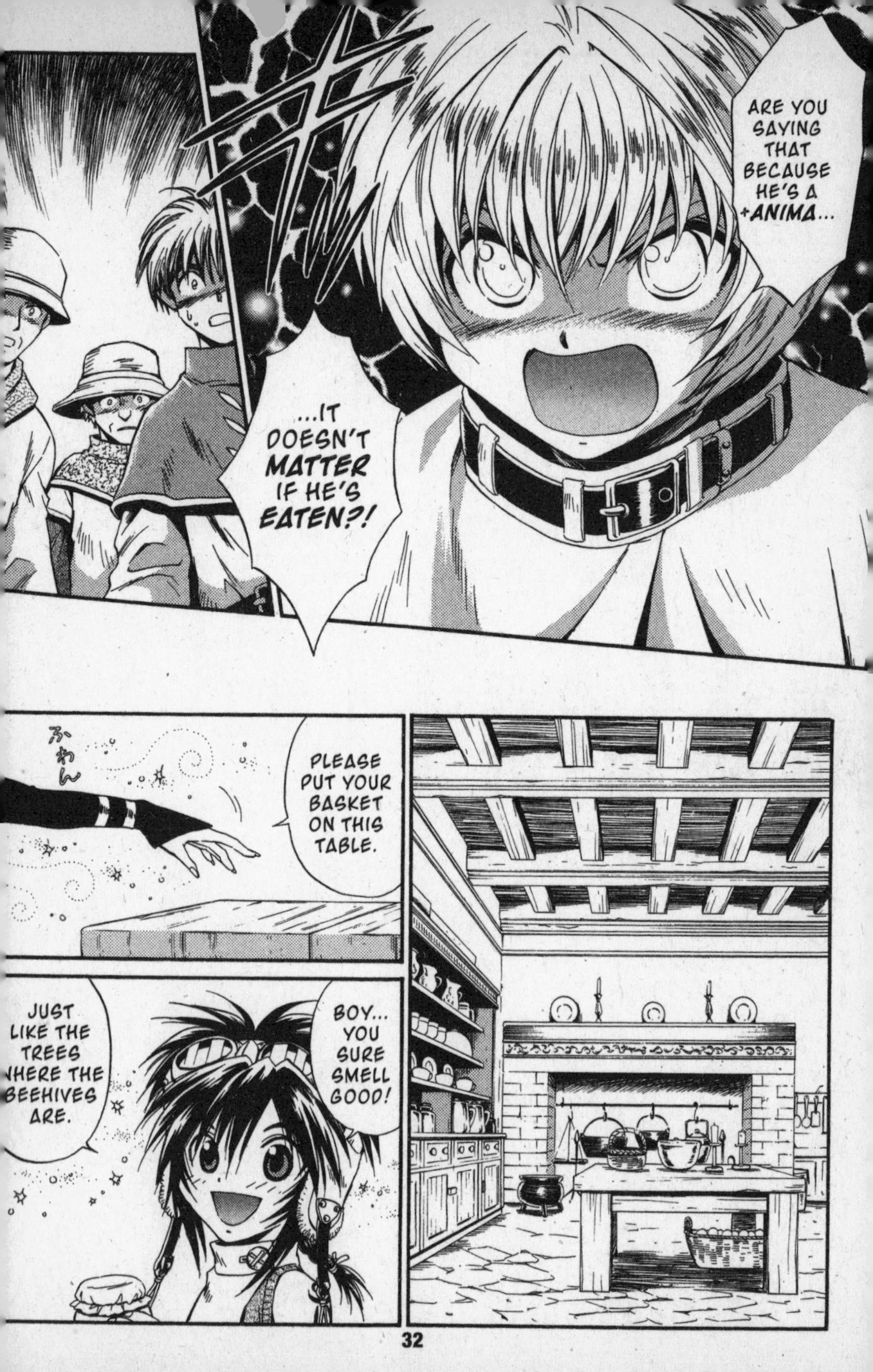
ARE YOU SAYING THAT BECAUSE HE'S A +ANIMA...
...IT DOESN'T MATTER IF HE'S EATEN?!
ふわん
PLEASE PUT YOUR BASKET ON THIS TABLE.
BOY... YOU SURE SMELL GOOD!
JUST LIKE THE TREES WHERE THE BEEHIVES ARE.

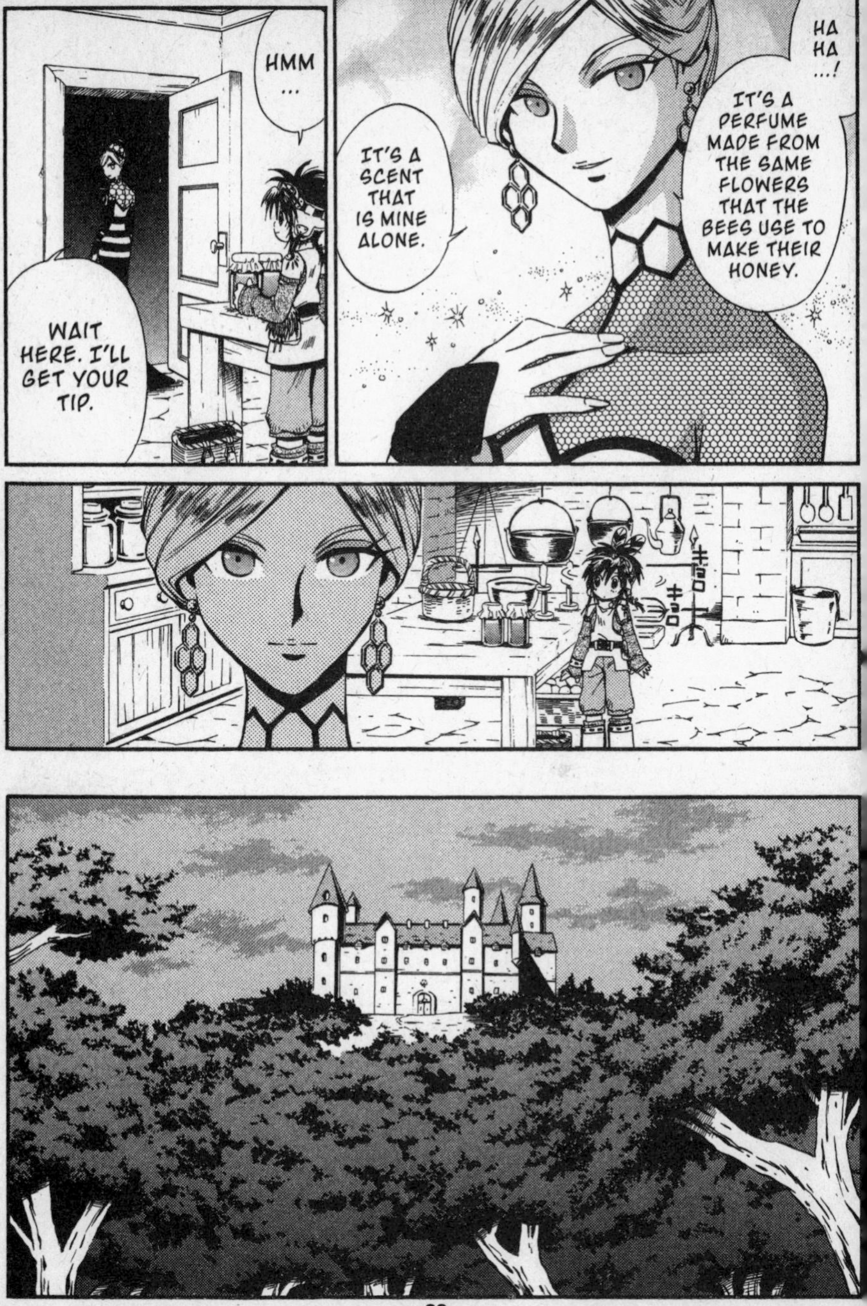
HA HA ...!
IT'S A PERFUME MADE FROM THE SAME FLOWERS THAT THE BEES USE TO MAKE THEIR HONEY.
IT'S A SCENT THAT IS MINE ALONE.
HMM ...
WAIT HERE. I'LL GET YOUR TIP.
キョロ キョロ

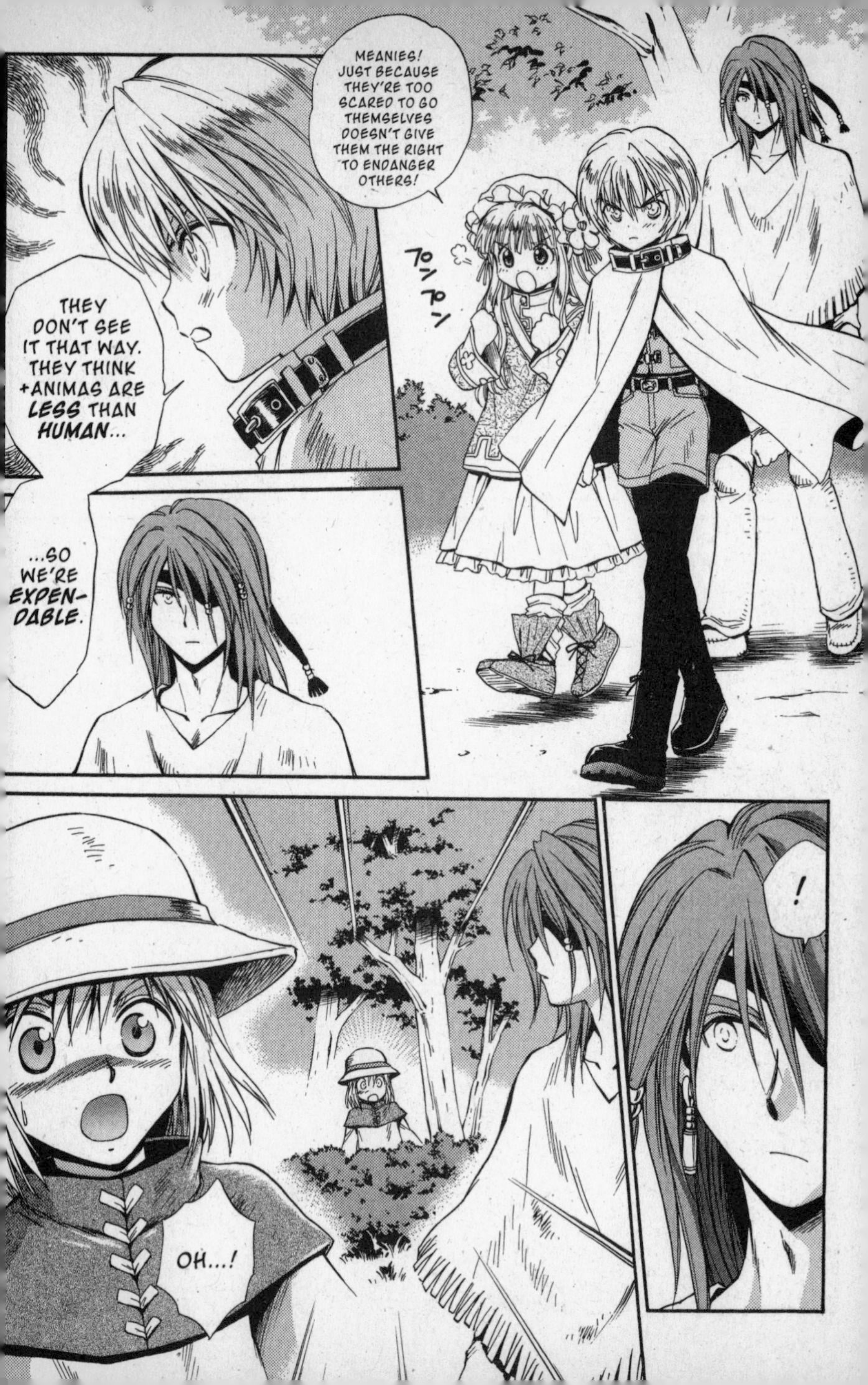
MEANIES! JUST BECAUSE THEY'RE TOO SCARED TO GO THEMSELVES DOESN'T GIVE THEM THE RIGHT TO ENDANGER OTHERS!
プンプン
THEY DON'T SEE IT THAT WAY. THEY THINK +ANIMAS ARE **LESS** THAN **HUMAN**...
...SO WE'RE **EXPENDABLE**.
!
OH...!

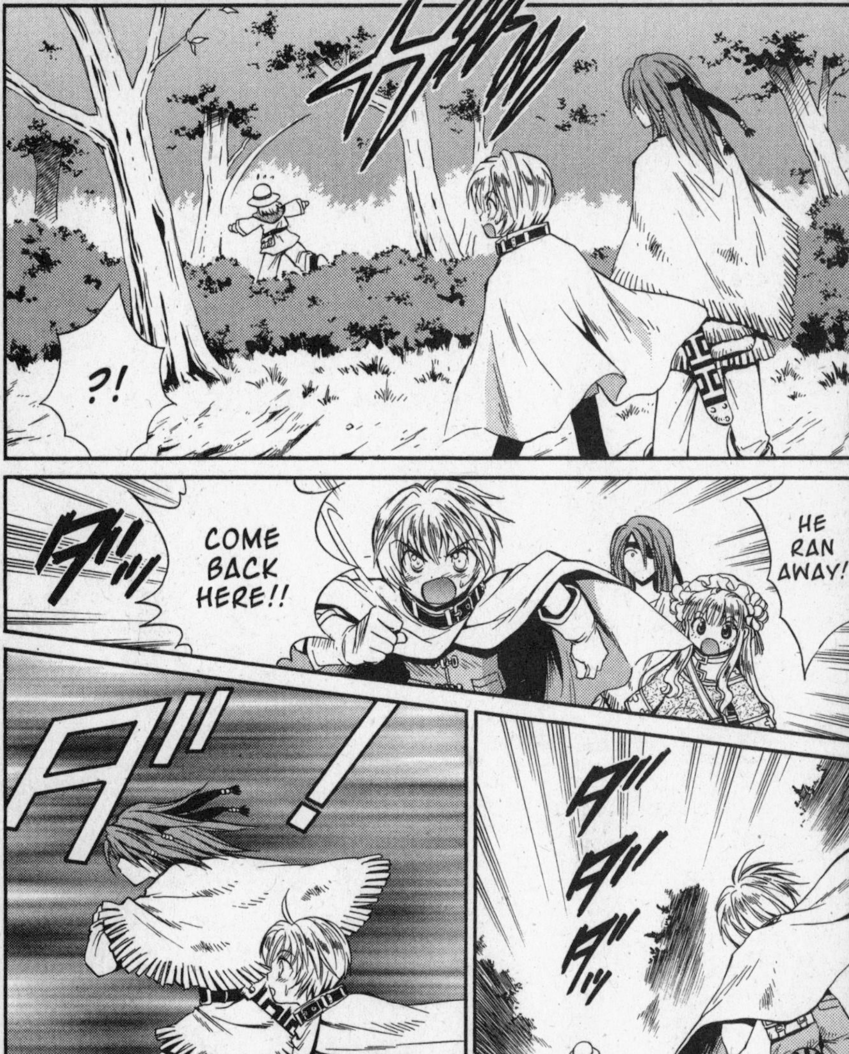
?!
HE RAN AWAY!
COME BACK HERE!!
!

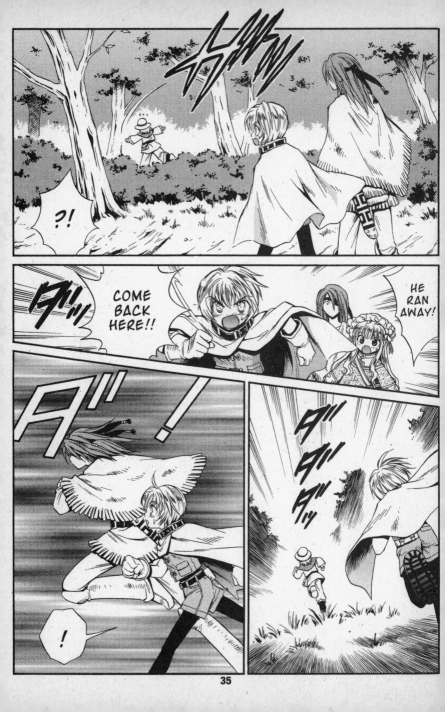

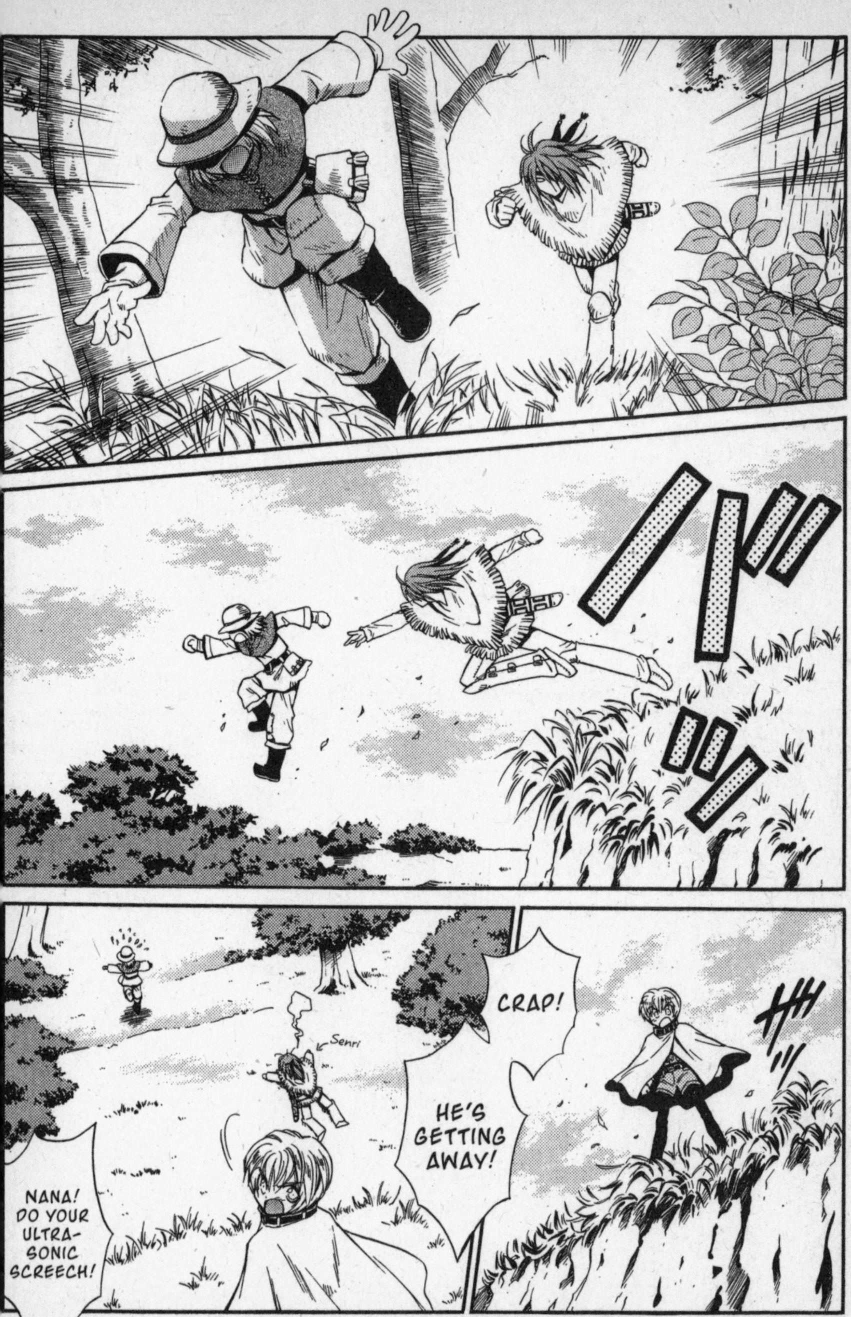
バッ
CRAP!
HE'S GETTING AWAY!
Senri
NANA! DO YOUR ULTRA-SONIC SCREECH!

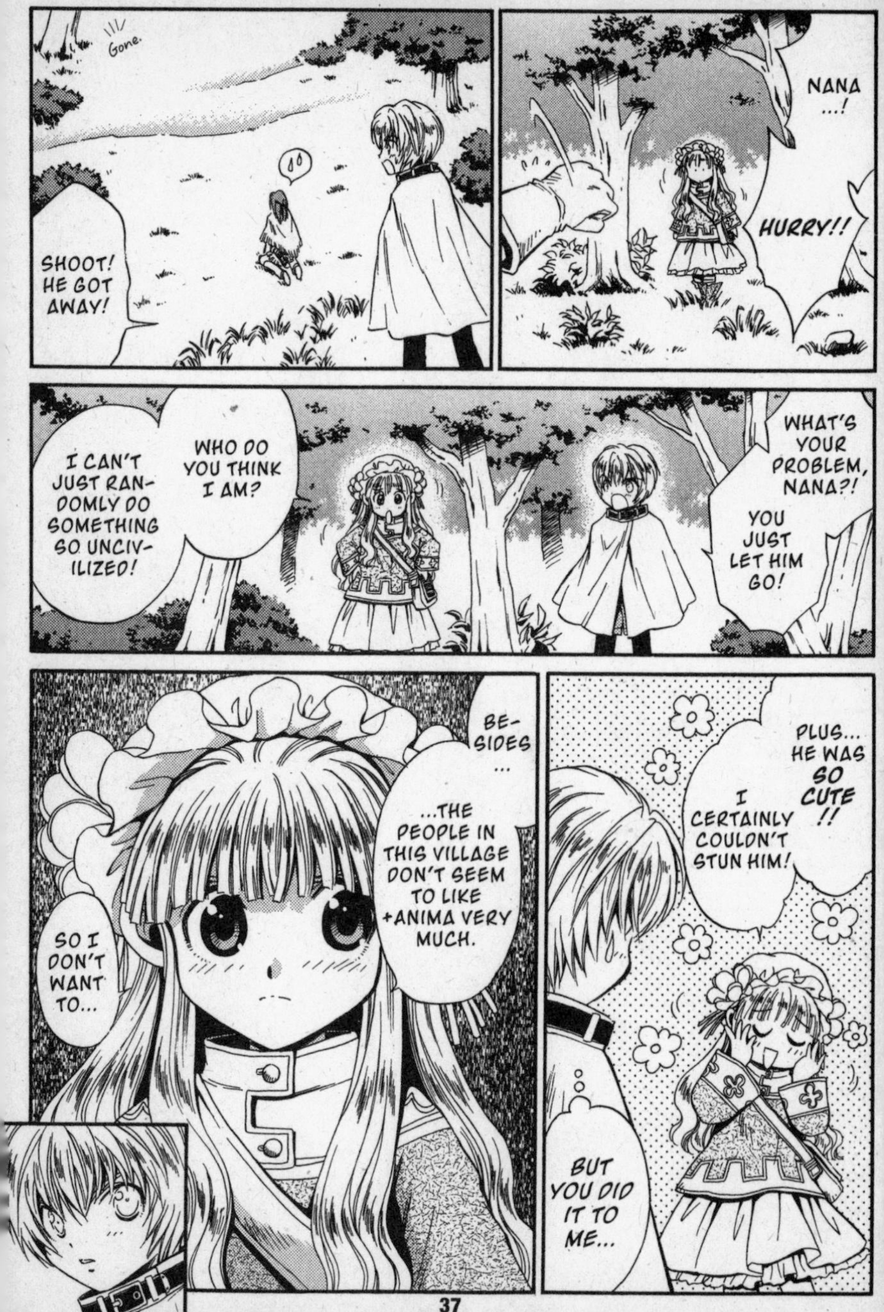
NANA ...!
HURRY!!
Gone.
SHOOT! HE GOT AWAY!
WHAT'S YOUR PROBLEM, NANA?!
YOU JUST LET HIM GO!
WHO DO YOU THINK I AM?
I CAN'T JUST RANDOMLY DO SOMETHING SO UNCIVILIZED!
PLUS... HE WAS SO CUTE!!
I CERTAINLY COULDN'T STUN HIM!
BUT YOU DID IT TO ME...
BESIDES...
...THE PEOPLE IN THIS VILLAGE DON'T SEEM TO LIKE +ANIMA VERY MUCH.
SO I DON'T WANT TO...

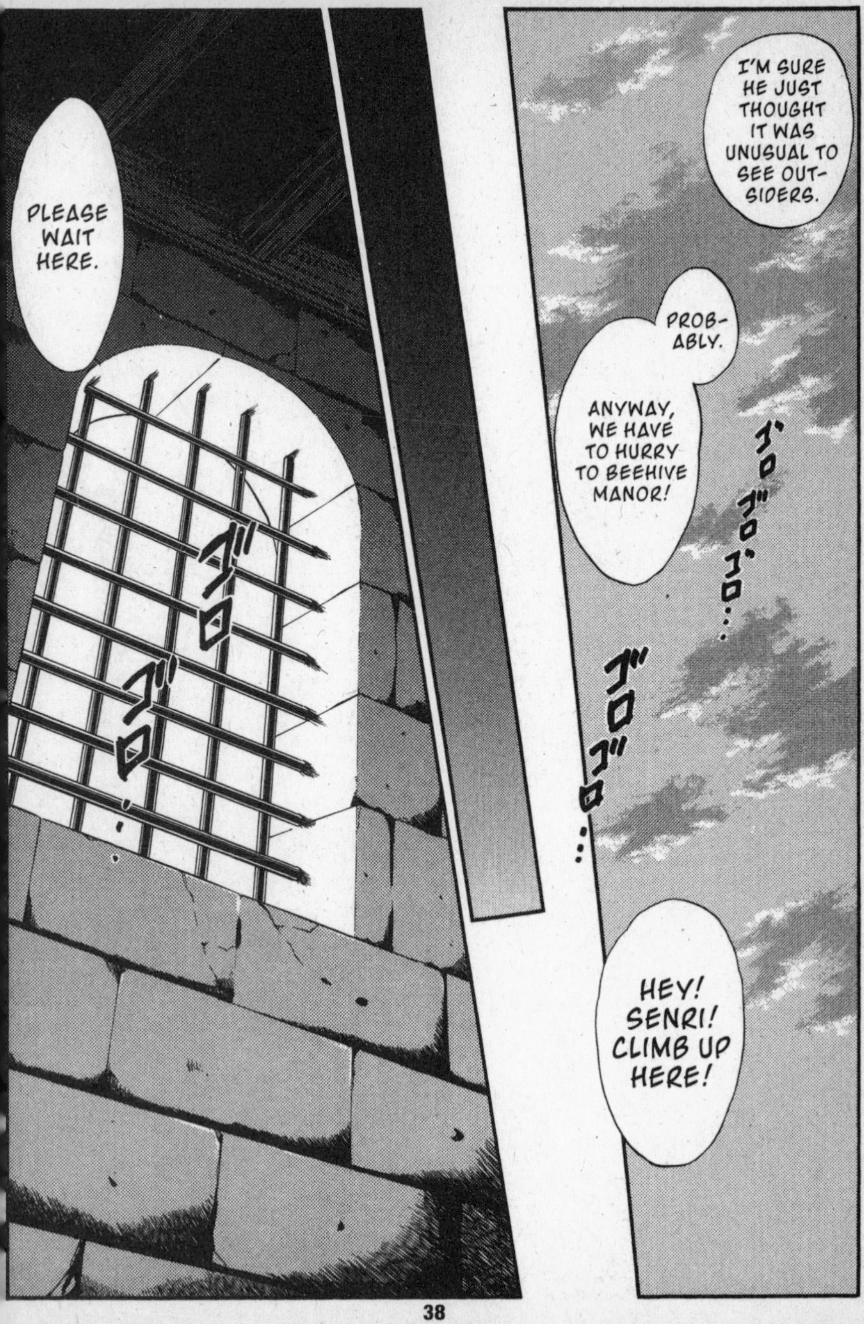
I'M SURE HE JUST THOUGHT IT WAS UNUSUAL TO SEE OUTSIDERS.
PROBABLY.
ANYWAY, WE HAVE TO HURRY TO BEEHIVE MANOR!
ゴロゴロ、ゴロ…
ゴロゴロ…
HEY! SENRI! CLIMB UP HERE!
PLEASE WAIT HERE.
ゴロゴロ!

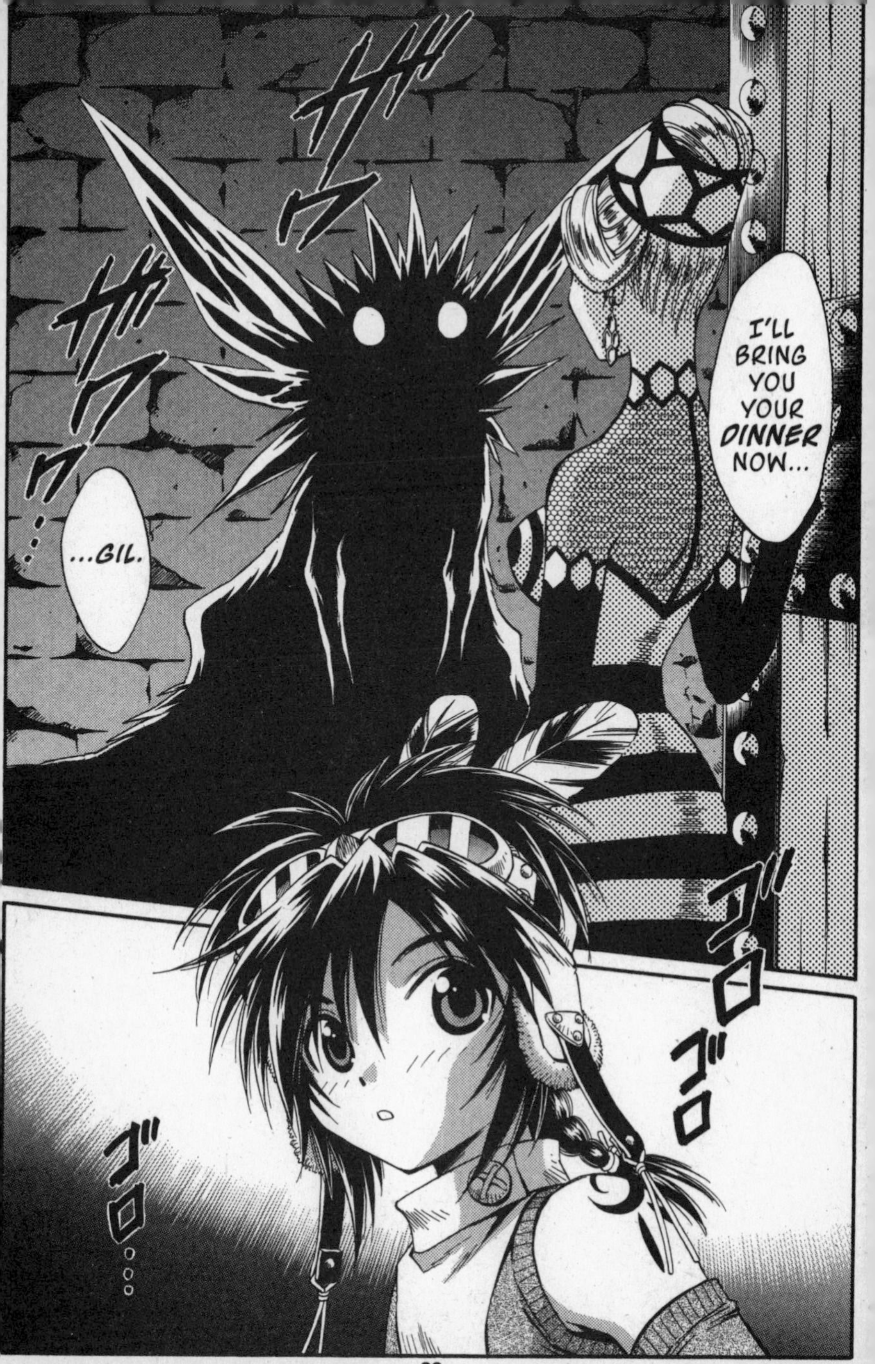
I'LL BRING YOU YOUR DINNER NOW...
...GIL.
ゴロ
ゴロ
ゴロ。。。

What's this?

Chapter 7
The Secret of Beehive Manor—Part 2

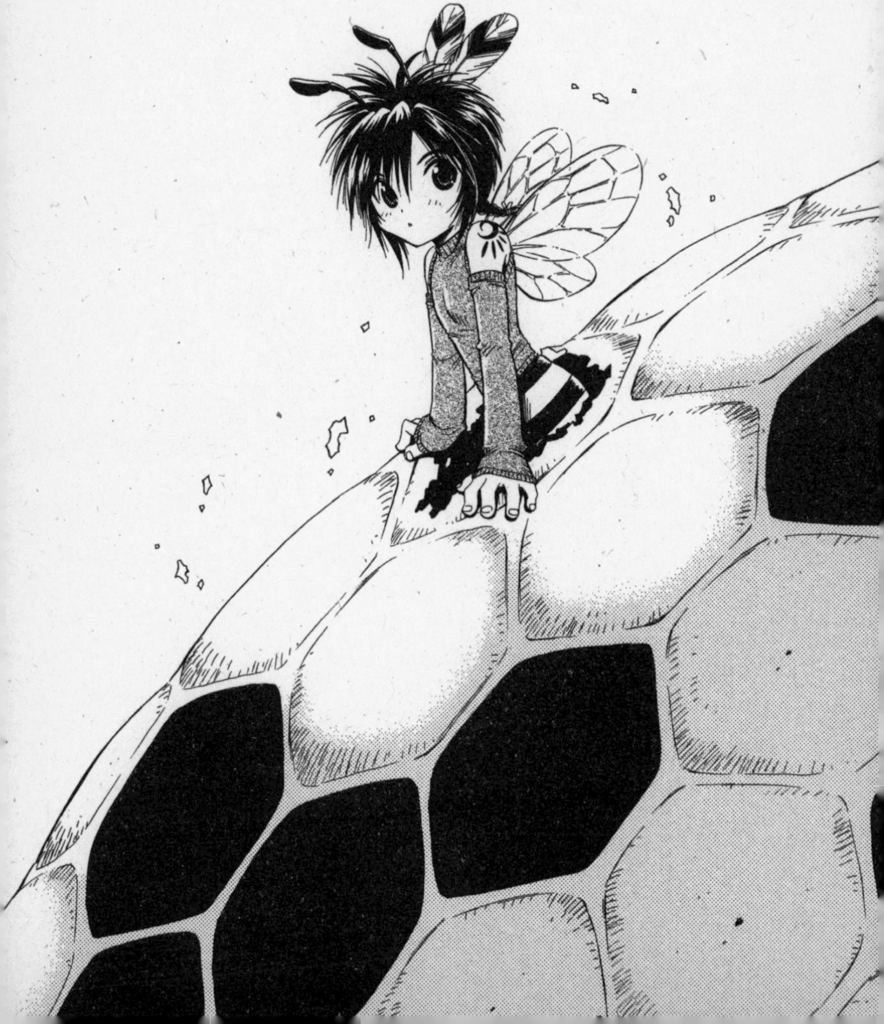

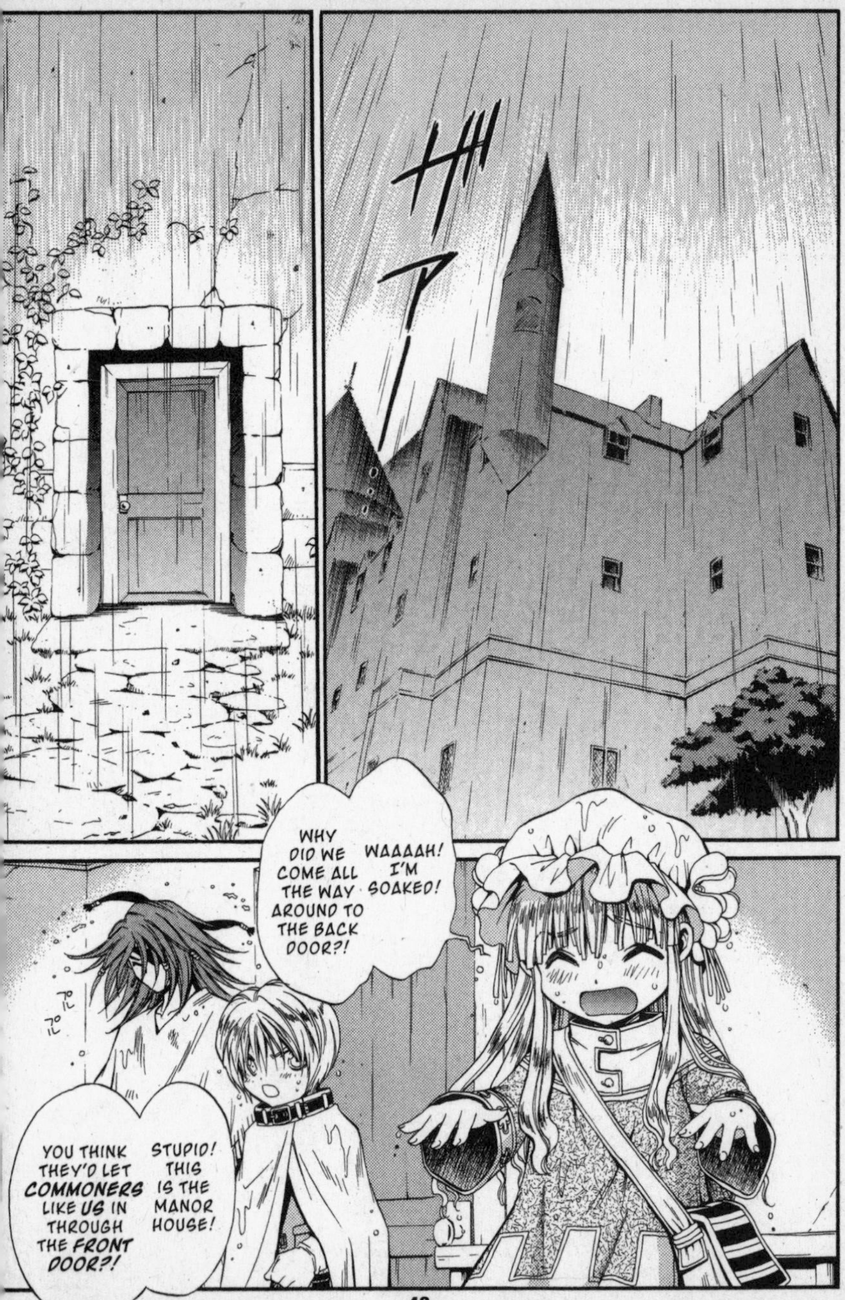
ザアー
WAAAAH! I'M SOAKED!
WHY DID WE COME ALL THE WAY AROUND TO THE BACK DOOR?!
STUPID! THIS IS THE MANOR HOUSE!
YOU THINK THEY'D LET COMMONERS LIKE US IN THROUGH THE FRONT DOOR?!
プルプル

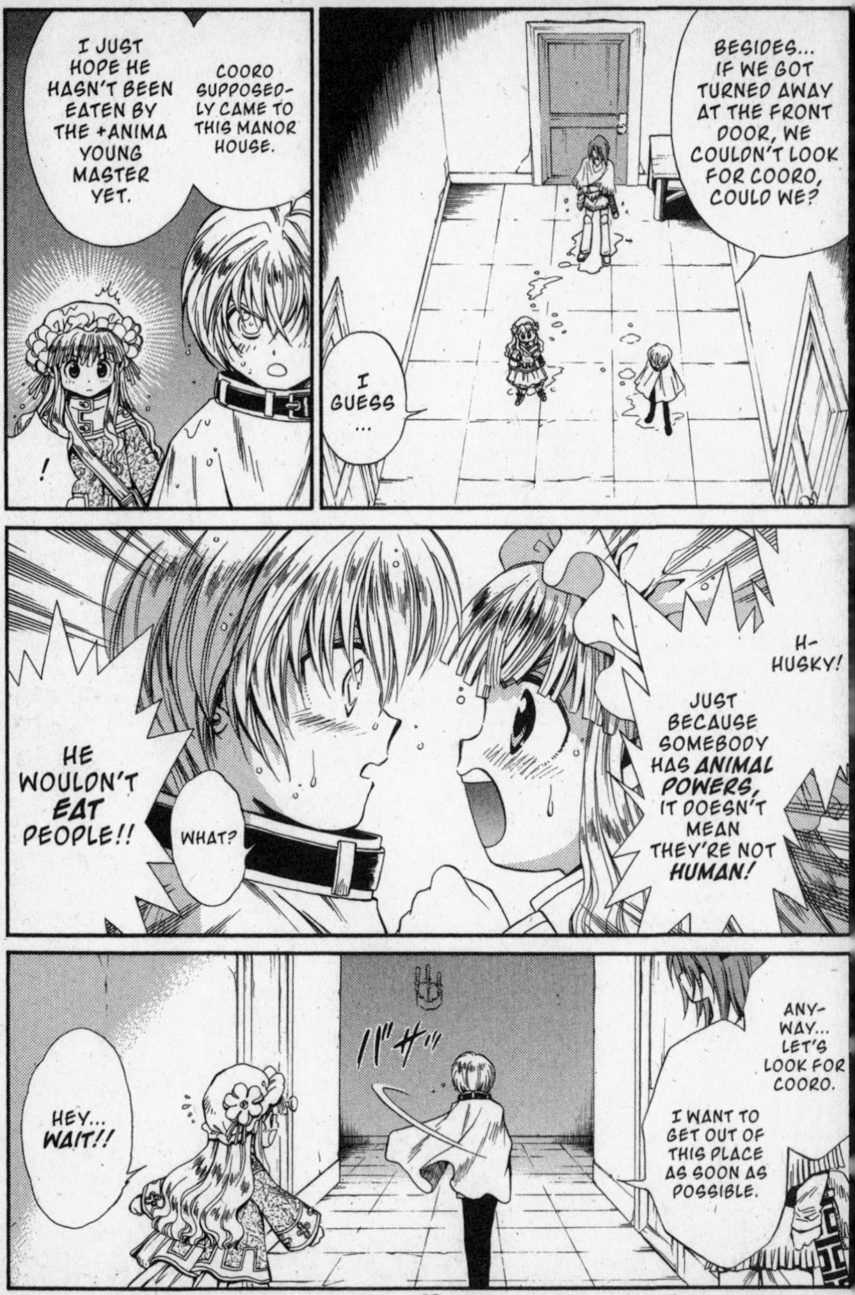
BESIDES... IF WE GOT TURNED AWAY AT THE FRONT DOOR, WE COULDN'T LOOK FOR COORO, COULD WE?
I GUESS ...
COORO SUPPOSED-LY CAME TO THIS MANOR HOUSE.
I JUST HOPE HE HASN'T BEEN EATEN BY THE +ANIMA YOUNG MASTER YET.
!
H-HUSKY!
JUST BECAUSE SOMEBODY HAS ANIMAL POWERS, IT DOESN'T MEAN THEY'RE NOT HUMAN!
WHAT?
HE WOULDN'T EAT PEOPLE!!
ANY-WAY... LET'S LOOK FOR COORO.
I WANT TO GET OUT OF THIS PLACE AS SOON AS POSSIBLE.
バサッ
HEY... WAIT!!

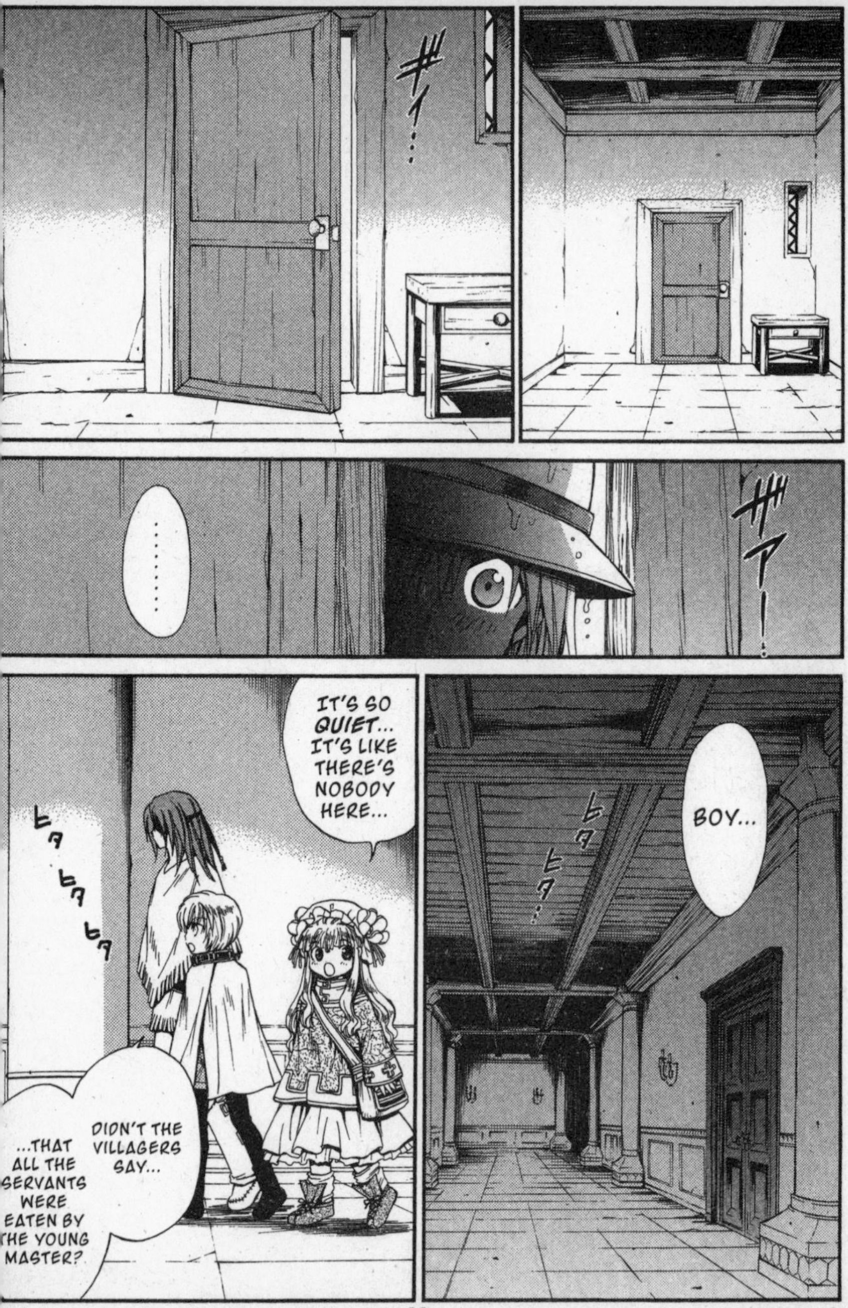
ギィ…
ザァー…!
……
BOY...
ヒタ ヒタ…
IT'S SO QUIET... IT'S LIKE THERE'S NOBODY HERE...
ヒタ ヒタ ヒタ
DIDN'T THE VILLAGERS SAY...
...THAT ALL THE SERVANTS WERE EATEN BY THE YOUNG MASTER?

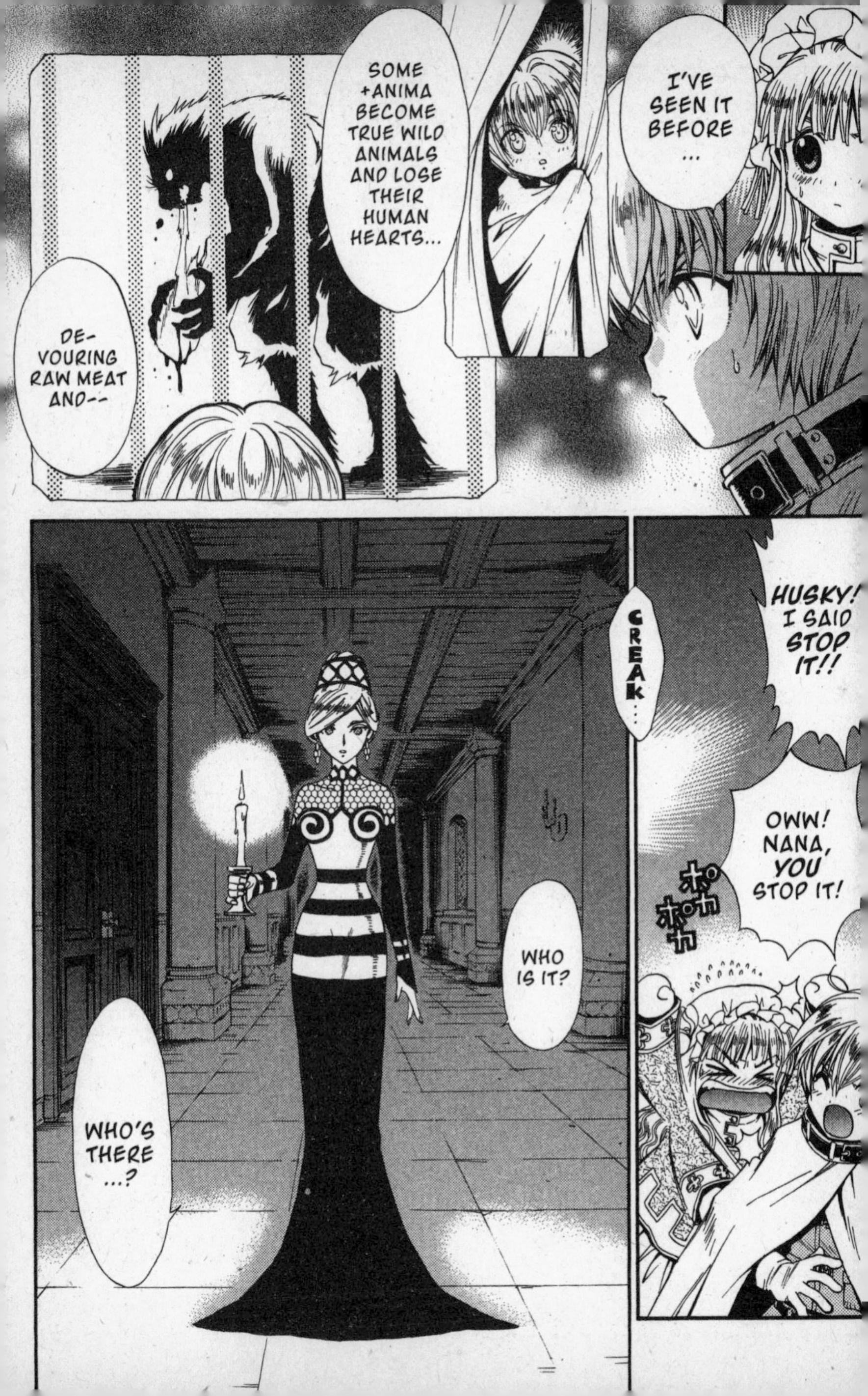
I'VE SEEN IT BEFORE ...
SOME +ANIMA BECOME TRUE WILD ANIMALS AND LOSE THEIR HUMAN HEARTS...
DE-VOURING RAW MEAT AND--
HUSKY! I SAID STOP IT!!
OWW! NANA, YOU STOP IT!
ポカ
ポカ
CREAK...
WHO IS IT?
WHO'S THERE ...?

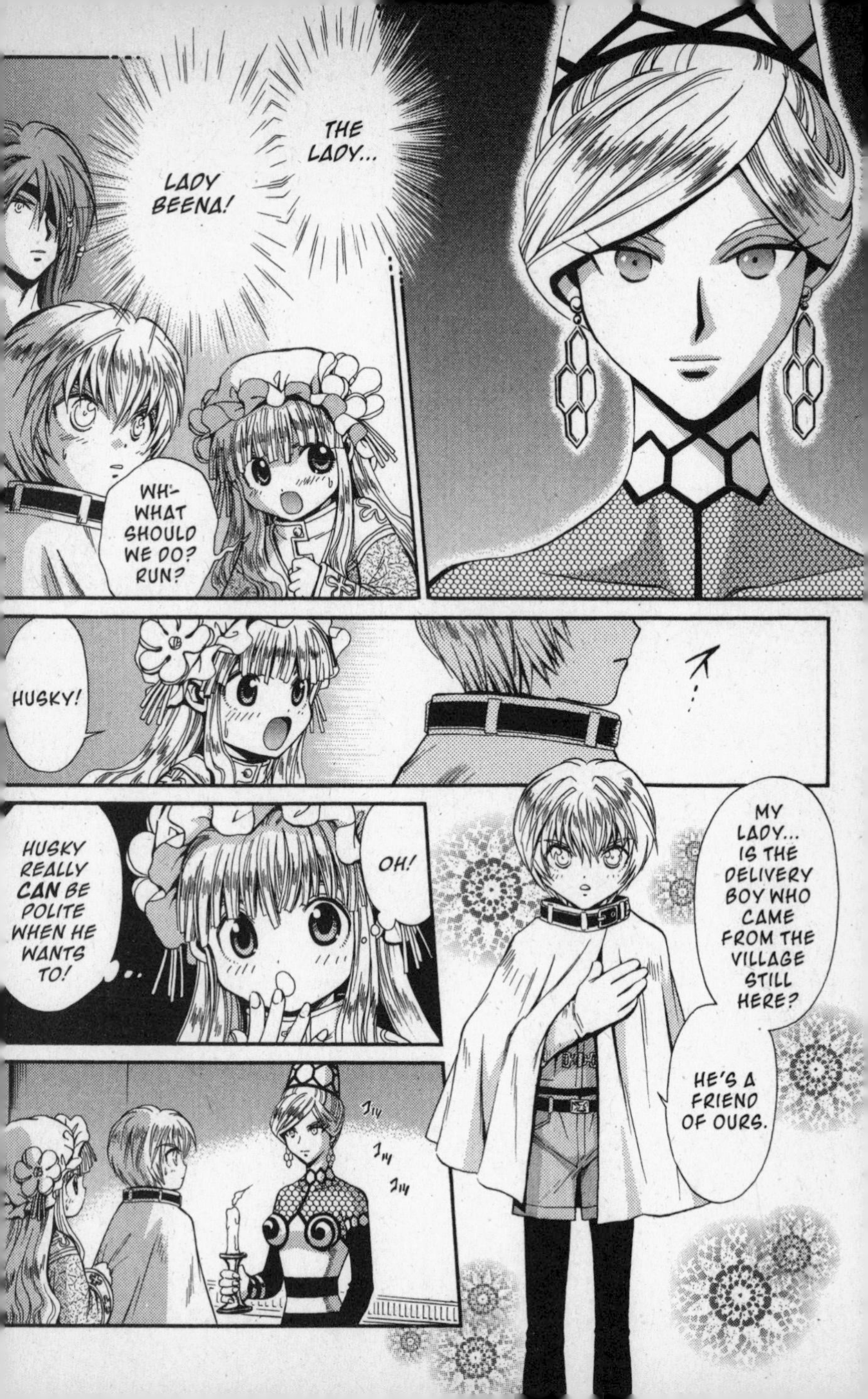
THE LADY...
LADY BEENA!
WH- WHAT SHOULD WE DO? RUN?
HUSKY!
MY LADY... IS THE DELIVERY BOY WHO CAME FROM THE VILLAGE STILL HERE?
HE'S A FRIEND OF OURS.
OH!
HUSKY REALLY CAN BE POLITE WHEN HE WANTS TO!

I SEE...

THEN PLEASE WAIT HERE IN THIS ROOM.

I'LL BE WITH YOU AFTER I'VE TAKEN CARE OF SOME... BUSINESS.

YOU AND THAT OTHER BOY... YOU'RE NOT FROM BEENA VILLAGE, ARE YOU?

BUT WE'RE LEAVING SOON, SO WE CAME TO GET HIM.

HE WAS ASKED TO MAKE A DELIVERY AS WE WERE PASSING THROUGH.

?!

OPEN UP!

WHAT ARE YOU GOING TO DO TO COORO?!

IT'S LOCKED!

47

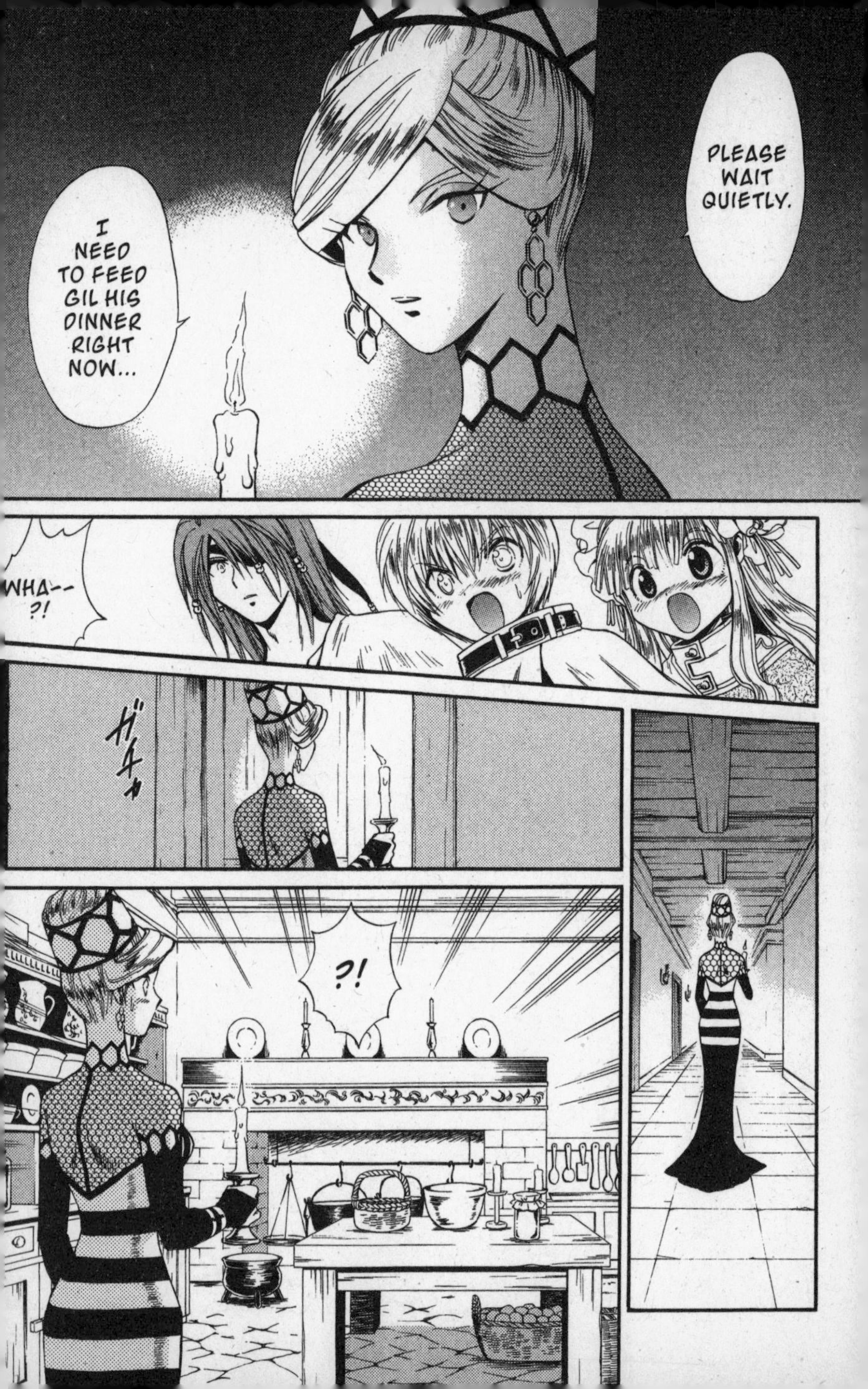
PLEASE WAIT QUIETLY.
I NEED TO FEED GIL HIS DINNER RIGHT NOW...
WHA-- ?!
ガチャ
?!

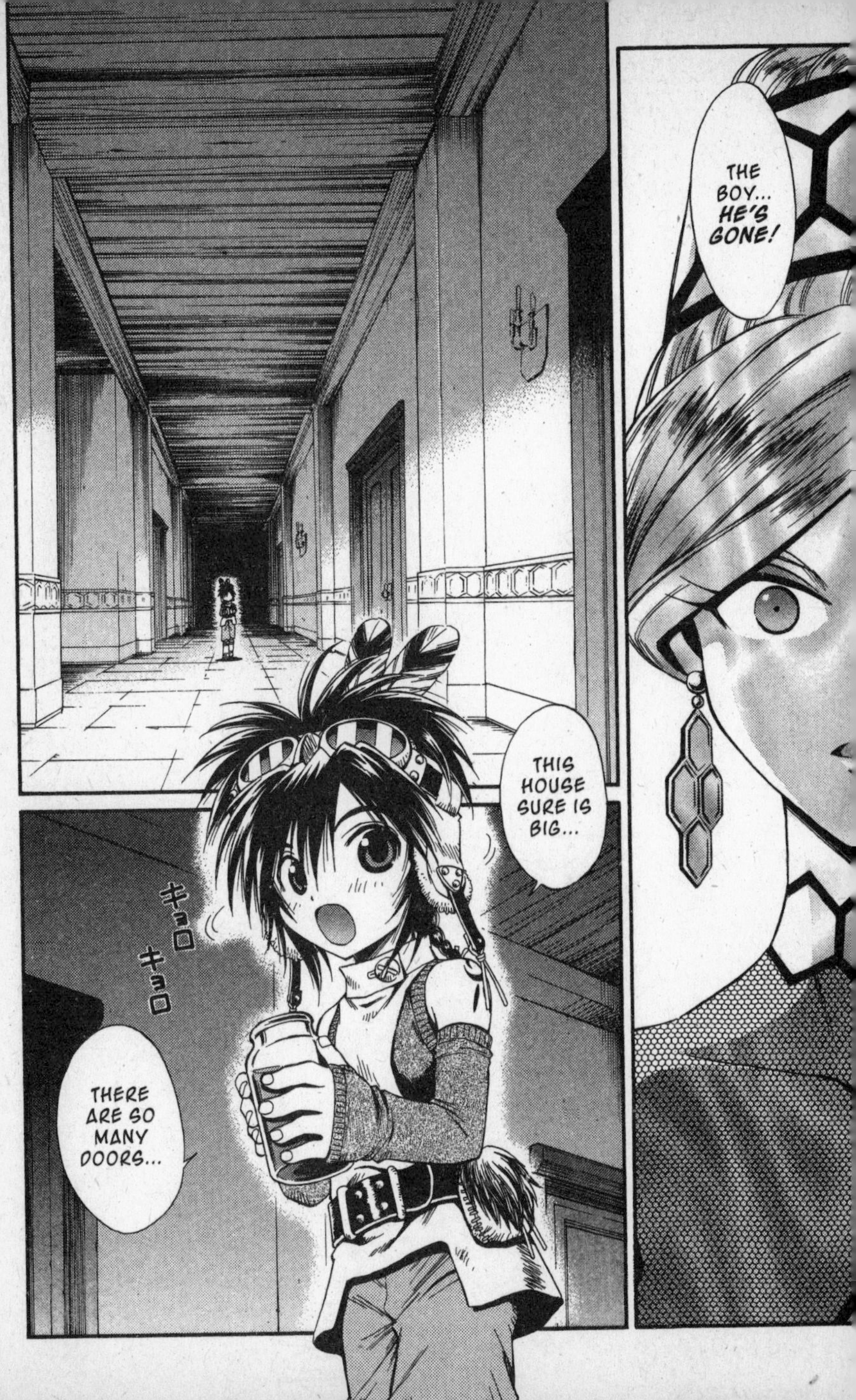
THE BOY... HE'S GONE!
THIS HOUSE SURE IS BIG...
キョロ キョロ
THERE ARE SO MANY DOORS...

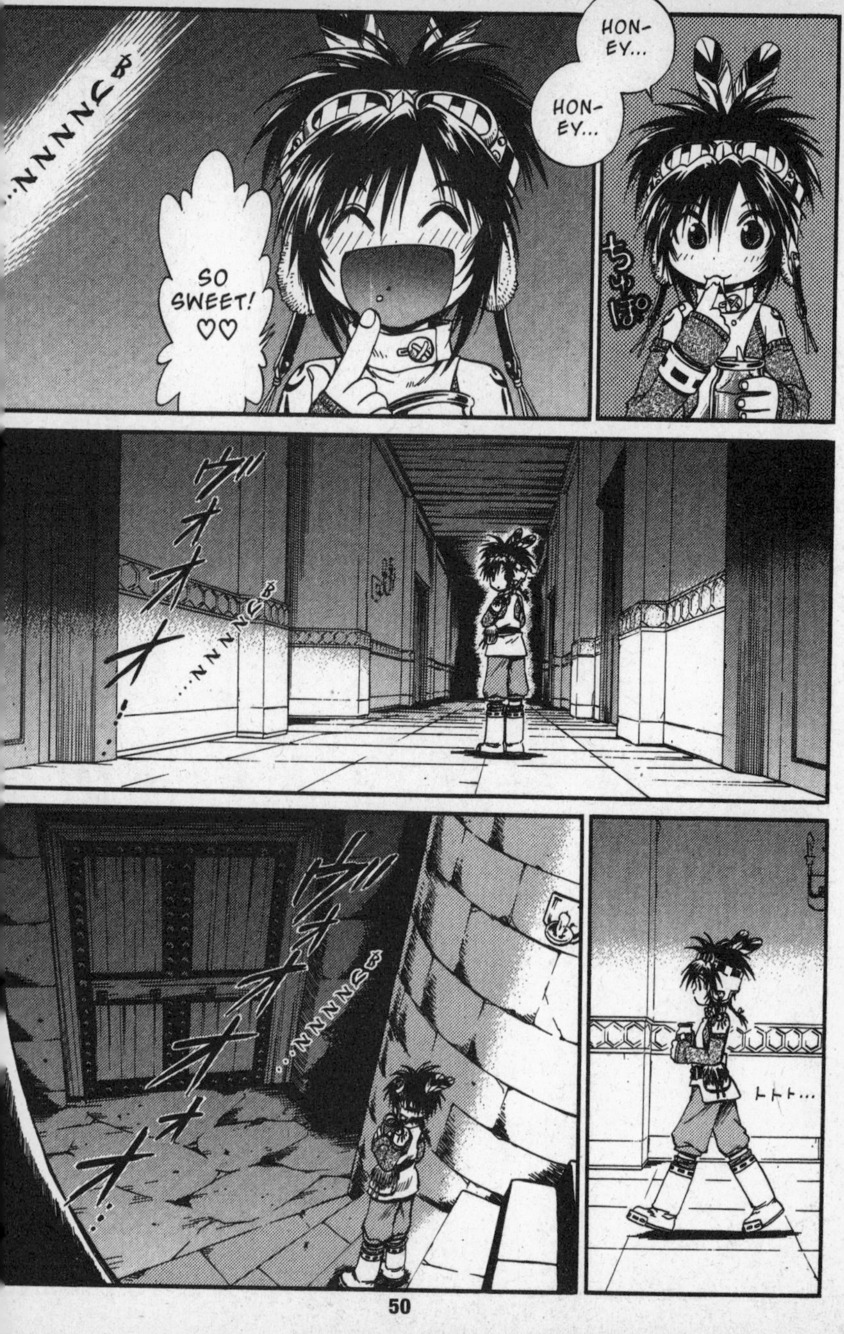
HON-EY...
HON-EY...
ちゅぽ
...NNNNGB
SO SWEET! ♡♡
ヴォオオオ…!!
...NNNNGB
トトト...
ヴォオオオオオ…
...NNNNGB

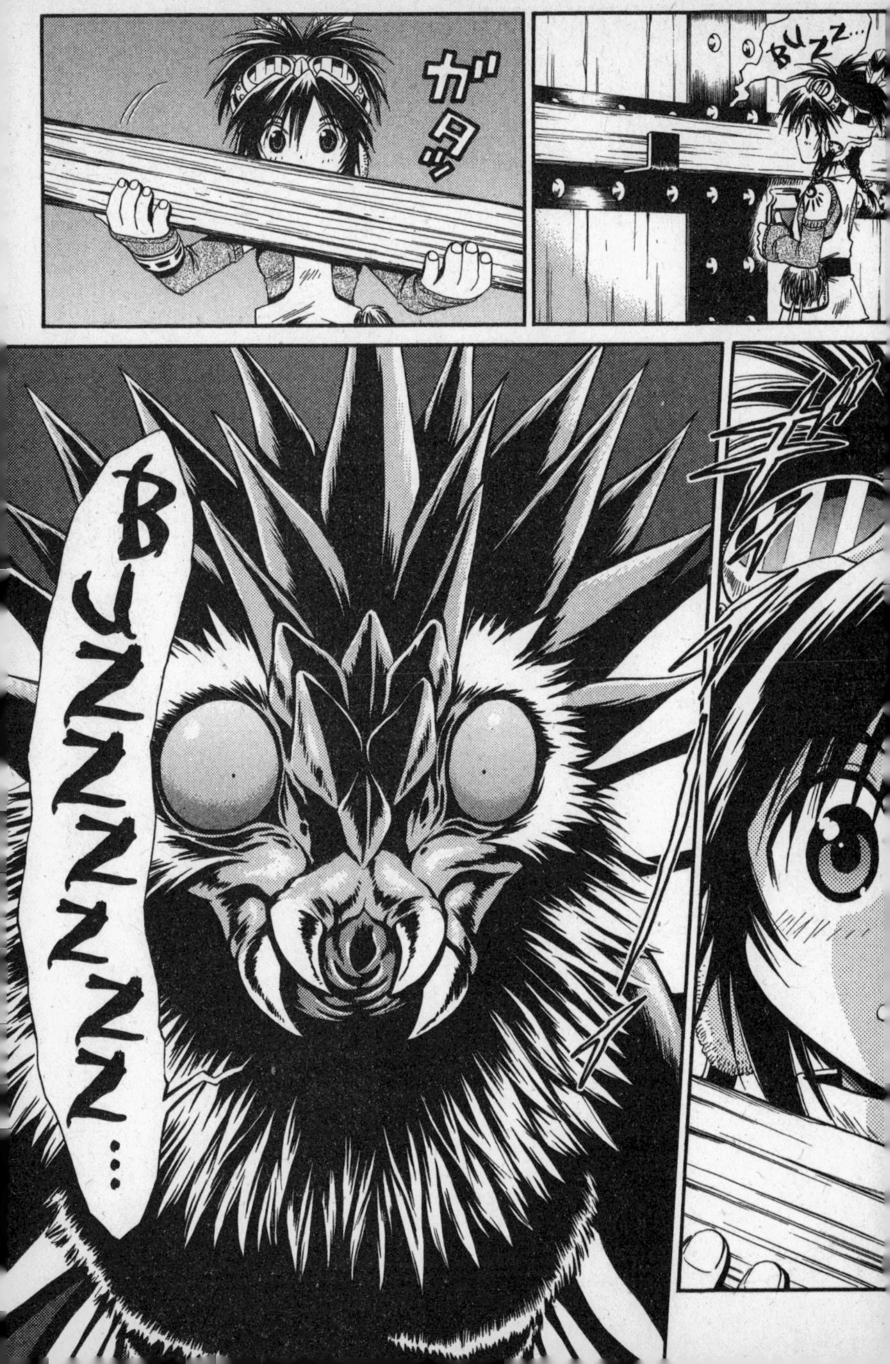
BUZZ...
ガタッ
BUZZZZZZ...

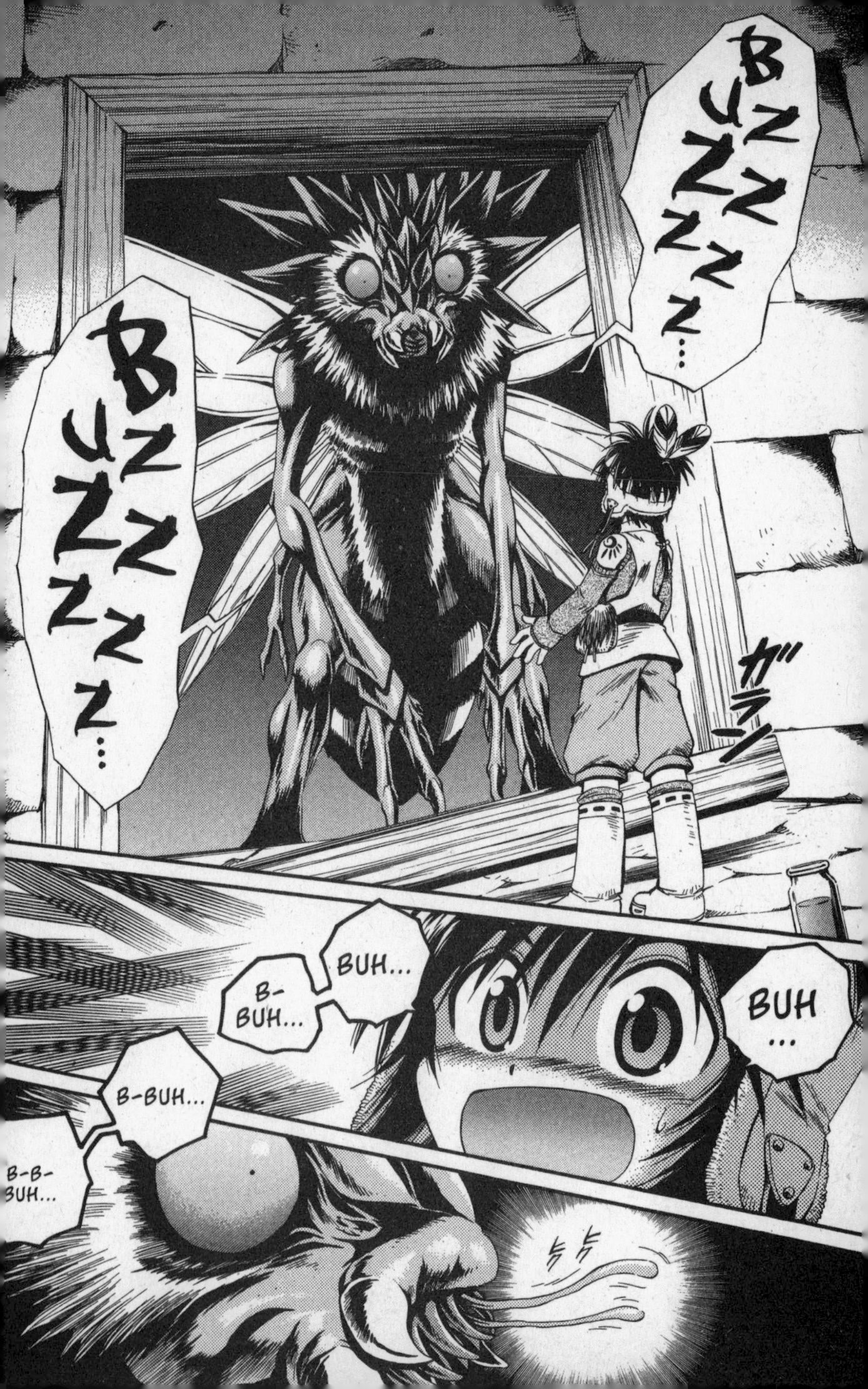
BUZZZZZZZ...
BUZZZZZZZ...
ガラン
BUH ...
BUH...
B-BUH...
B-BUH...
B-B-BUH...

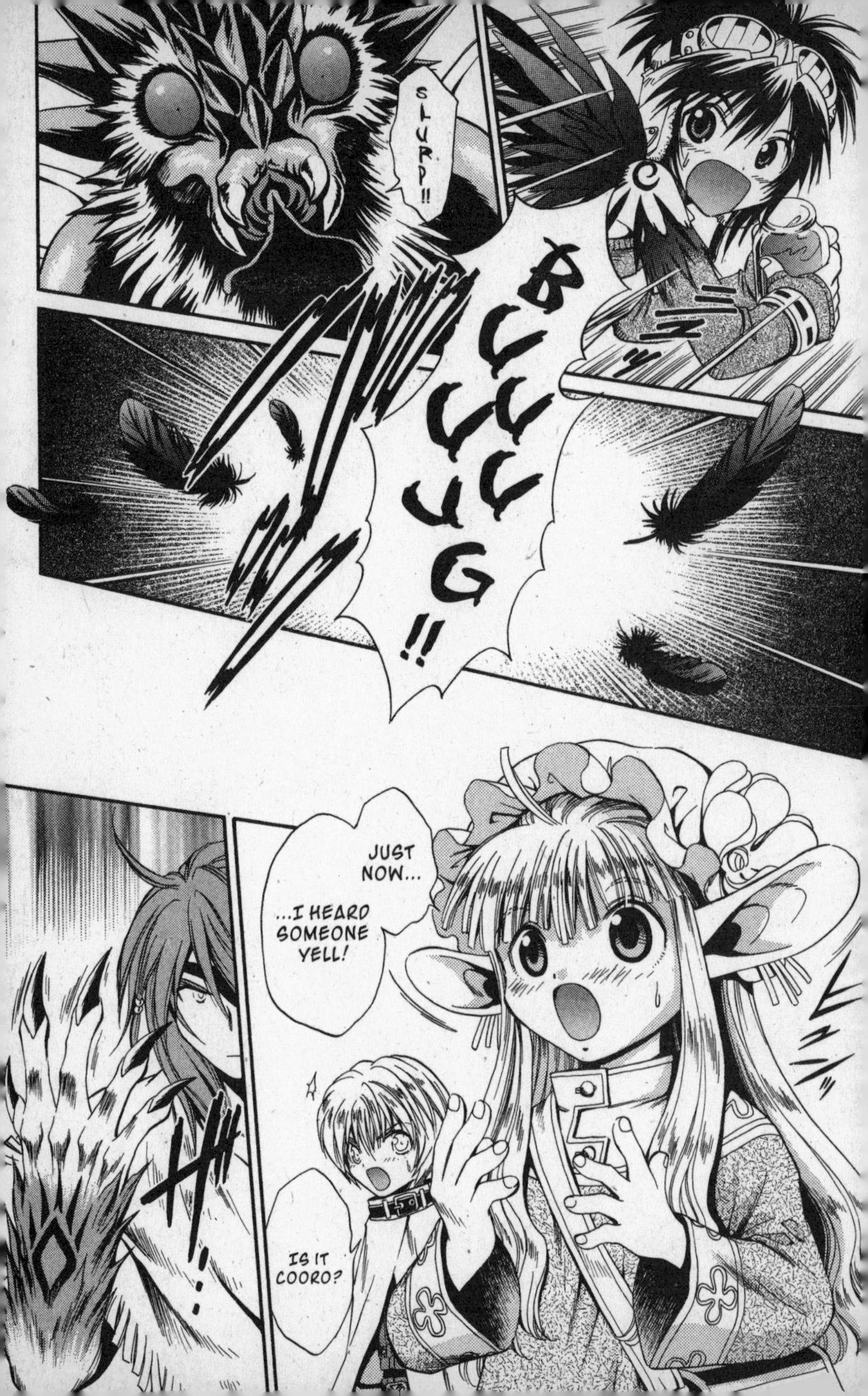
SLURP!!
BUUUUUUG!!
JUST NOW...
...I HEARD SOMEONE YELL!
IS IT COORO?

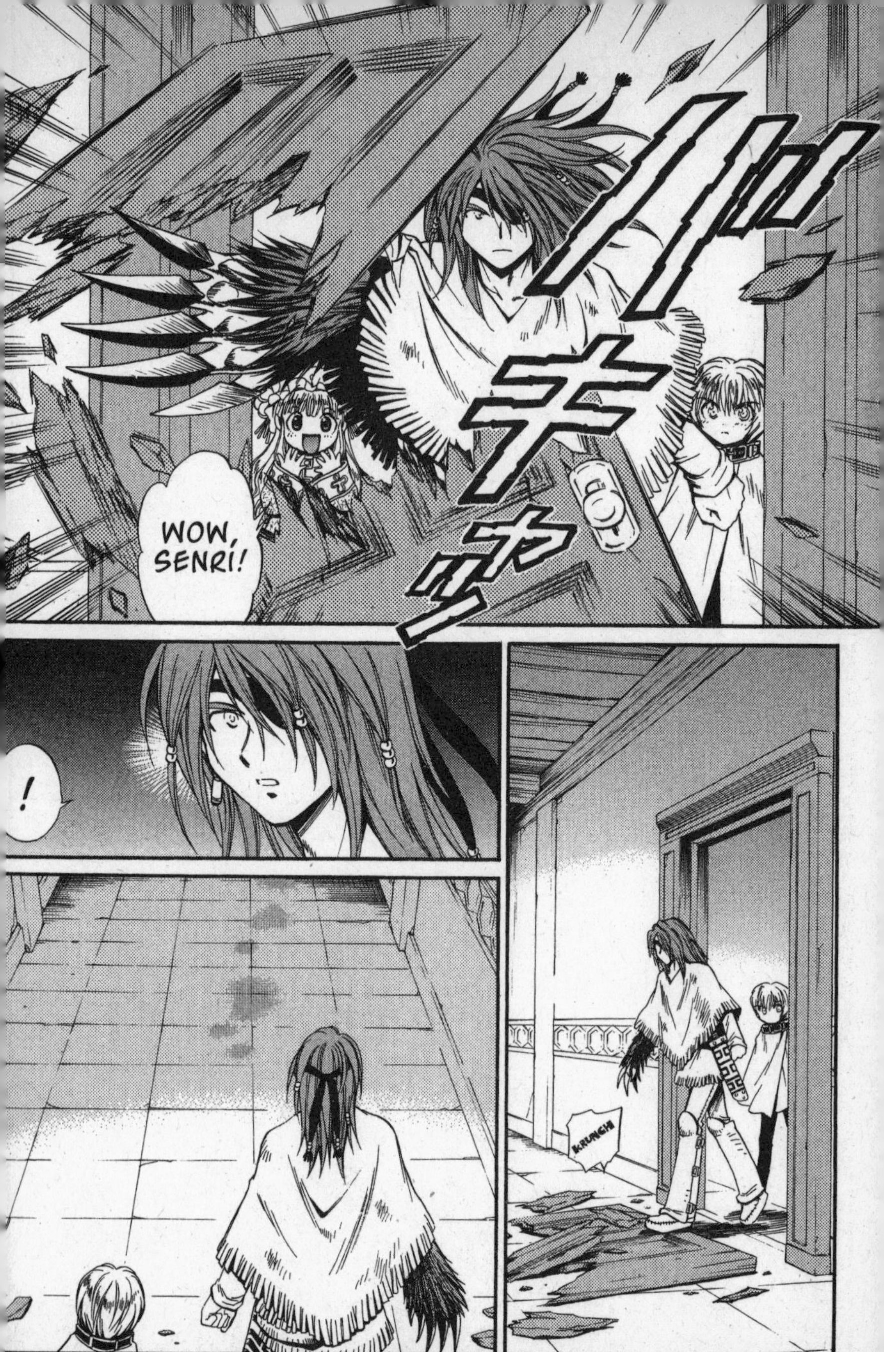
バキャッ
WOW, SENRI!
KRUNCH
!

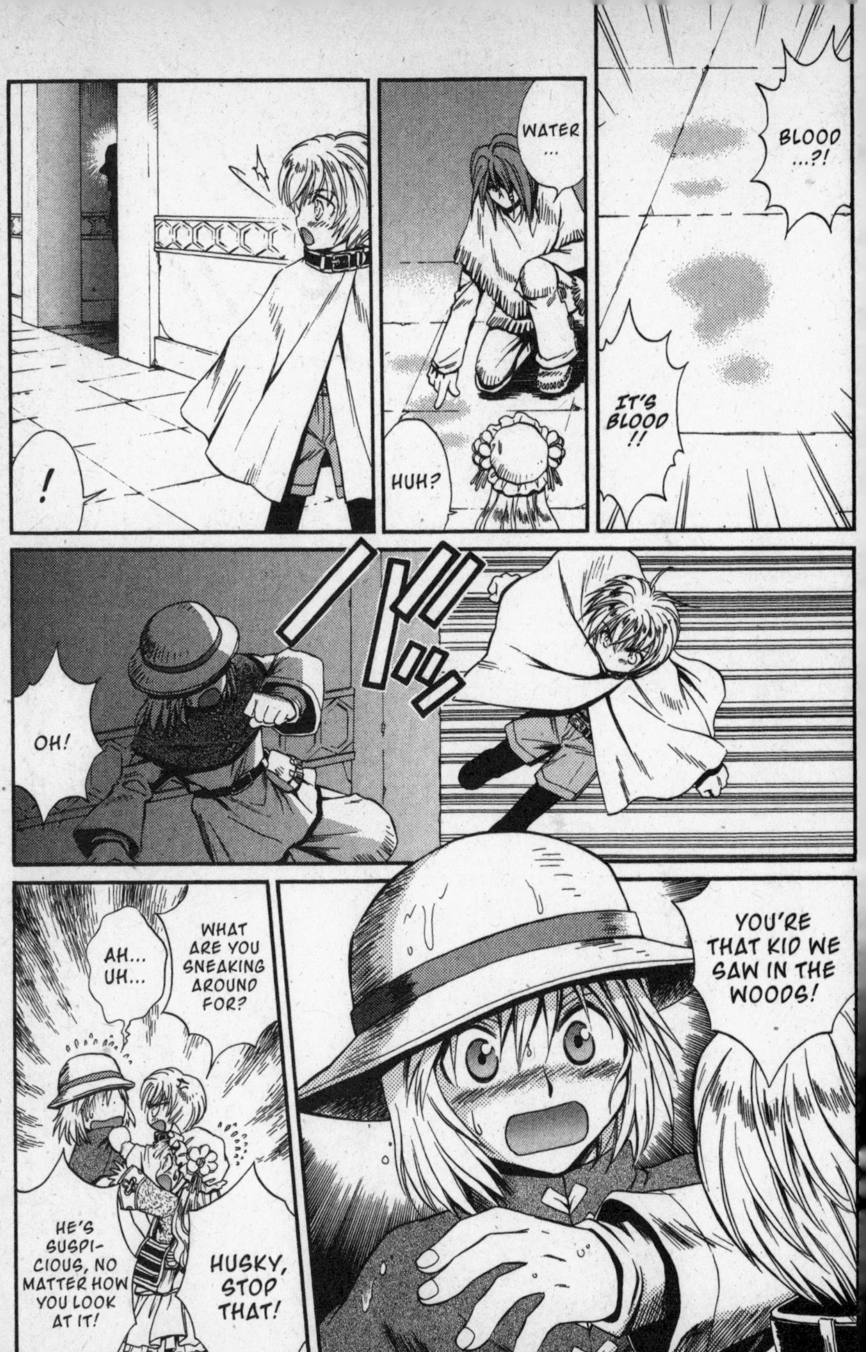
BLOOD ...?!
IT'S BLOOD !!
WATER ...
HUH?
!
OH!
YOU'RE THAT KID WE SAW IN THE WOODS!
WHAT ARE YOU SNEAKING AROUND FOR?
AH... UH...
HUSKY, STOP THAT!
HE'S SUSPI- CIOUS, NO MATTER HOW YOU LOOK AT IT!

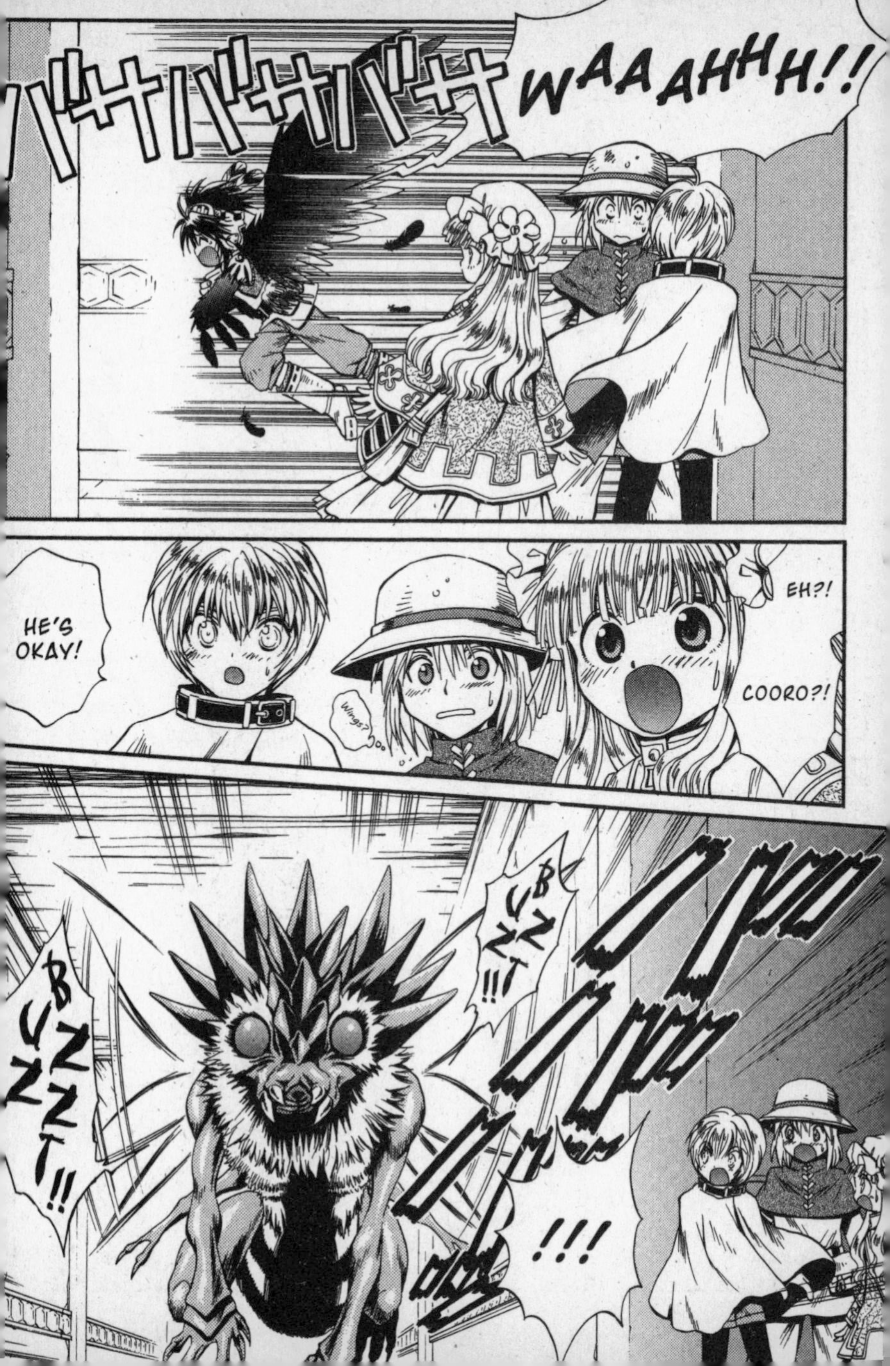

WAAAHHHH!!
EH?!
COORO?!
Wings?
HE'S OKAY!
BUZZT!!!
!!!
BUZZZT!!

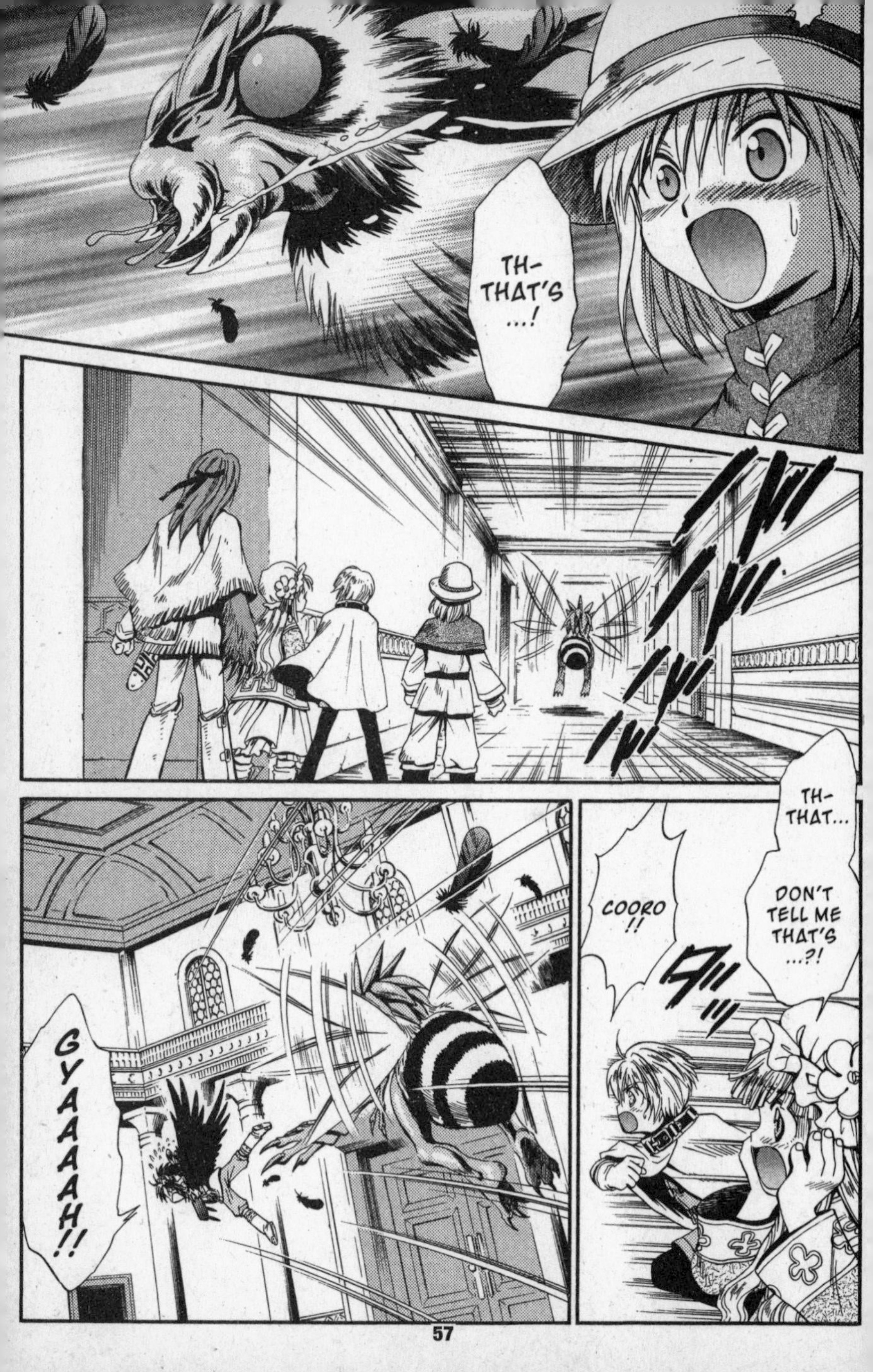
TH-
THAT'S
...!
TH-
THAT...
DON'T
TELL ME
THAT'S
...?!
COORO
!!
GYAAAAH!!

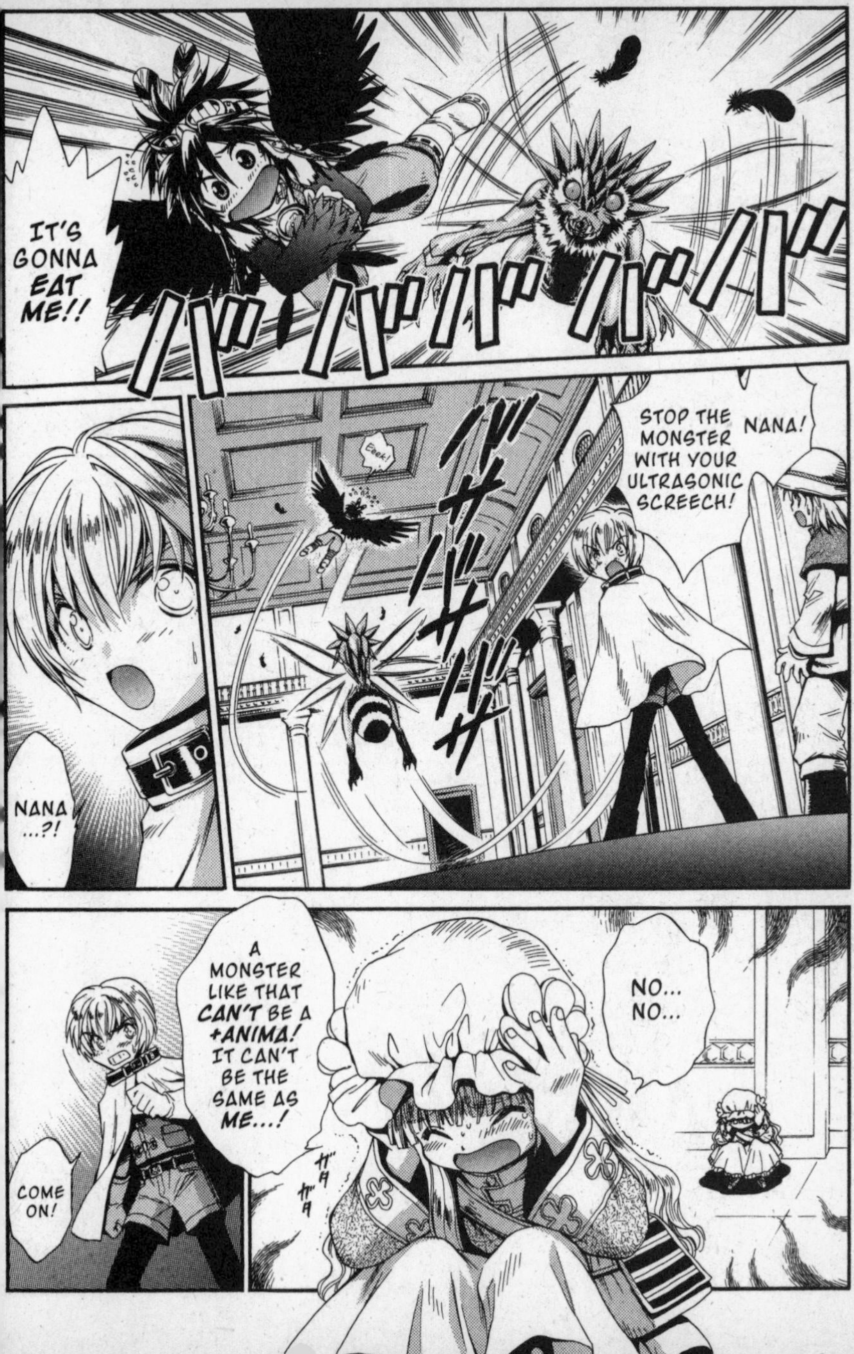
IT'S GONNA EAT ME!!
NANA!
STOP THE MONSTER WITH YOUR ULTRASONIC SCREECH!
Eeek!
NANA ...?!
NO... NO...
A MONSTER LIKE THAT CAN'T BE A +ANIMA! IT CAN'T BE THE SAME AS ME...!
ガタ ガタ
COME ON!

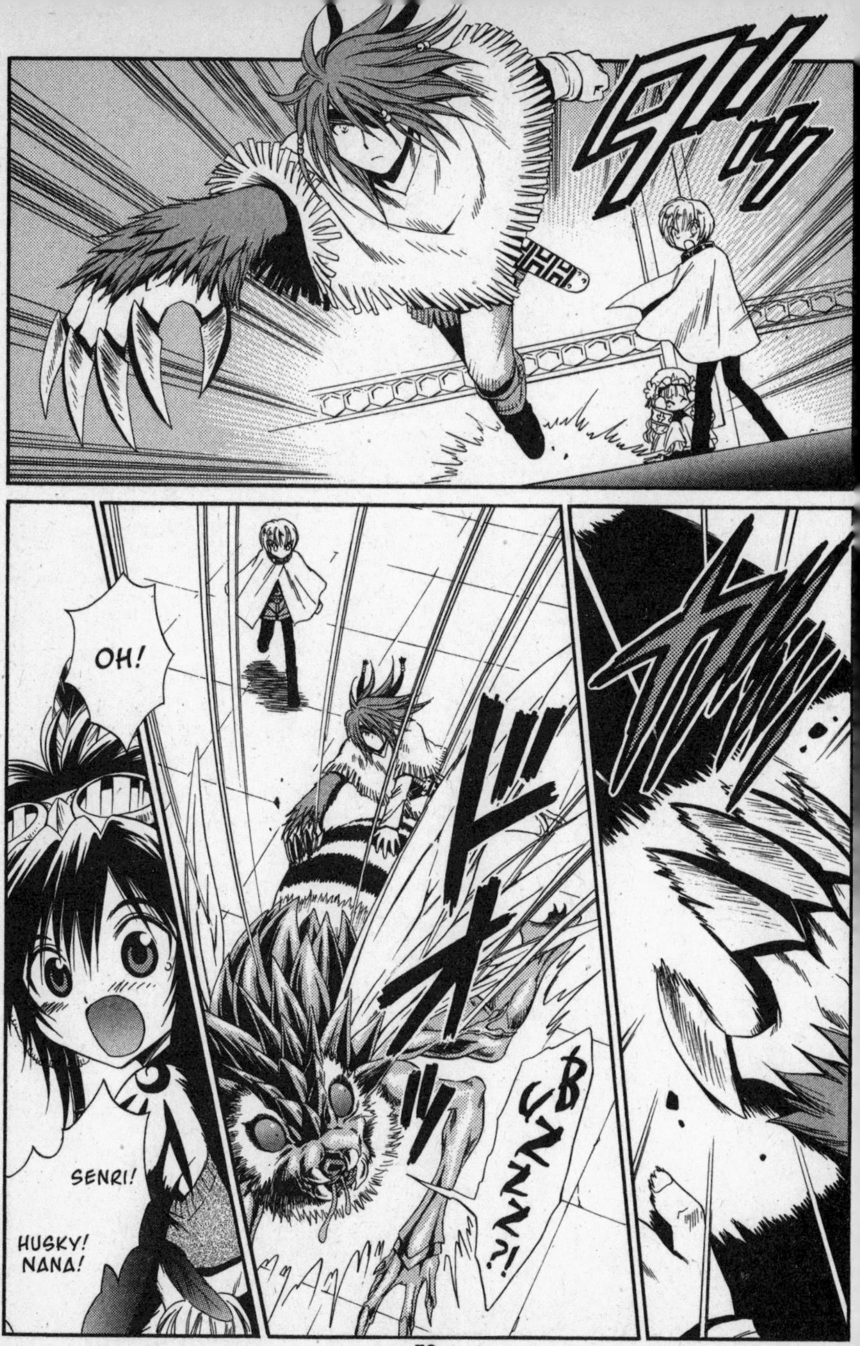
BUZZZZ?!
OH!
SENRI!
HUSKY! NANA!

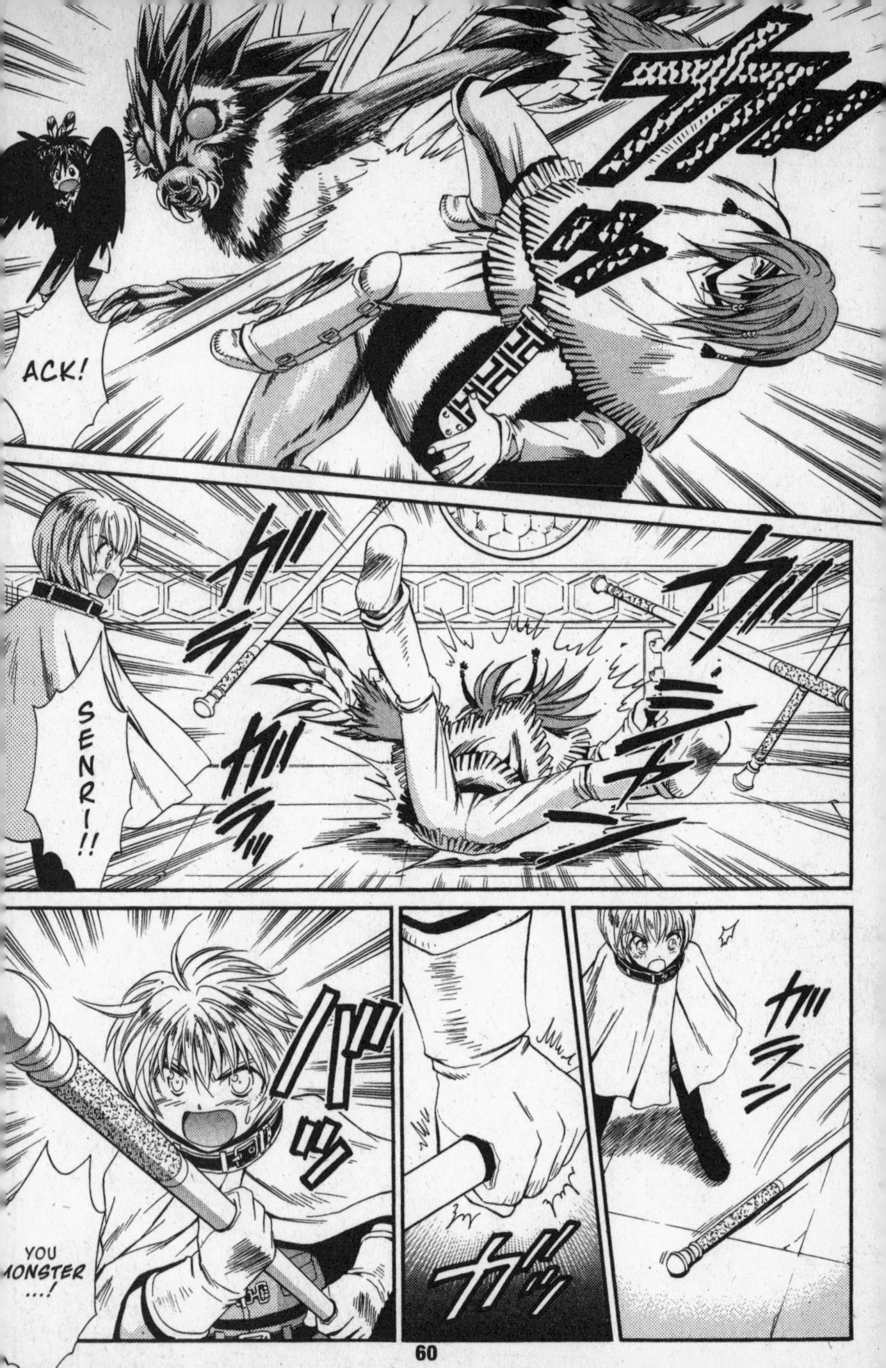

ACK!
SENRI!!
YOU MONSTER...!

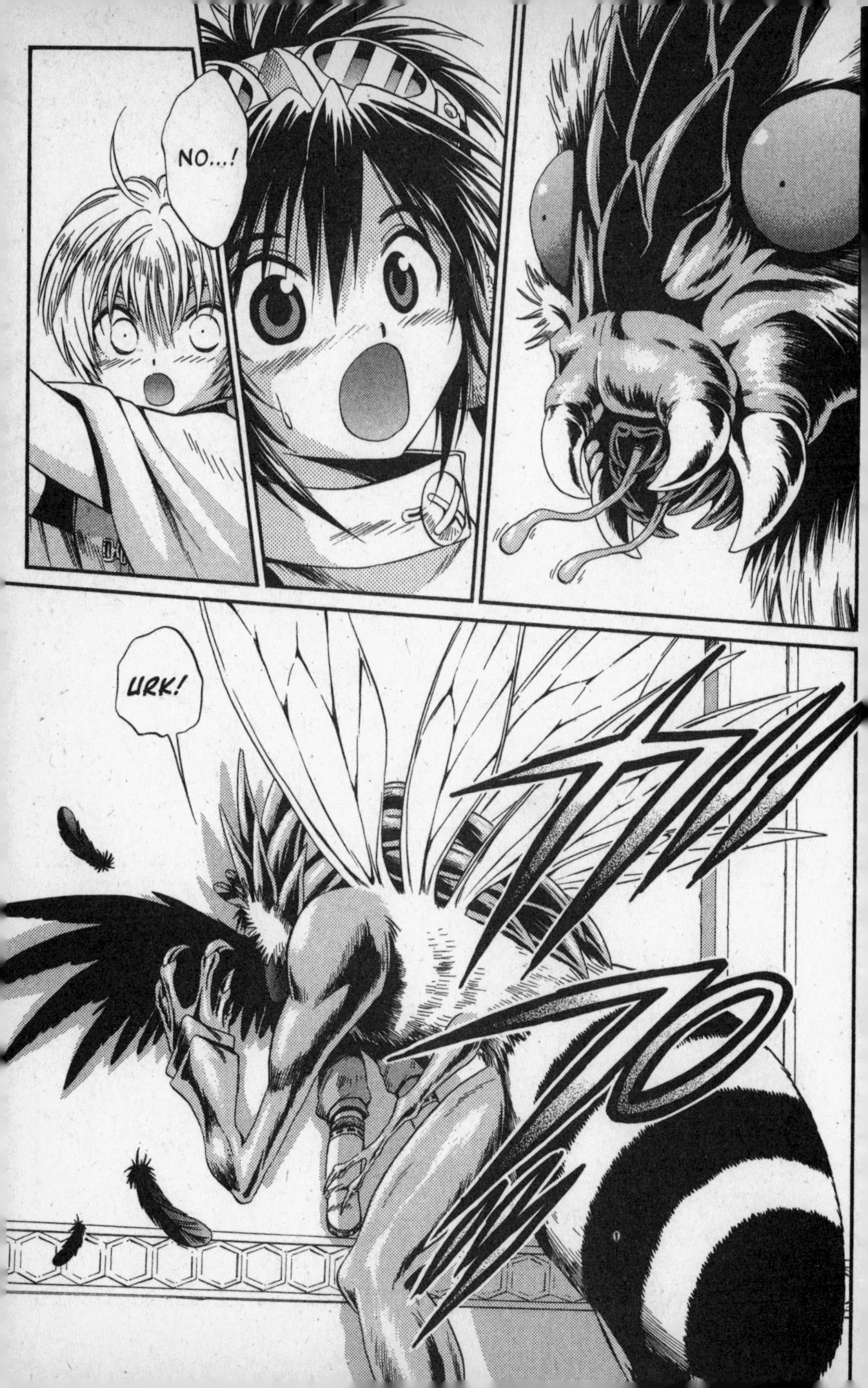
NO...!
URK!
SHHHHH

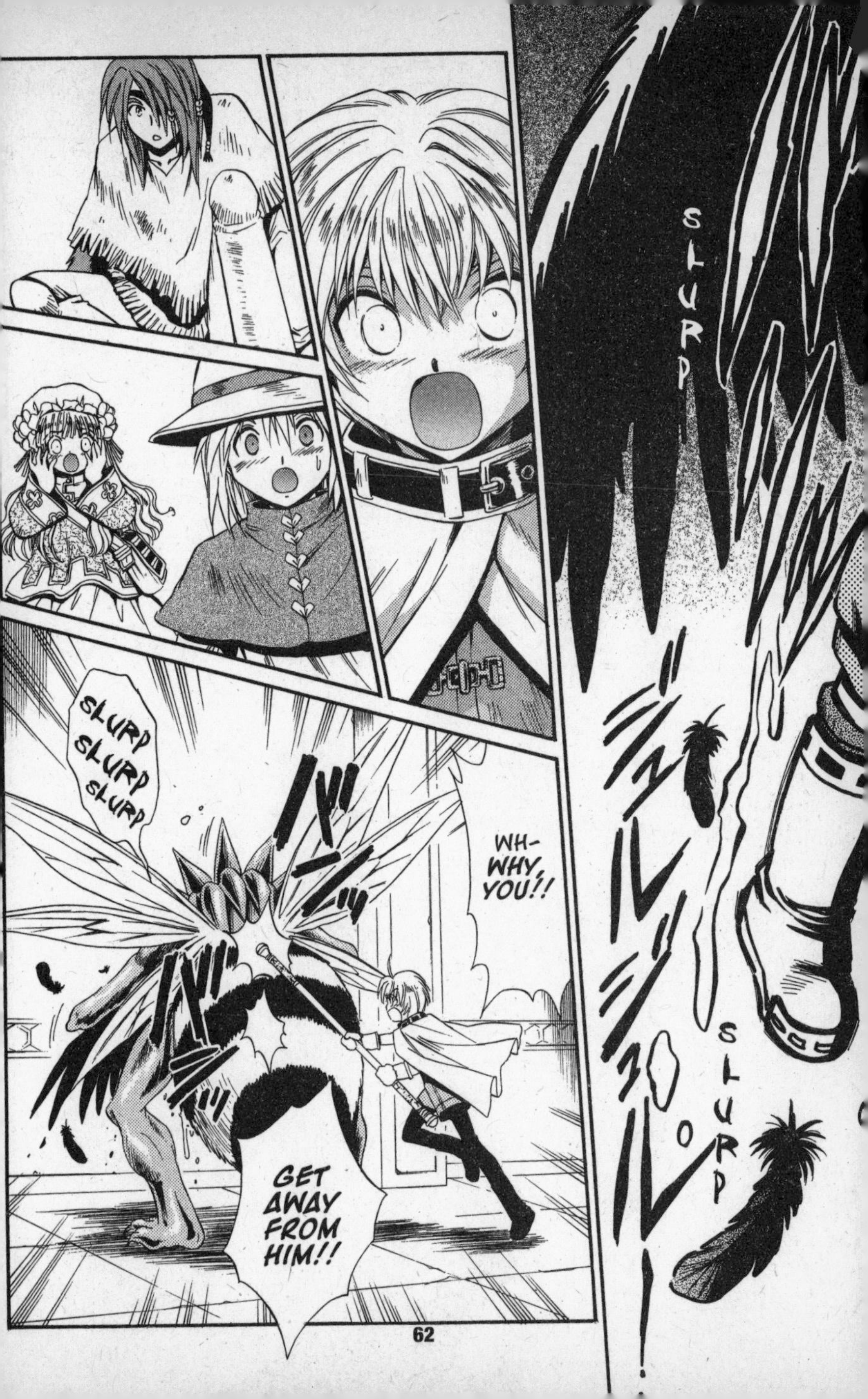
SLURP
SLURP
WH- WHY, YOU!!
SLURP SLURP SLURP
GET AWAY FROM HIM!!

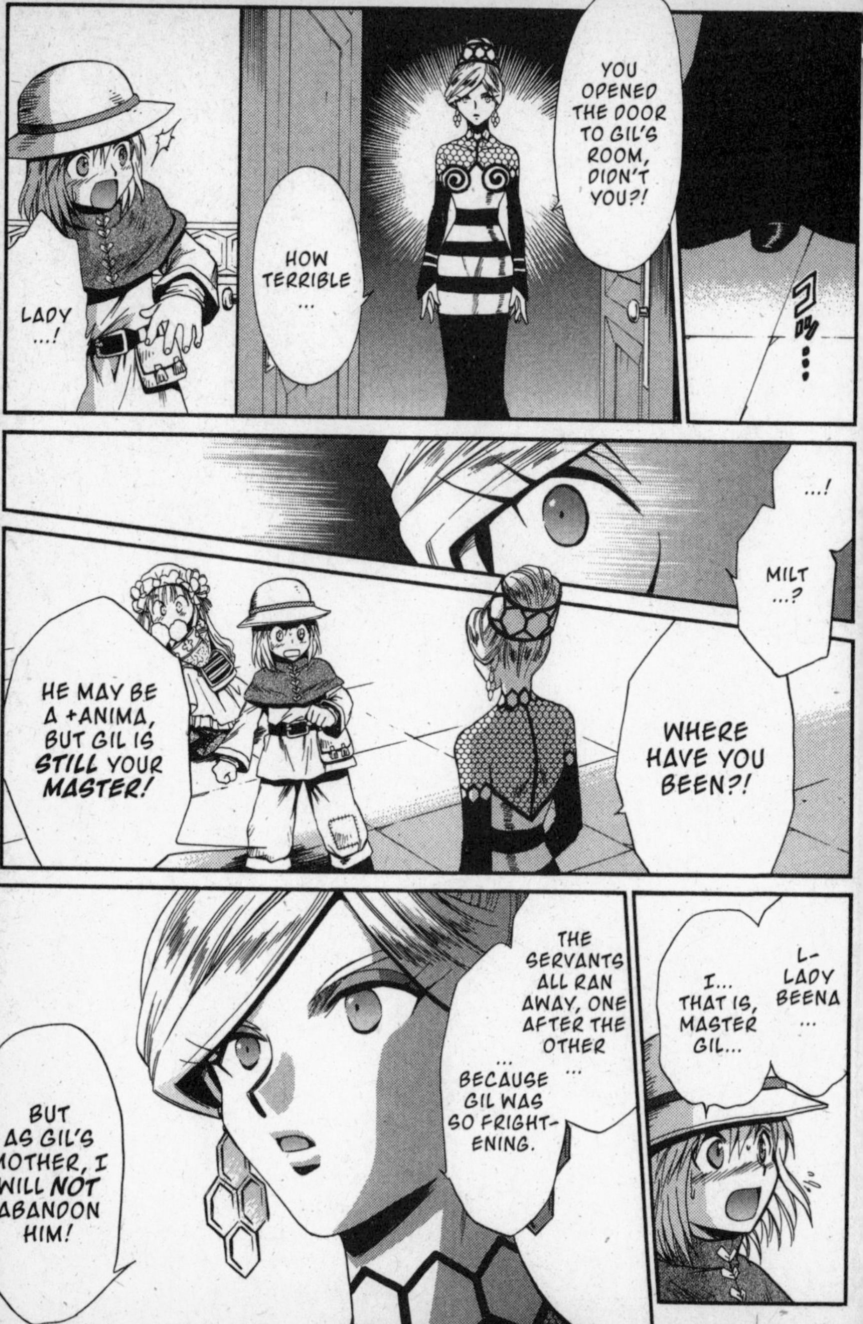
YOU OPENED THE DOOR TO GIL'S ROOM, DIDN'T YOU?!
HOW TERRIBLE ...
LADY ...!
...!
MILT ...?
WHERE HAVE YOU BEEN?!
HE MAY BE A +ANIMA, BUT GIL IS **STILL** YOUR **MASTER!**
L- LADY BEENA ...
I... THAT IS, MASTER GIL...
THE SERVANTS ALL RAN AWAY, ONE AFTER THE OTHER ...
... BECAUSE GIL WAS SO FRIGHT-ENING.
BUT AS GIL'S MOTHER, I WILL **NOT** ABANDON HIM!

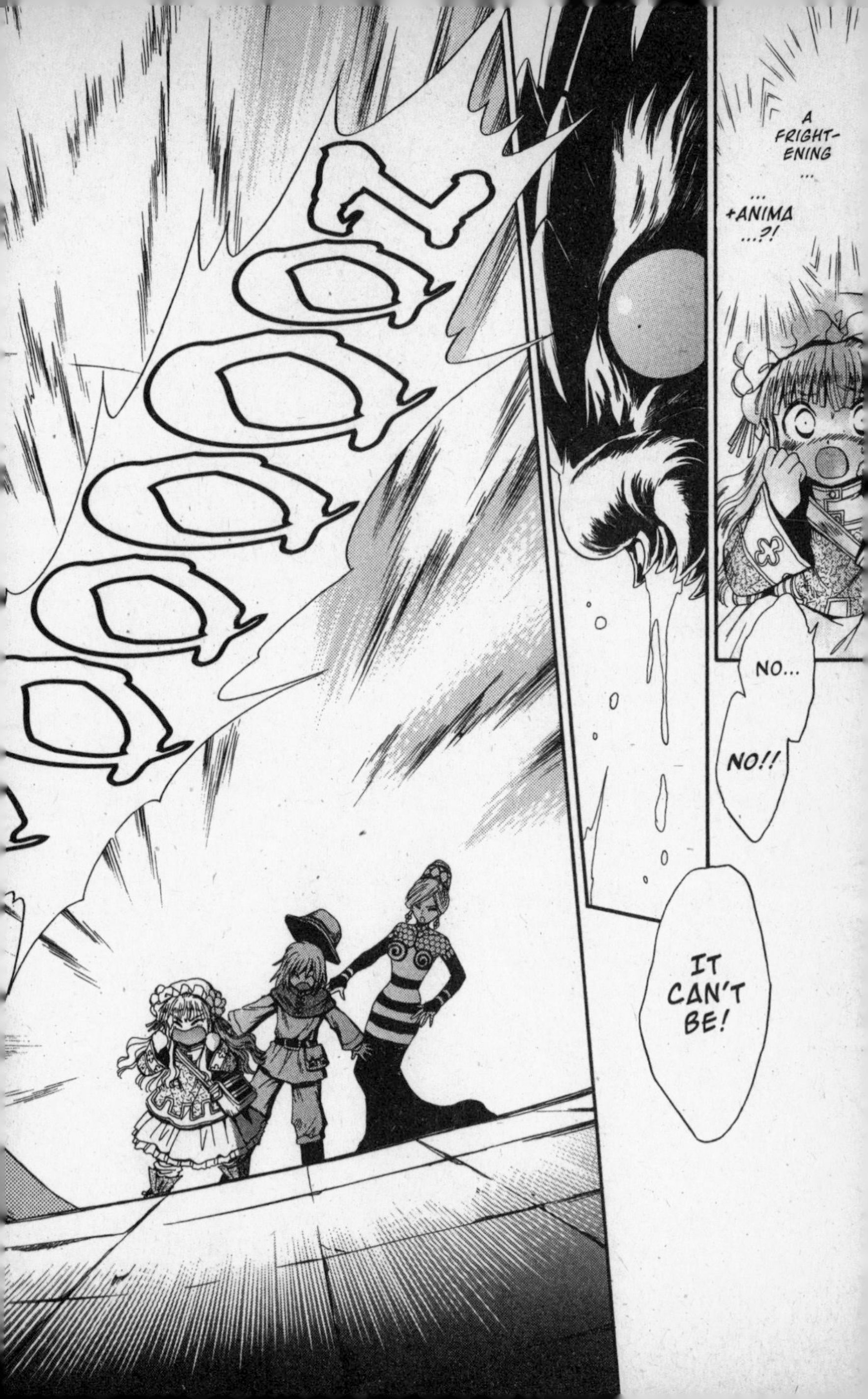
A FRIGHTENING ...
... +ANIMA ...?!
NO...
NO!!
IT CAN'T BE!

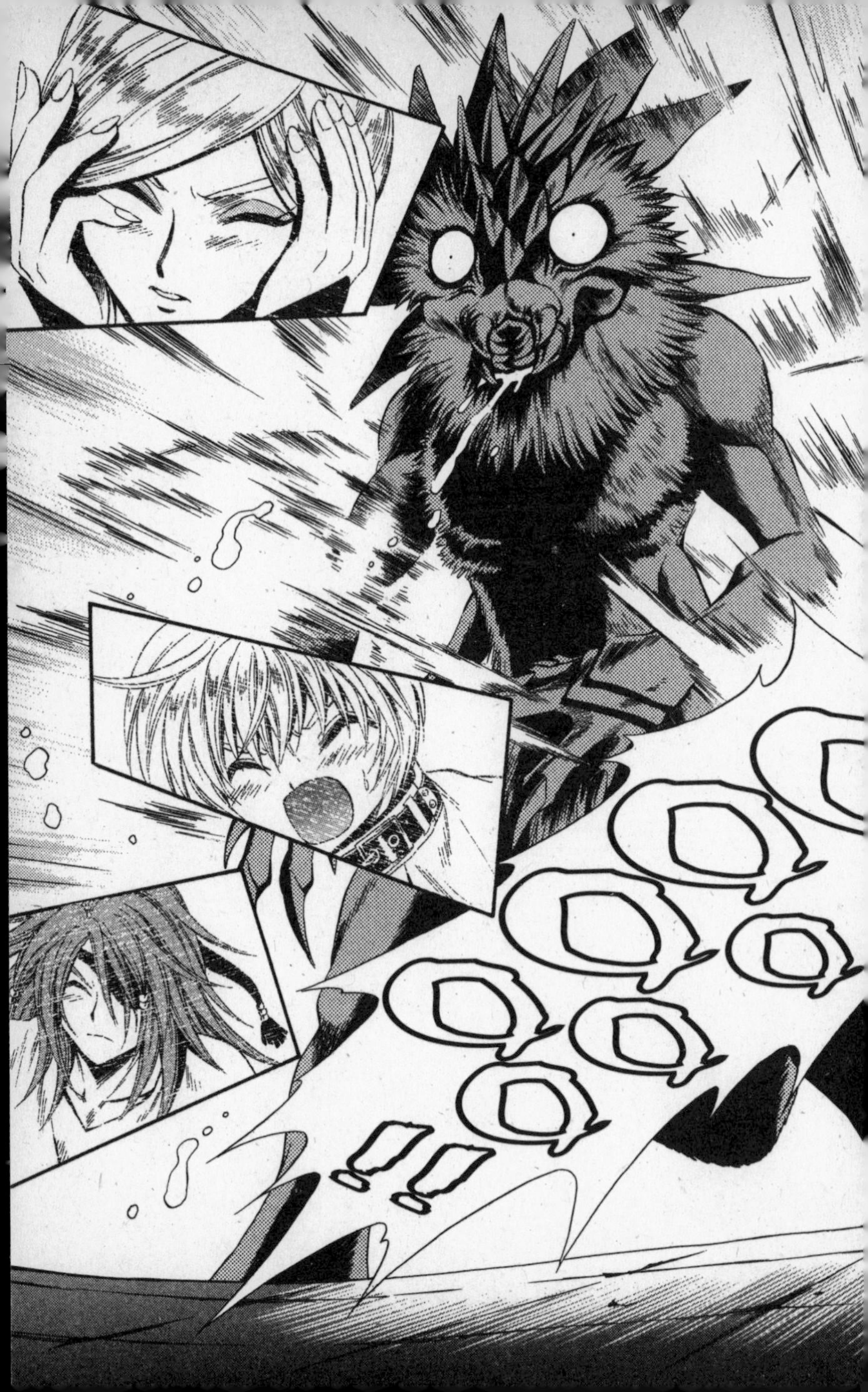
OOOOOOO!!

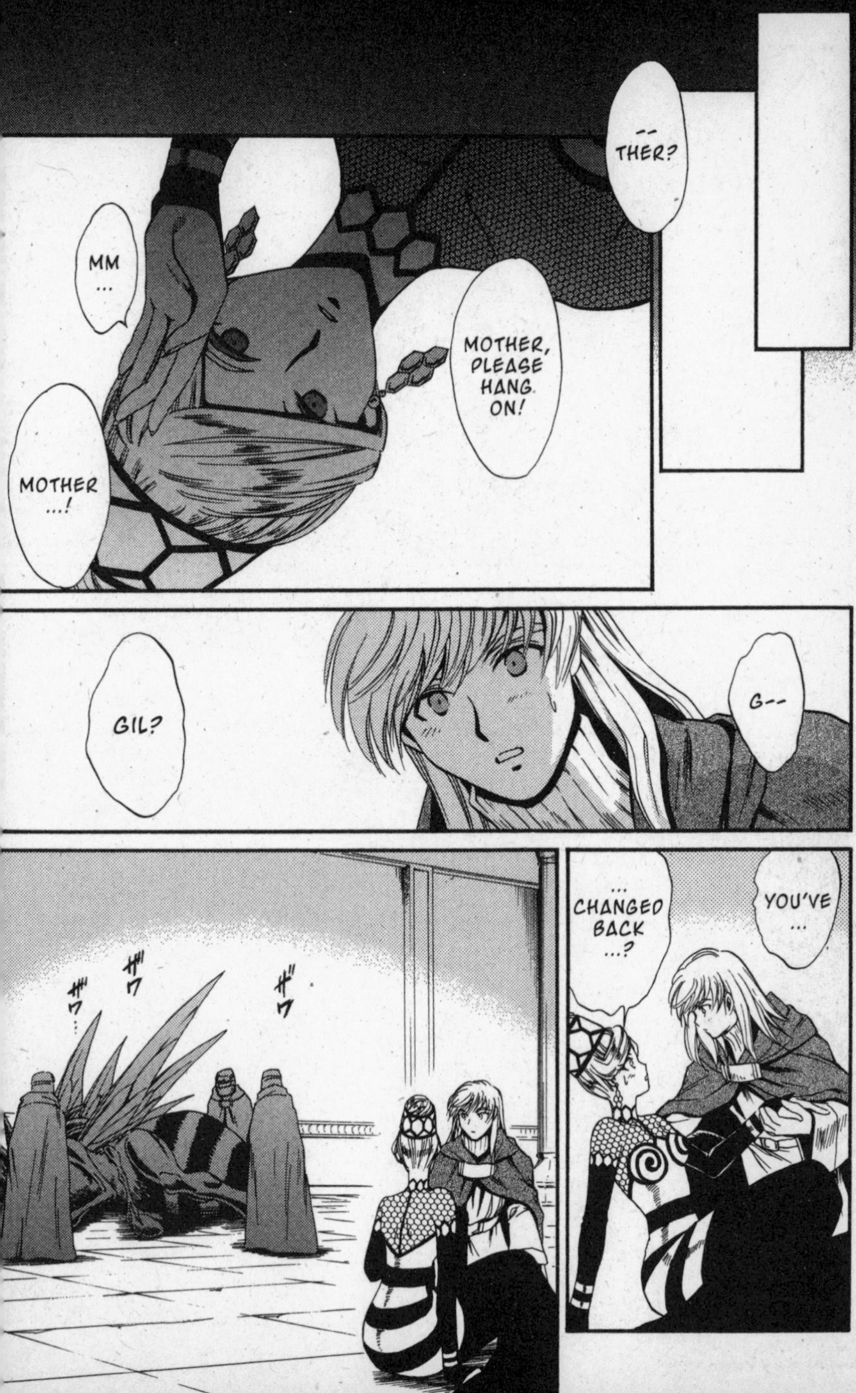
--THER?
MOTHER, PLEASE HANG ON!
MM ...
MOTHER ...!
G--
GIL?
YOU'VE ...
... CHANGED BACK ...?
ザワ
ザワ
ザワ...

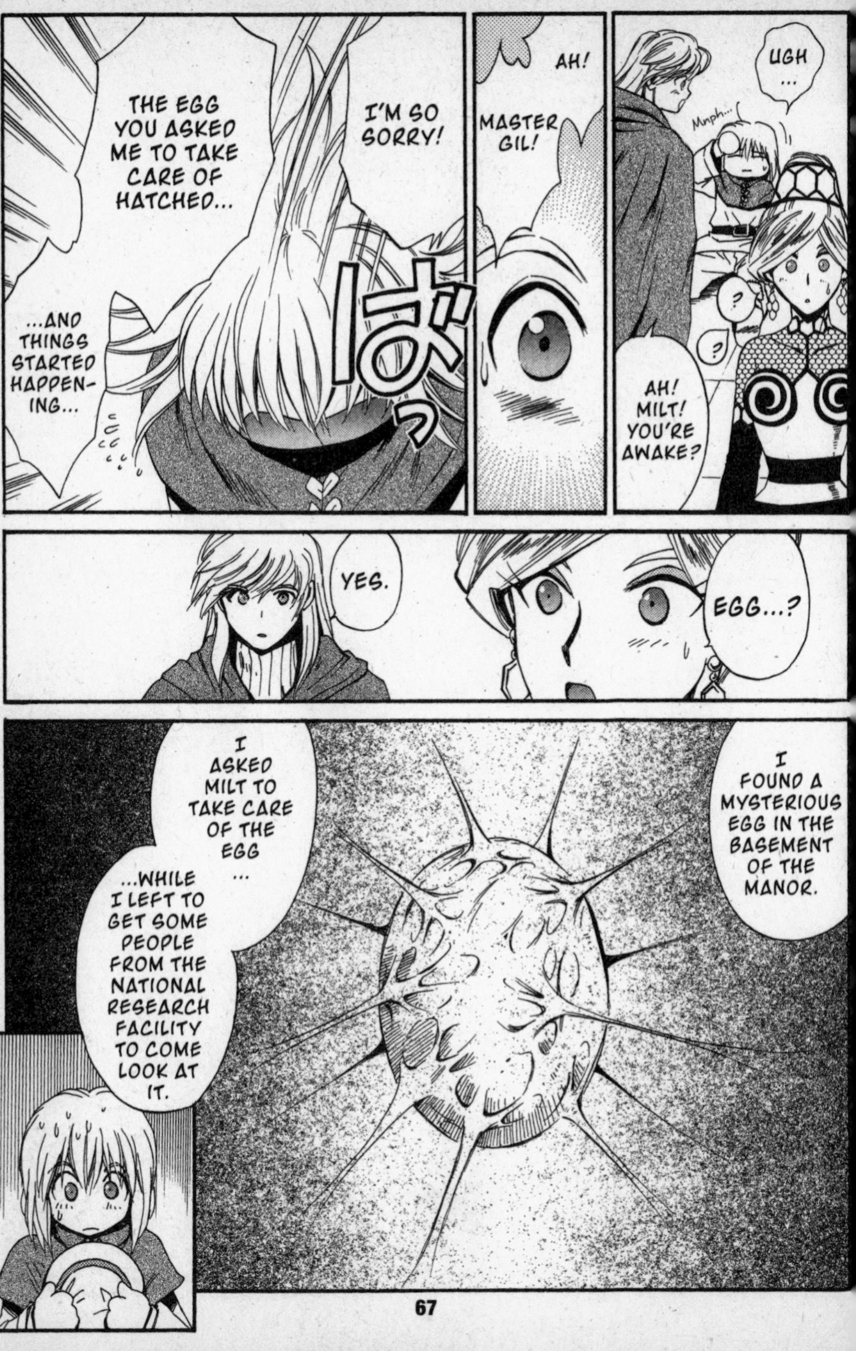
UGH ...
Mnph...
?
?
AH! MILT! YOU'RE AWAKE?
AH!
MASTER GIL!
ばっ
I'M SO SORRY!
THE EGG YOU ASKED ME TO TAKE CARE OF HATCHED...
...AND THINGS STARTED HAPPENING...
EGG...?
YES.
I FOUND A MYSTERIOUS EGG IN THE BASEMENT OF THE MANOR.
I ASKED MILT TO TAKE CARE OF THE EGG ...
...WHILE I LEFT TO GET SOME PEOPLE FROM THE NATIONAL RESEARCH FACILITY TO COME LOOK AT IT.

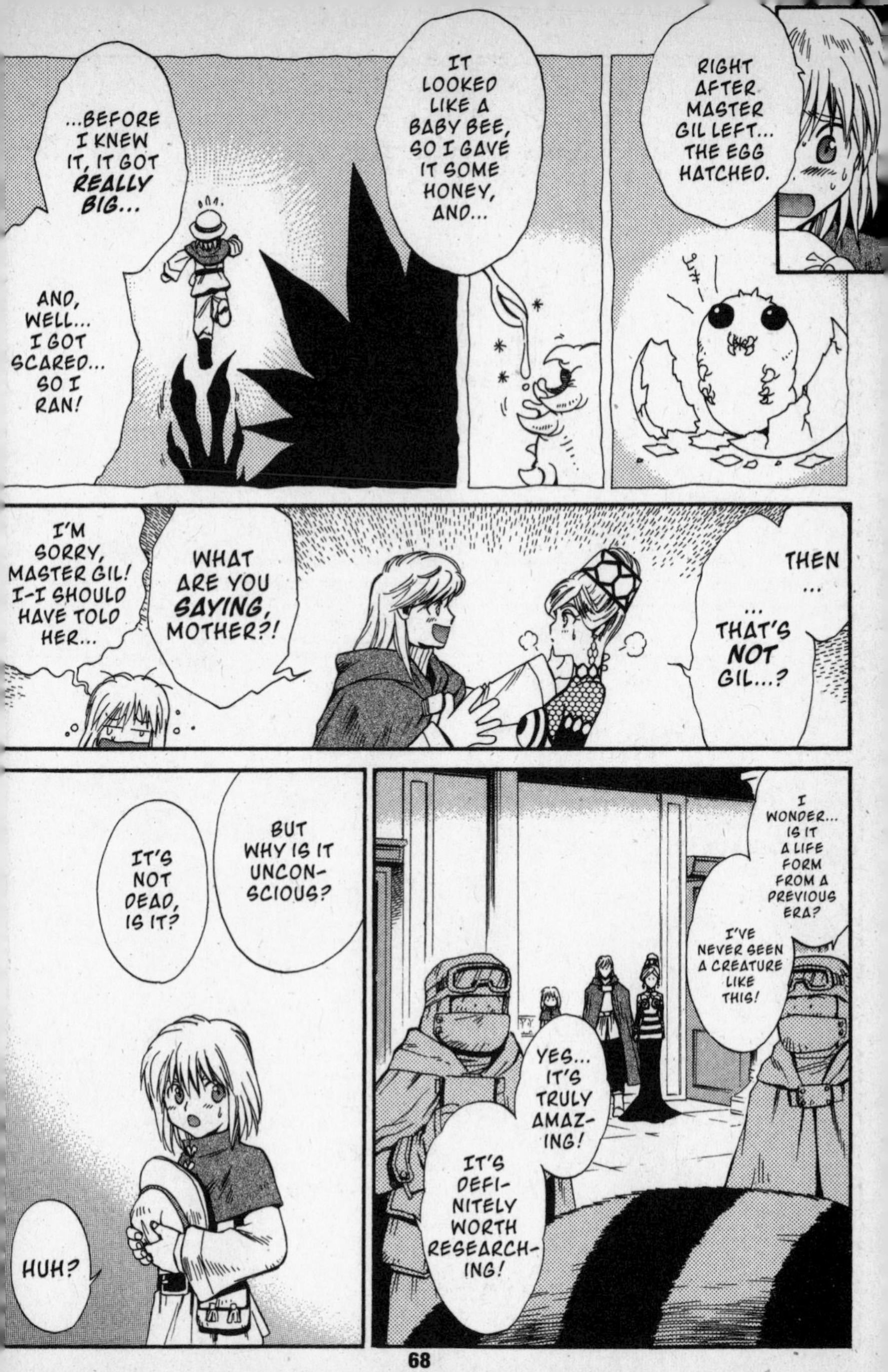
RIGHT AFTER MASTER GIL LEFT... THE EGG HATCHED.
IT LOOKED LIKE A BABY BEE, SO I GAVE IT SOME HONEY, AND...
...BEFORE I KNEW IT, IT GOT REALLY BIG...
AND, WELL... I GOT SCARED... SO I RAN!
THEN ... ... THAT'S NOT GIL...?
WHAT ARE YOU SAYING, MOTHER?!
I'M SORRY, MASTER GIL! I-I SHOULD HAVE TOLD HER...
I WONDER... IS IT A LIFE FORM FROM A PREVIOUS ERA?
I'VE NEVER SEEN A CREATURE LIKE THIS!
YES... IT'S TRULY AMAZ-ING!
IT'S DEFI-NITELY WORTH RESEARCH-ING!
BUT WHY IS IT UNCON-SCIOUS?
IT'S NOT DEAD, IS IT?
HUH?

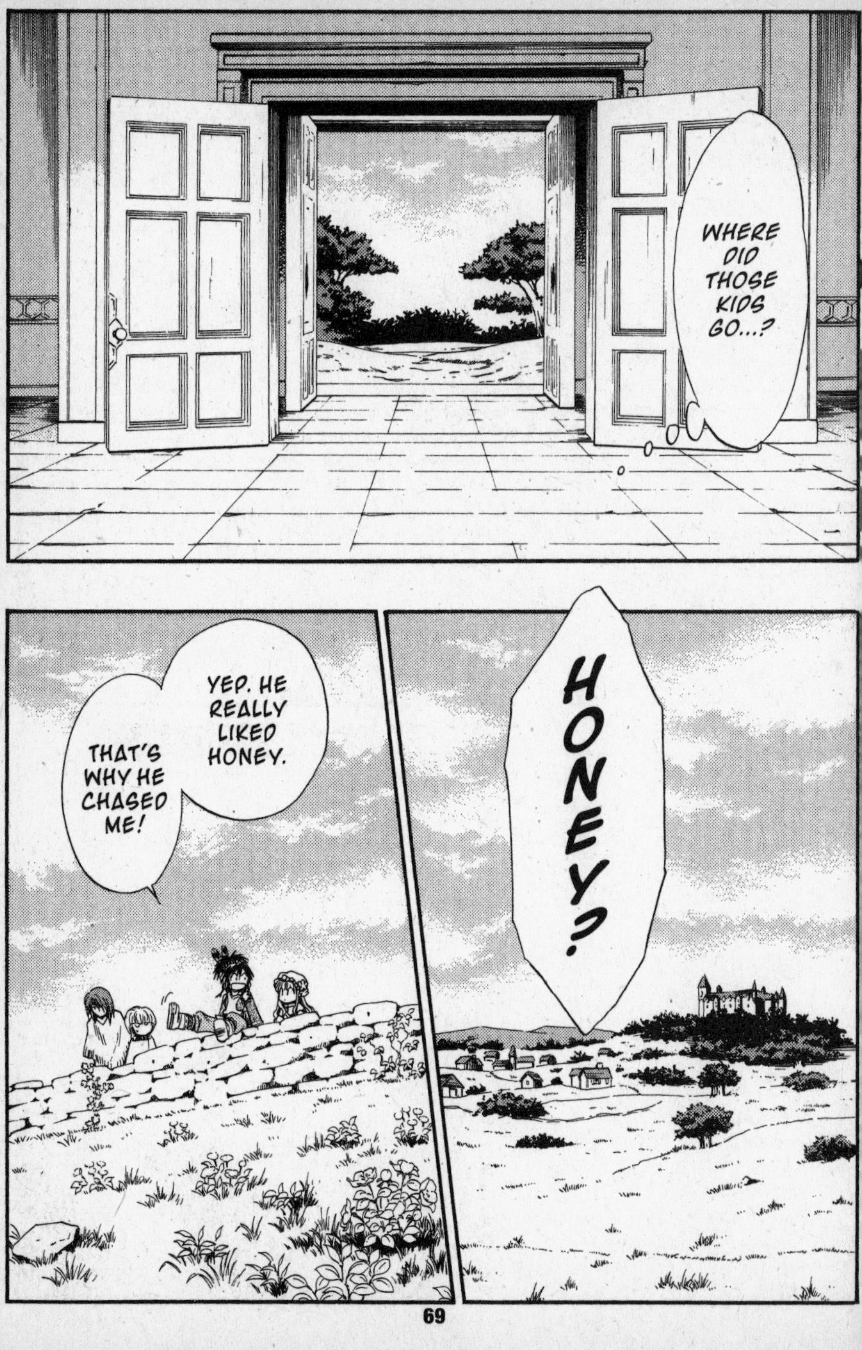
WHERE DID THOSE KIDS GO...?
HONEY?
YEP. HE REALLY LIKED HONEY.
THAT'S WHY HE CHASED ME!

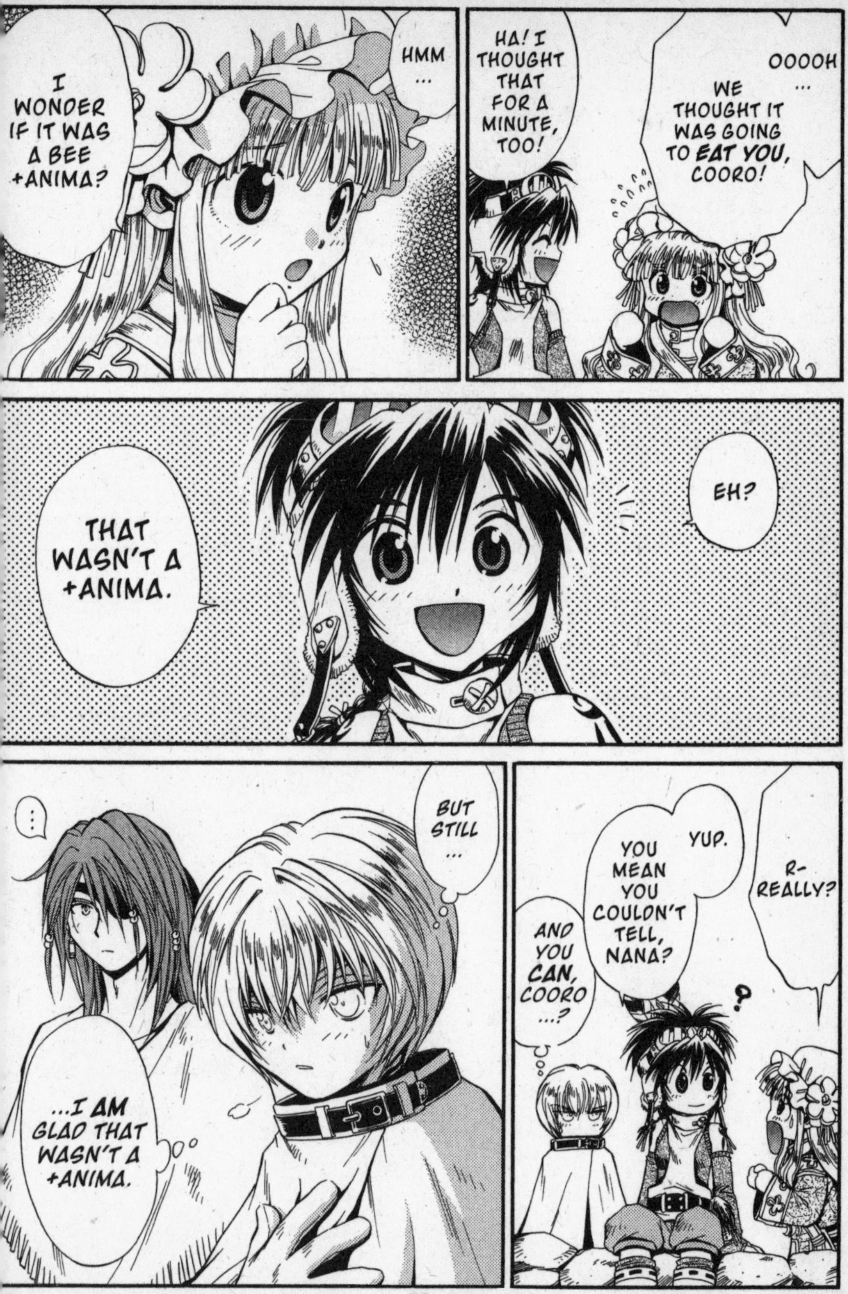
OOOOH ...
WE THOUGHT IT WAS GOING TO **EAT YOU**, COORO!
HA! I THOUGHT THAT FOR A MINUTE, TOO!
HMM ...
I WONDER IF IT WAS A BEE +ANIMA?
EH?
THAT WASN'T A +ANIMA.
R-REALLY?
YUP.
YOU MEAN YOU COULDN'T TELL, NANA?
AND YOU **CAN**, COORO ...?
BUT STILL ...
...
...I AM GLAD THAT WASN'T A +ANIMA.

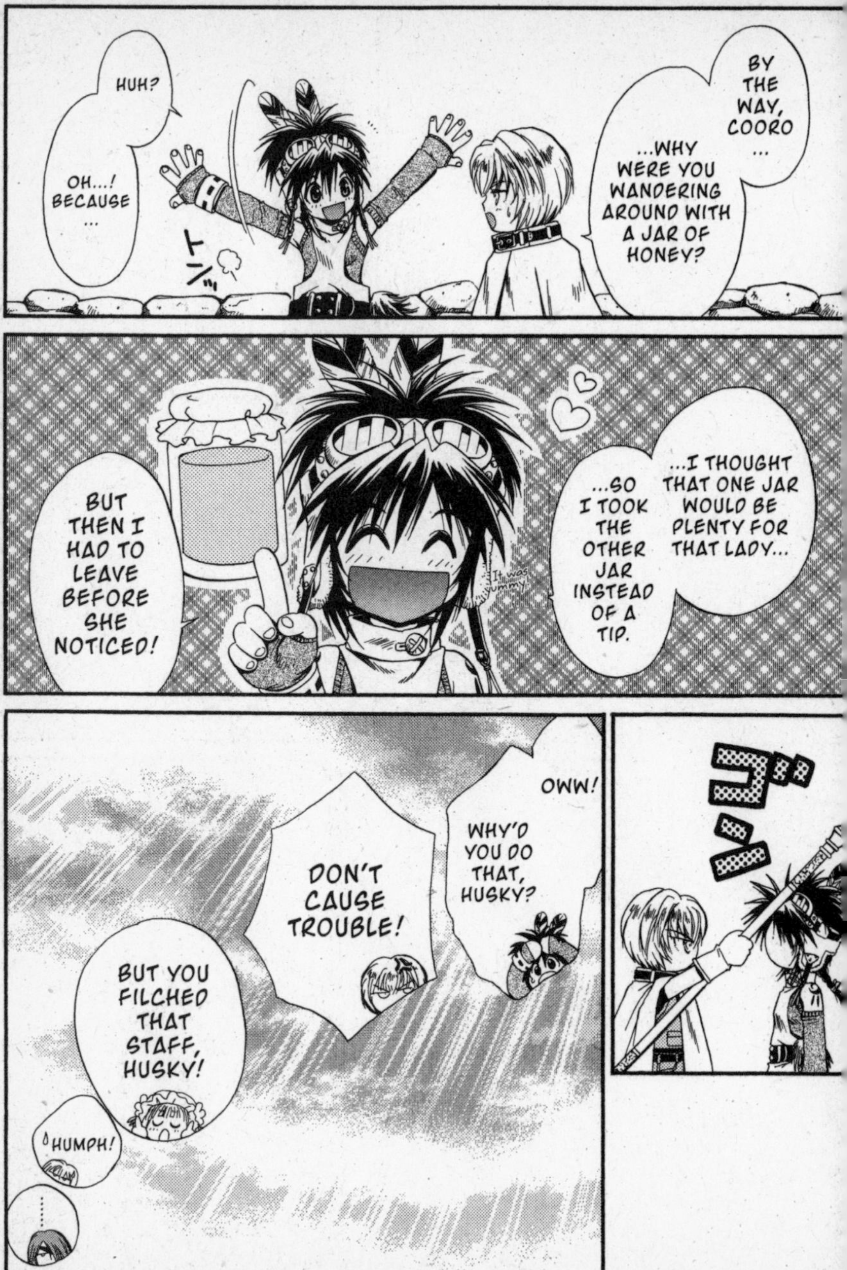
BY THE WAY, COORO ...
...WHY WERE YOU WANDERING AROUND WITH A JAR OF HONEY?
HUH?
OH...! BECAUSE ...
...I THOUGHT THAT ONE JAR WOULD BE PLENTY FOR THAT LADY...
...SO I TOOK THE OTHER JAR INSTEAD OF A TIP.
It was yummy!
BUT THEN I HAD TO LEAVE BEFORE SHE NOTICED!
OWW!
WHY'D YOU DO THAT, HUSKY?
DON'T CAUSE TROUBLE!
BUT YOU FILCHED THAT STAFF, HUSKY!
HUMPH!
......

Favorite dish!

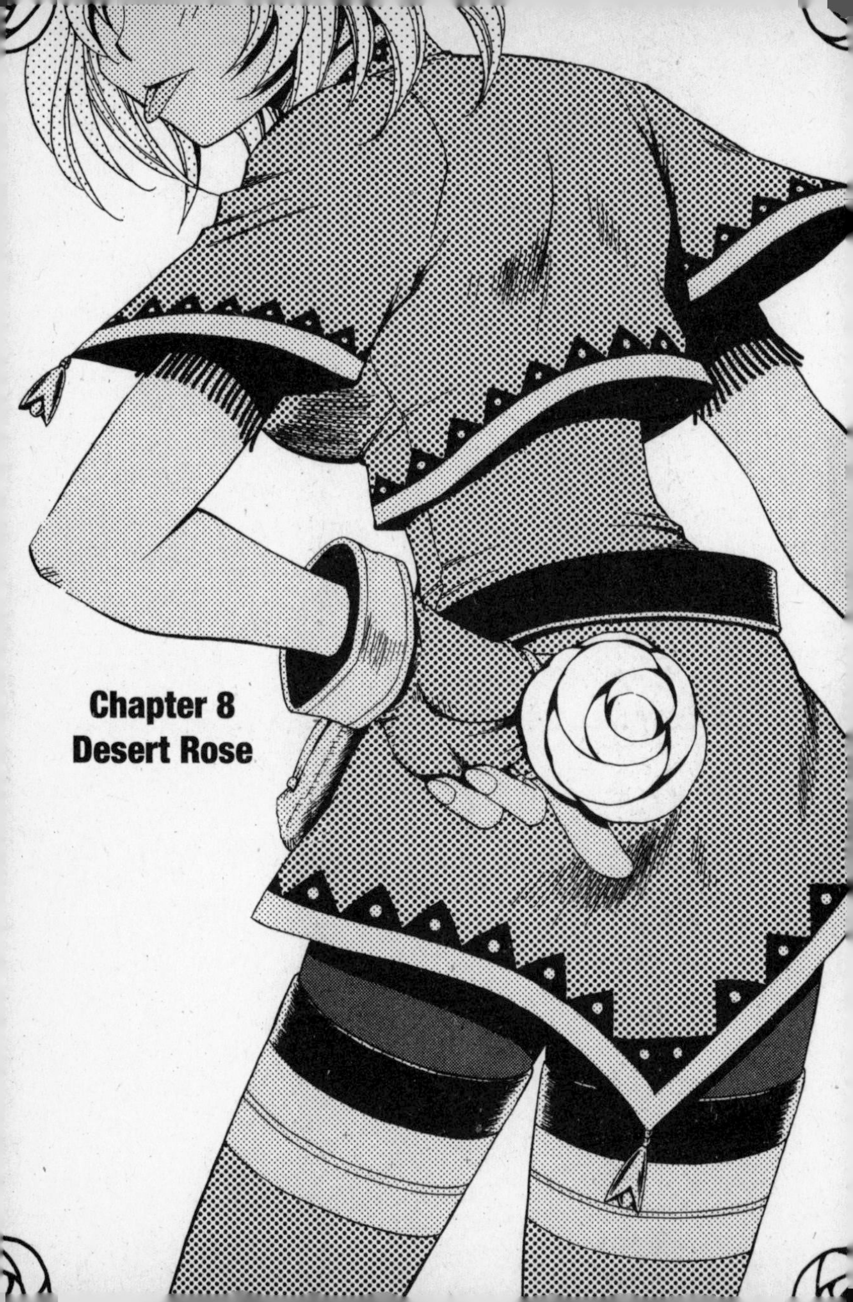

Chapter 8
Desert Rose

=SIGH=

SUMMER'S ALMOST OVER.

THE OCEAN'S IN THE SOUTH, ISN'T IT?

I'VE NEVER SEEN THE OCEAN...

HAVE YOU, SENRI?

YEAH! WE WOULDN'T WANT TO FREEZE TO DEATH!

LET'S GO SOUTH BEFORE WINTER STARTS.

SOUTH SLANG TOWN

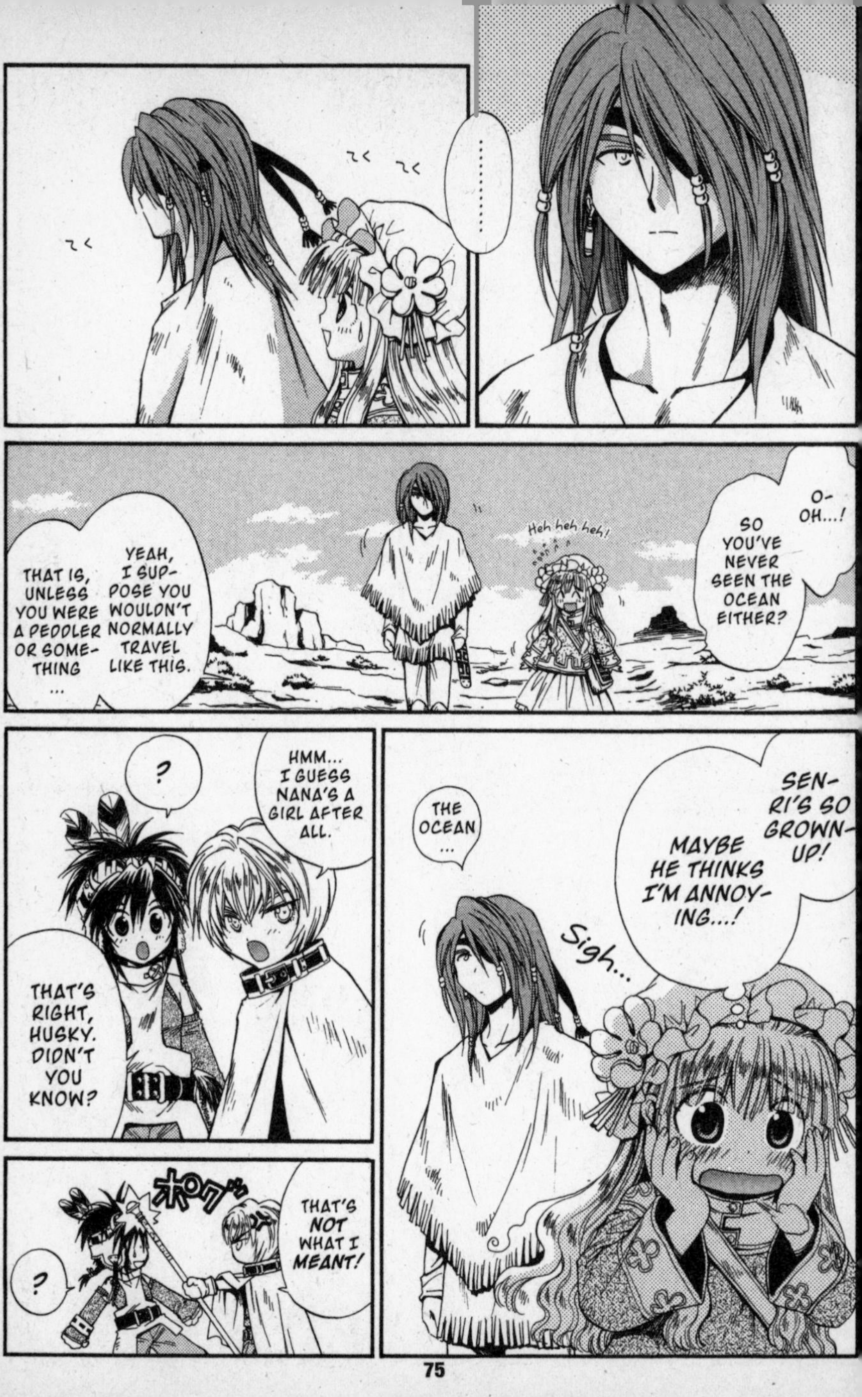
……
O-OH…!
SO YOU'VE NEVER SEEN THE OCEAN EITHER?
Heh heh heh!
YEAH, I SUP-POSE YOU WOULDN'T NORMALLY TRAVEL LIKE THIS.
THAT IS, UNLESS YOU WERE A PEDDLER OR SOME-THING …
SEN-RI'S SO GROWN-UP!
MAYBE HE THINKS I'M ANNOY-ING…!
THE OCEAN …
Sigh…
HMM… I GUESS NANA'S A GIRL AFTER ALL.
?
THAT'S RIGHT, HUSKY. DIDN'T YOU KNOW?
THAT'S NOT WHAT I MEANT!
?

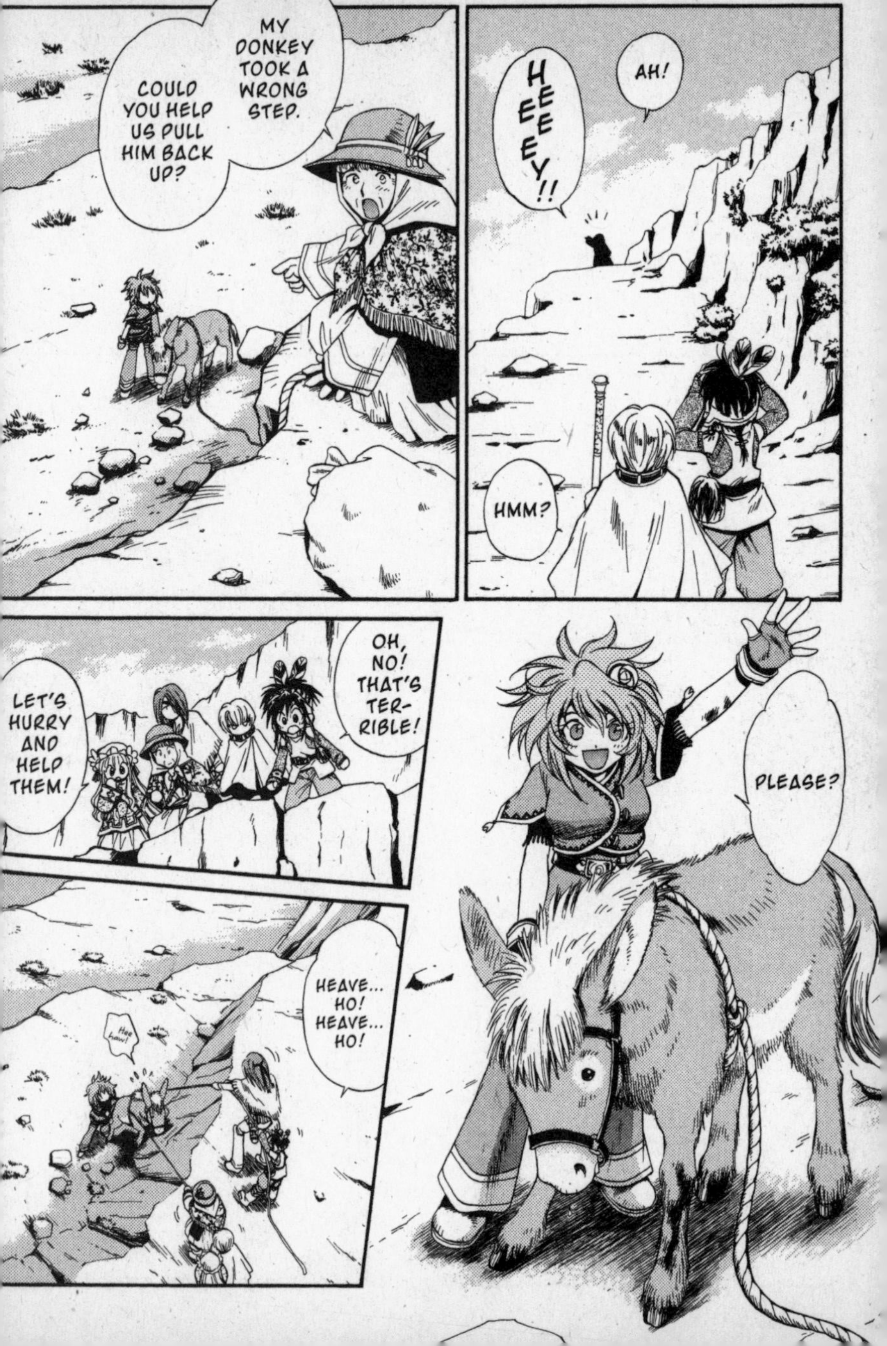
AH!
HEEEEY!!
HMM?
MY DONKEY TOOK A WRONG STEP.
COULD YOU HELP US PULL HIM BACK UP?
PLEASE?
OH, NO! THAT'S TER-RIBLE!
LET'S HURRY AND HELP THEM!
HEAVE... HO! HEAVE... HO!
Hee haw!

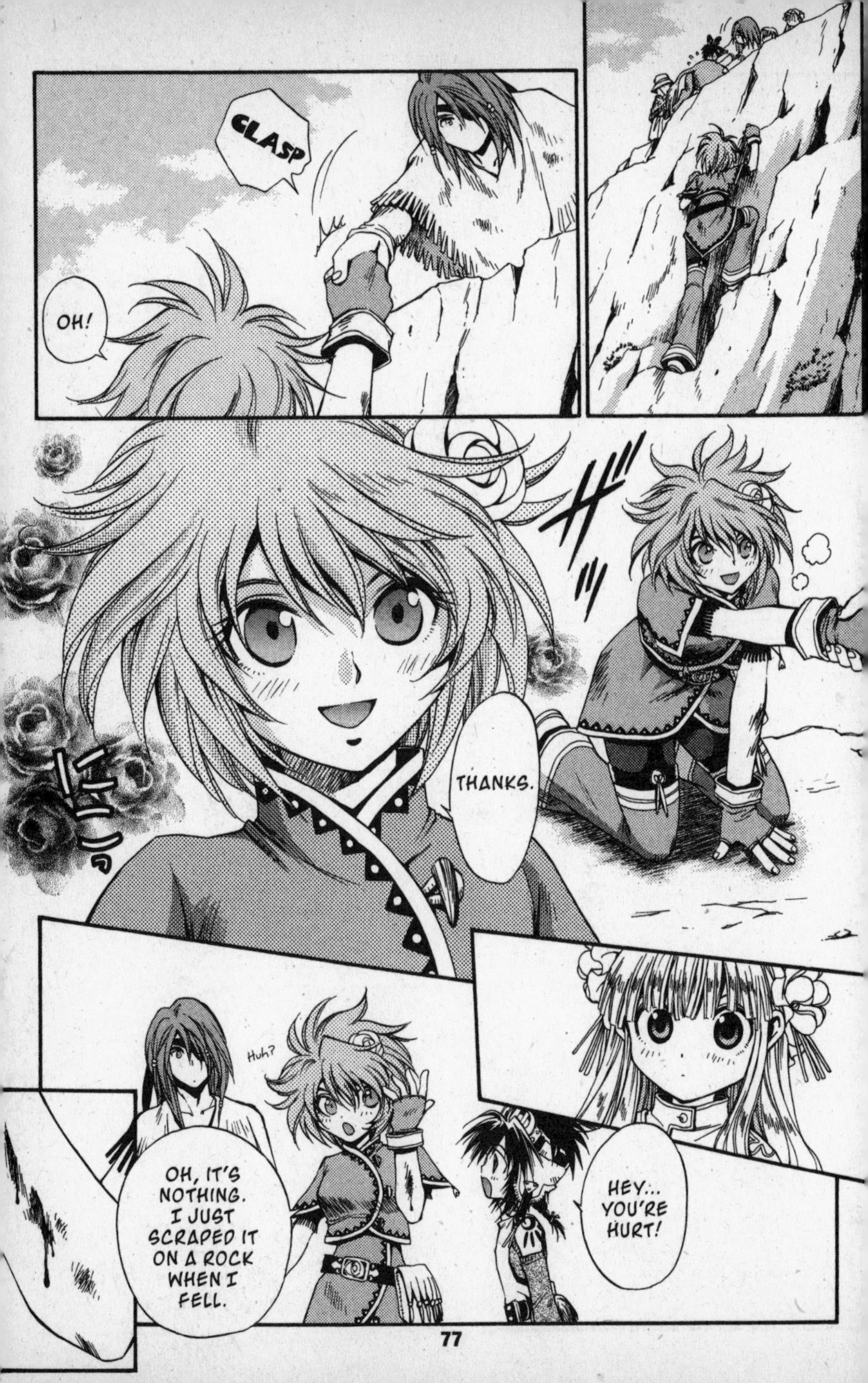
CLASP
OH!
THANKS.
HEY... YOU'RE HURT!
Huh?
OH, IT'S NOTHING. I JUST SCRAPED IT ON A ROCK WHEN I FELL.

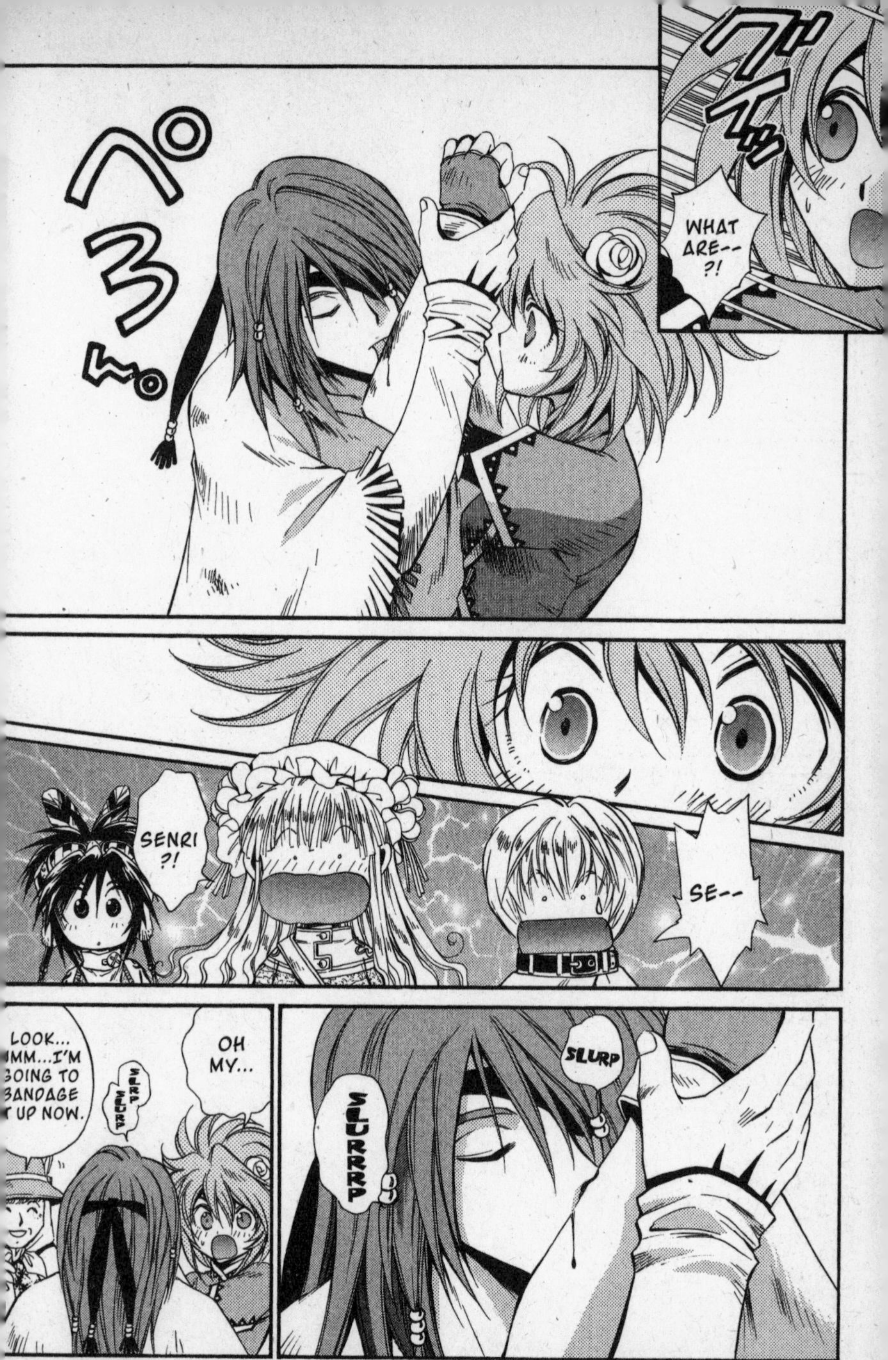

グイッ
WHAT ARE-- ?!
ぺろっ
SE--
SENRI ?!
SLURP
SLURRRP
OH MY...
SLURP SLURP
LOOK... MMM...I'M GOING TO BANDAGE IT UP NOW.

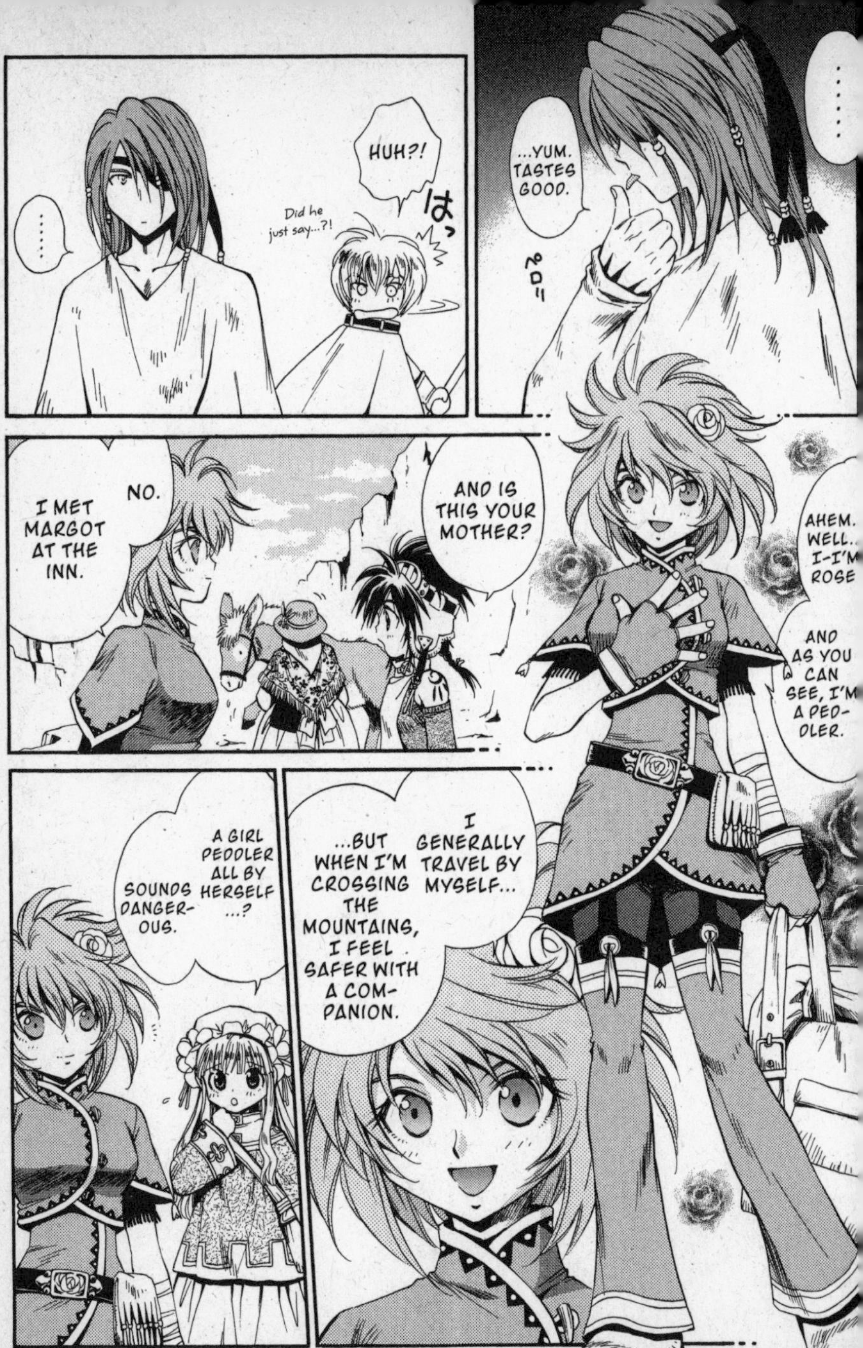

......
...YUM. TASTES GOOD.
ペロ
HUH?!
は
Did he just say...?!
......
AHEM. WELL. I-I'M ROSE
AND AS YOU CAN SEE, I'M A PEDDLER.
AND IS THIS YOUR MOTHER?
NO.
I MET MARGOT AT THE INN.
I GENERALLY TRAVEL BY MYSELF...
...BUT WHEN I'M CROSSING THE MOUNTAINS, I FEEL SAFER WITH A COMPANION.
A GIRL PEDDLER ALL BY HERSELF ...?
SOUNDS DANGEROUS.

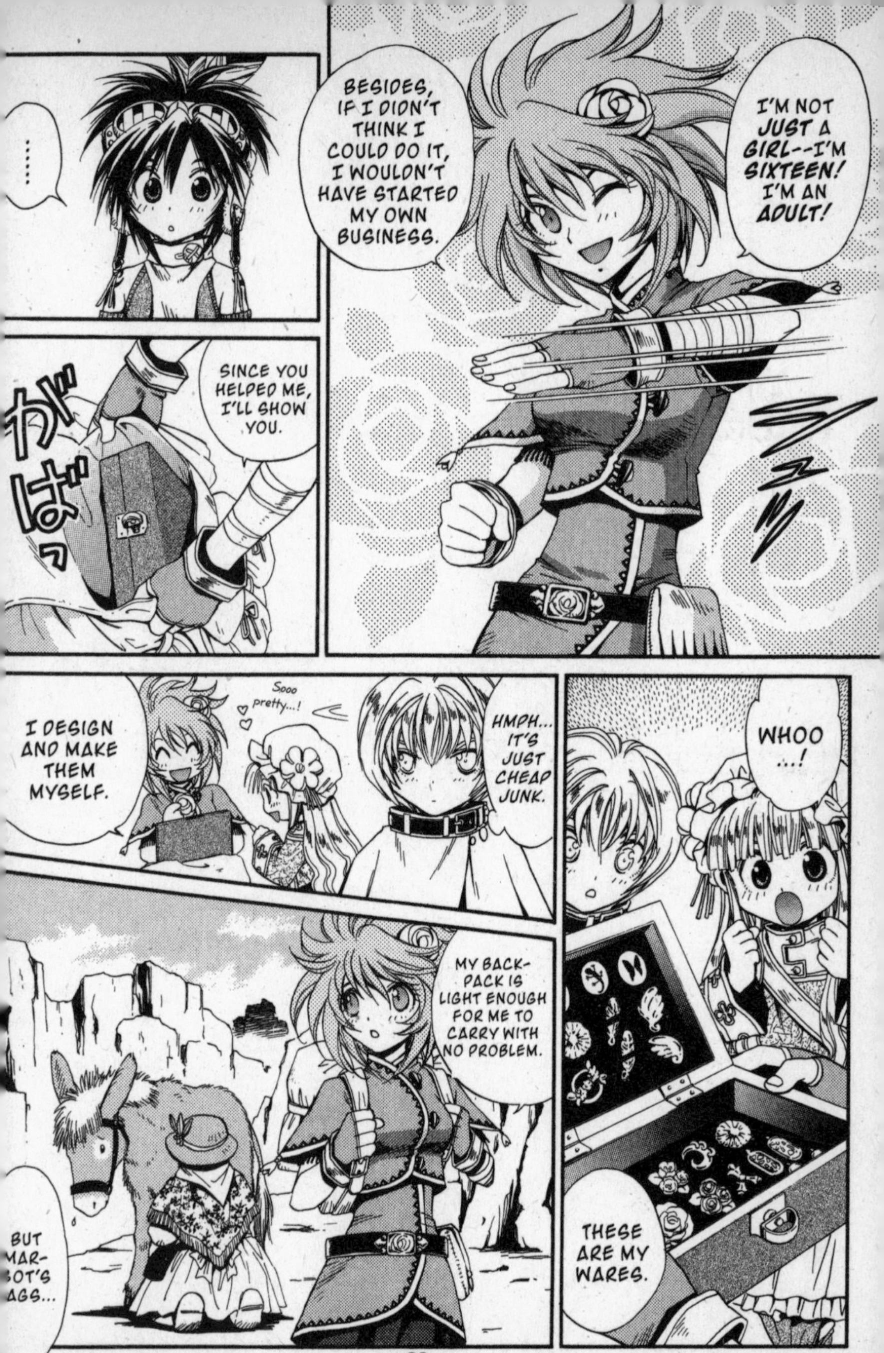

I'M NOT JUST A GIRL--I'M SIXTEEN! I'M AN ADULT!
BESIDES, IF I DIDN'T THINK I COULD DO IT, I WOULDN'T HAVE STARTED MY OWN BUSINESS.
......
SINCE YOU HELPED ME, I'LL SHOW YOU.
がばっ
WHOO ...!
THESE ARE MY WARES.
HMPH... IT'S JUST CHEAP JUNK.
Sooo pretty...!
I DESIGN AND MAKE THEM MYSELF.
MY BACK-PACK IS LIGHT ENOUGH FOR ME TO CARRY WITH NO PROBLEM.
BUT MAR- OT'S AGS...

OH! I KNOW!

Sigh...

I CAN'T MAKE HIM CARRY A HEAVY LOAD ACROSS THE MOUNTAIN WHEN HE'S HURT...

WILL YOU FOUR HELP ME AGAIN?

IF WE CAN JUST GET THESE THINGS TO THE VILLAGE ON THE OTHER SIDE OF THE NORTHERN RIDGE...

NORTH?! BUT WE'RE HEADING SOUTH! LOOK, WE CAN'T JUST--

OH, HUSKY...!

OF COURSE WE'LL HELP!

I'D BE WILLING TO PAY YOU THI MUCH.

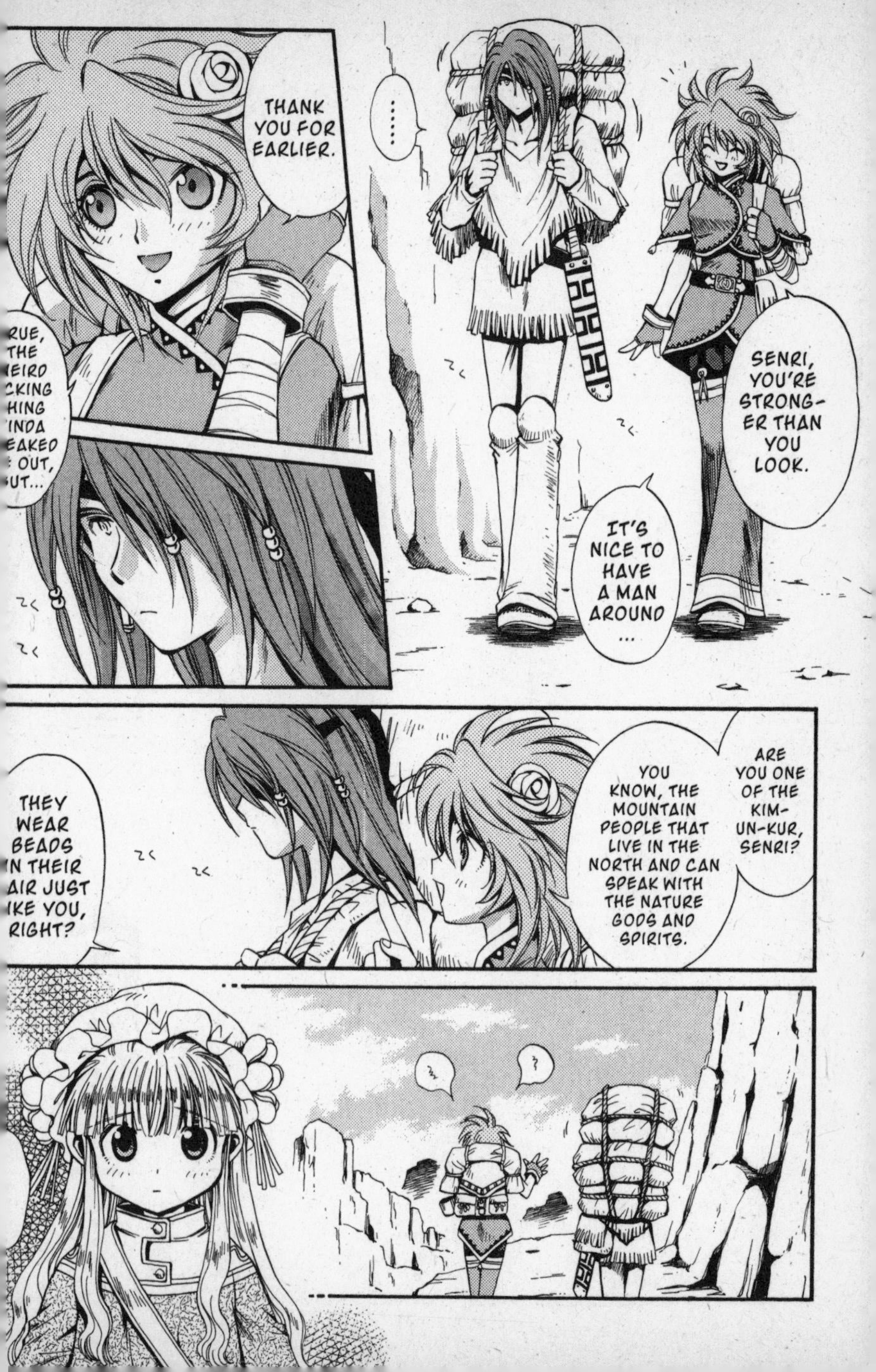
SENRI, YOU'RE STRONGER THAN YOU LOOK.
IT'S NICE TO HAVE A MAN AROUND ...
......
THANK YOU FOR EARLIER.
RUE, THE EIRD CKING HING INDA EAKED OUT, UT...
ARE YOU ONE OF THE KIM-UN-KUR, SENRI?
YOU KNOW, THE MOUNTAIN PEOPLE THAT LIVE IN THE NORTH AND CAN SPEAK WITH THE NATURE GODS AND SPIRITS.
THEY WEAR BEADS N THEIR AIR JUST IKE YOU, RIGHT?
?
?

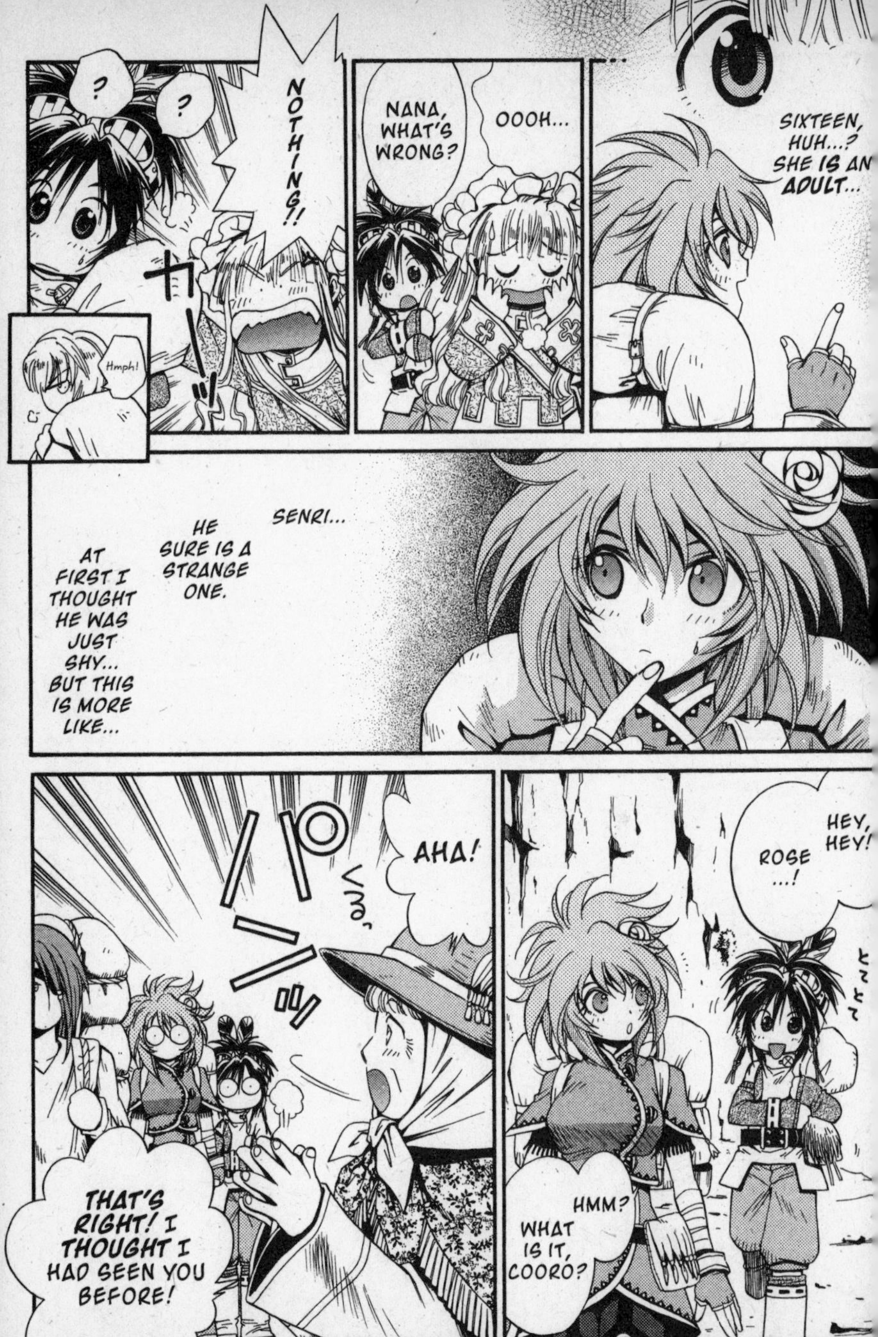

SIXTEEN, HUH...? SHE IS AN ADULT...
OOOH...
NANA, WHAT'S WRONG?
NOTHING!!
?
?
Hmph!
SENRI...
HE SURE IS A STRANGE ONE.
AT FIRST I THOUGHT HE WAS JUST SHY... BUT THIS IS MORE LIKE...
HEY, HEY!
ROSE ...!
HMM? WHAT IS IT, COORO?
AHA!
THAT'S RIGHT! I THOUGHT I HAD SEEN YOU BEFORE!

SENRI, YOU TRAVELED WITH A LARGE CARAVAN WHEN YOU WERE YOUNG, DIDN'T YOU?

I REMEMBER THOSE BEADS AND THE EYE PATCH!

YOU WERE ONLY ABOUT THIS BIG...

SO IT'S NOT LIKE THE TWO OF US TALKED MUCH...

I WAS ONLY WITH THE CARAVAN FOR TEN DAYS WHILE WE CROSSED THE PRAIRIE...

......

IS IT FULL OF NOTES? LIKE A DIARY OR SOMETHING?

HE *REALLY* PANICKED WHEN SAMMY TOOK IT.

OH, REALLY? NOW I'M CURIOUS, TOO.

OH! SENRI'S BOOK.

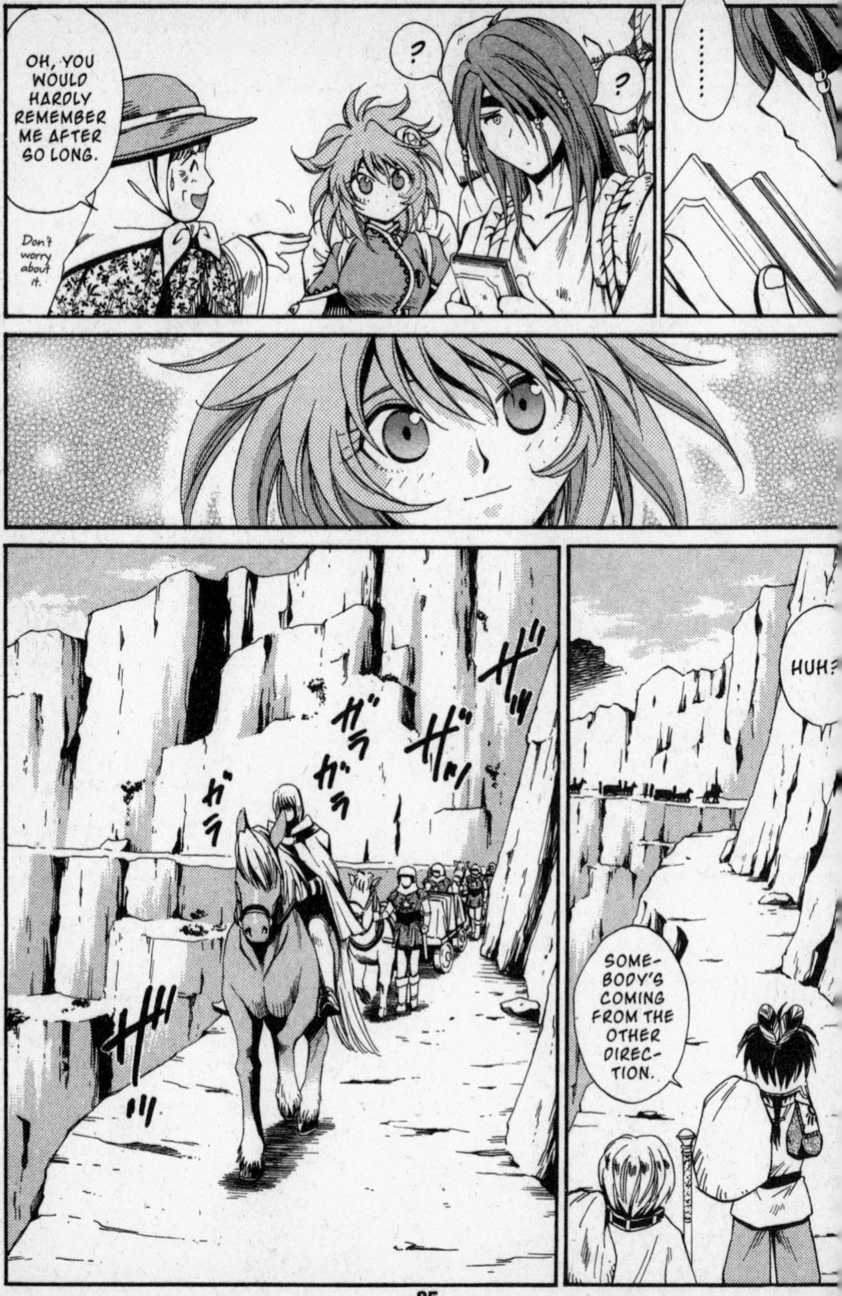
......
?
?
OH, YOU WOULD HARDLY REMEMBER ME AFTER SO LONG.
Don't worry about it.
HUH?
SOME-BODY'S COMING FROM THE OTHER DIREC-TION.

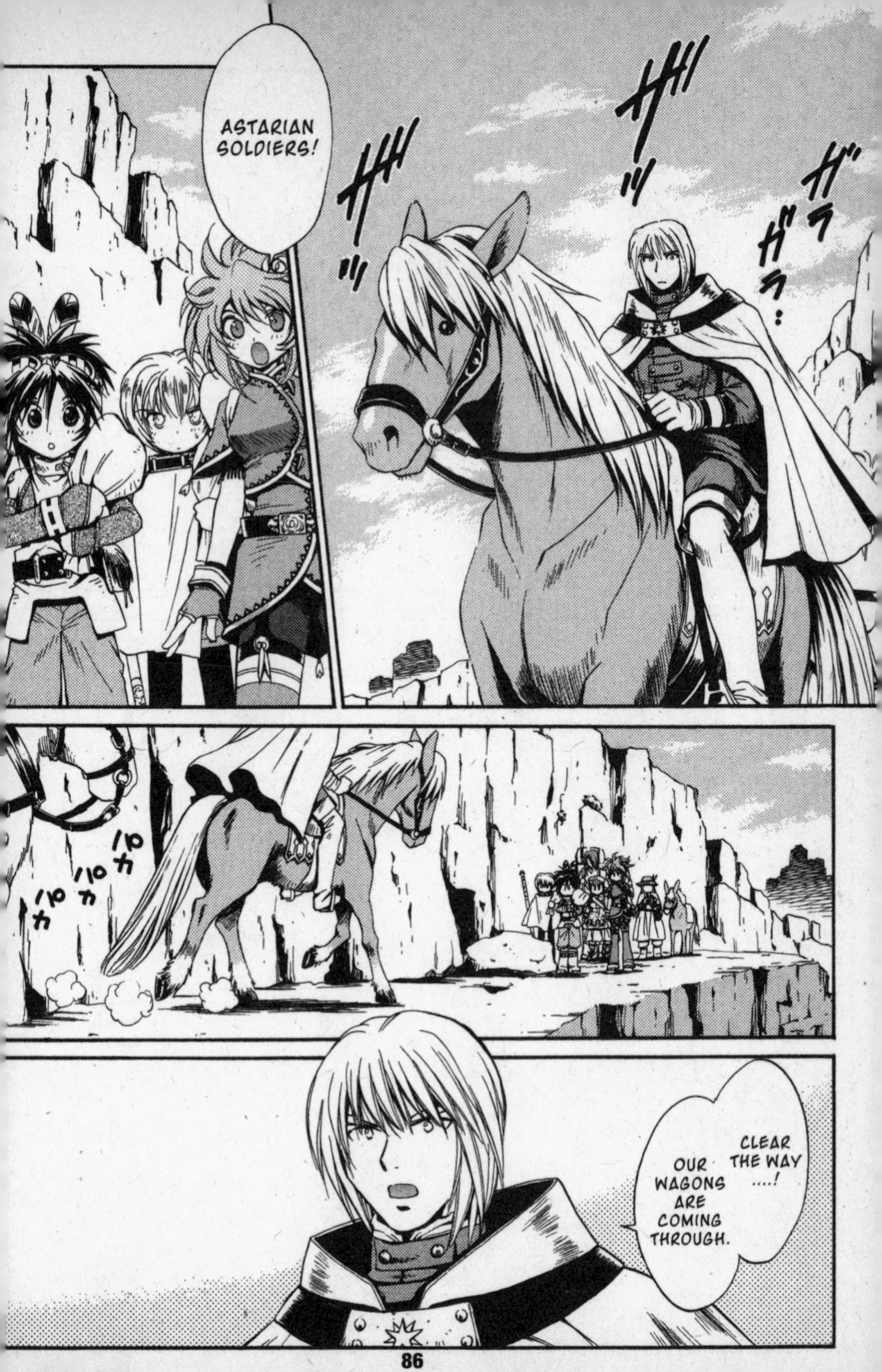

ガラ ガラ
ASTARIAN SOLDIERS!
パカ パカ パカ
CLEAR THE WAY .....!
OUR WAGONS ARE COMING THROUGH.

87

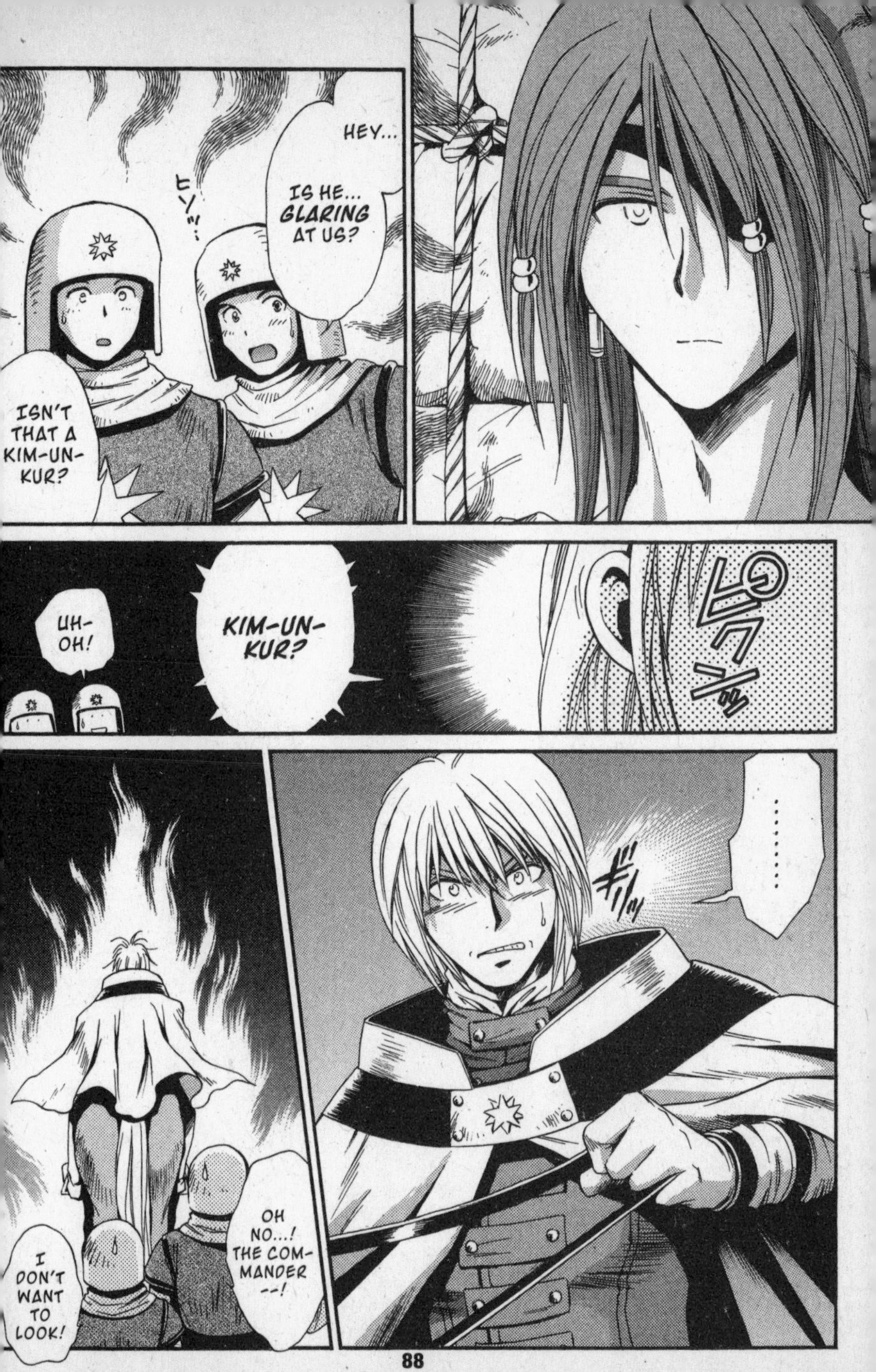
HEY...
IS HE... GLARING AT US?
ISN'T THAT A KIM-UN-KUR?
KIM-UN-KUR?
UH-OH!
......
OH NO...! THE COMMANDER--!
I DON'T WANT TO LOOK!

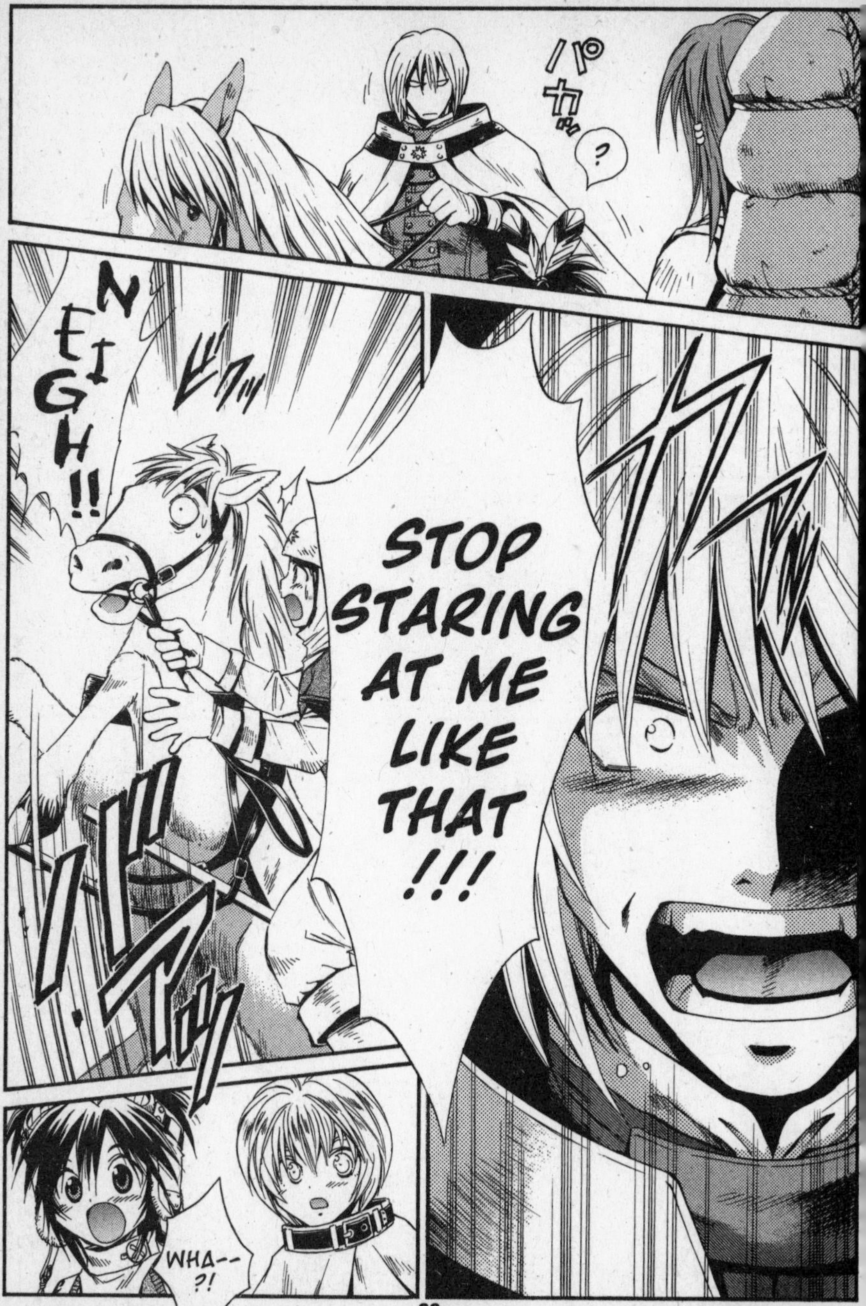
パカッ
?
STOP STARING AT ME LIKE THAT!!!
NEIGH!!
WHA-- ?!

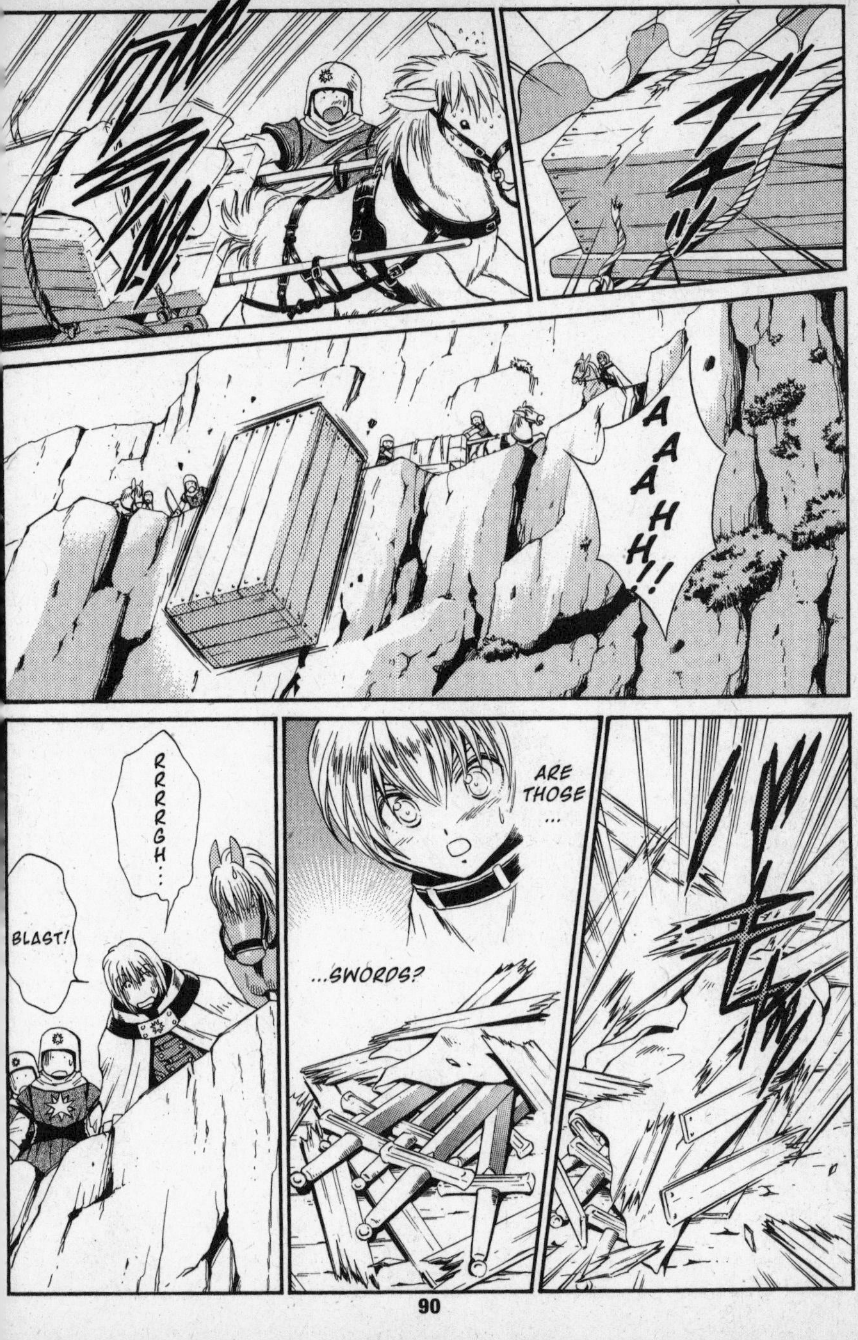
AAAAHH!!
ARE THOSE ...
...SWORDS?
RRRRGH...
BLAST!

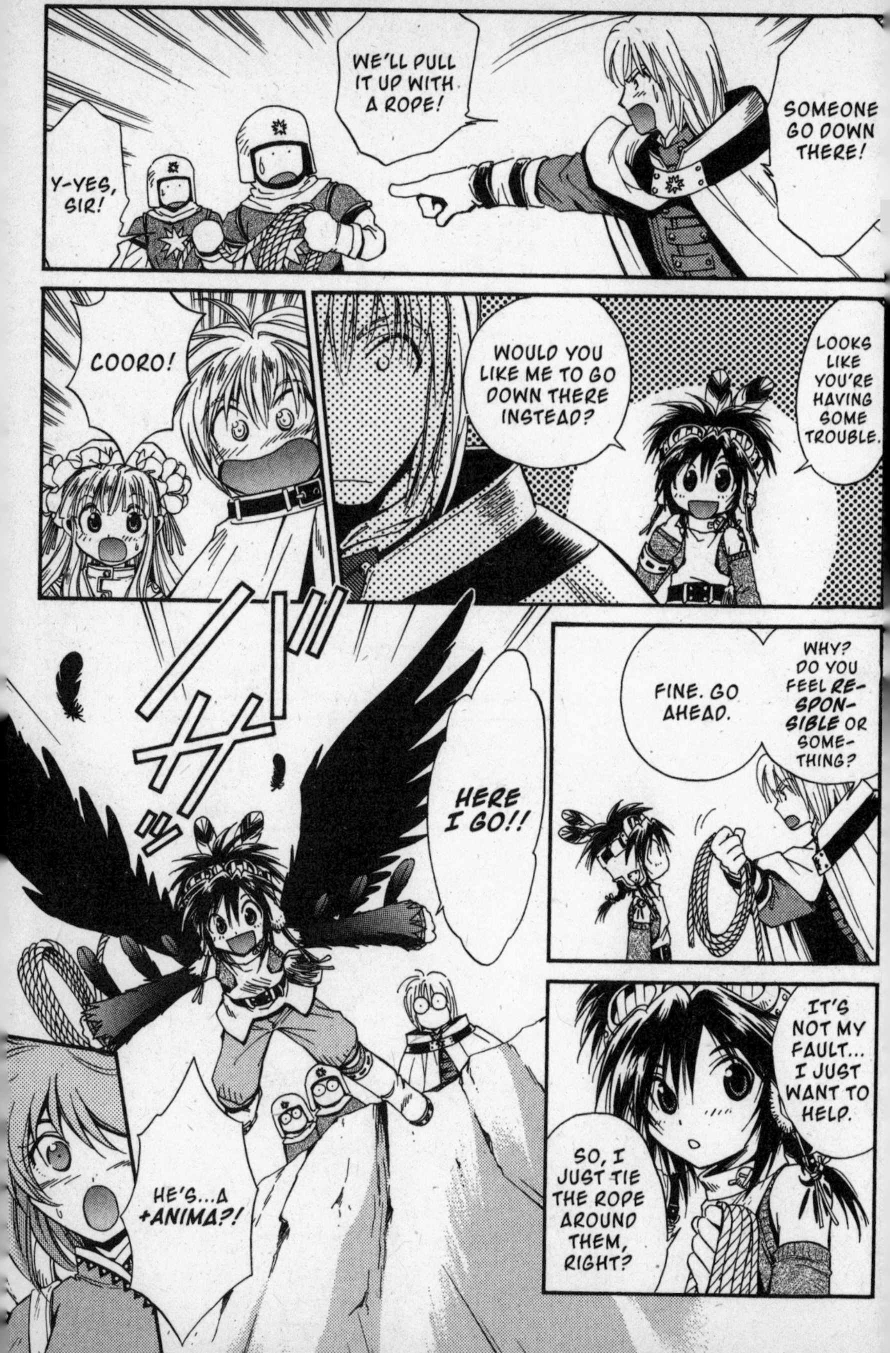
SOMEONE GO DOWN THERE!
WE'LL PULL IT UP WITH A ROPE!
Y-YES, SIR!
LOOKS LIKE YOU'RE HAVING SOME TROUBLE.
WOULD YOU LIKE ME TO GO DOWN THERE INSTEAD?
COORO!
WHY? DO YOU FEEL RE-SPON-SIBLE OR SOME-THING?
FINE. GO AHEAD.
IT'S NOT MY FAULT... I JUST WANT TO HELP.
SO, I JUST TIE THE ROPE AROUND THEM, RIGHT?
HERE I GO!!
HE'S...A +ANIMA?!

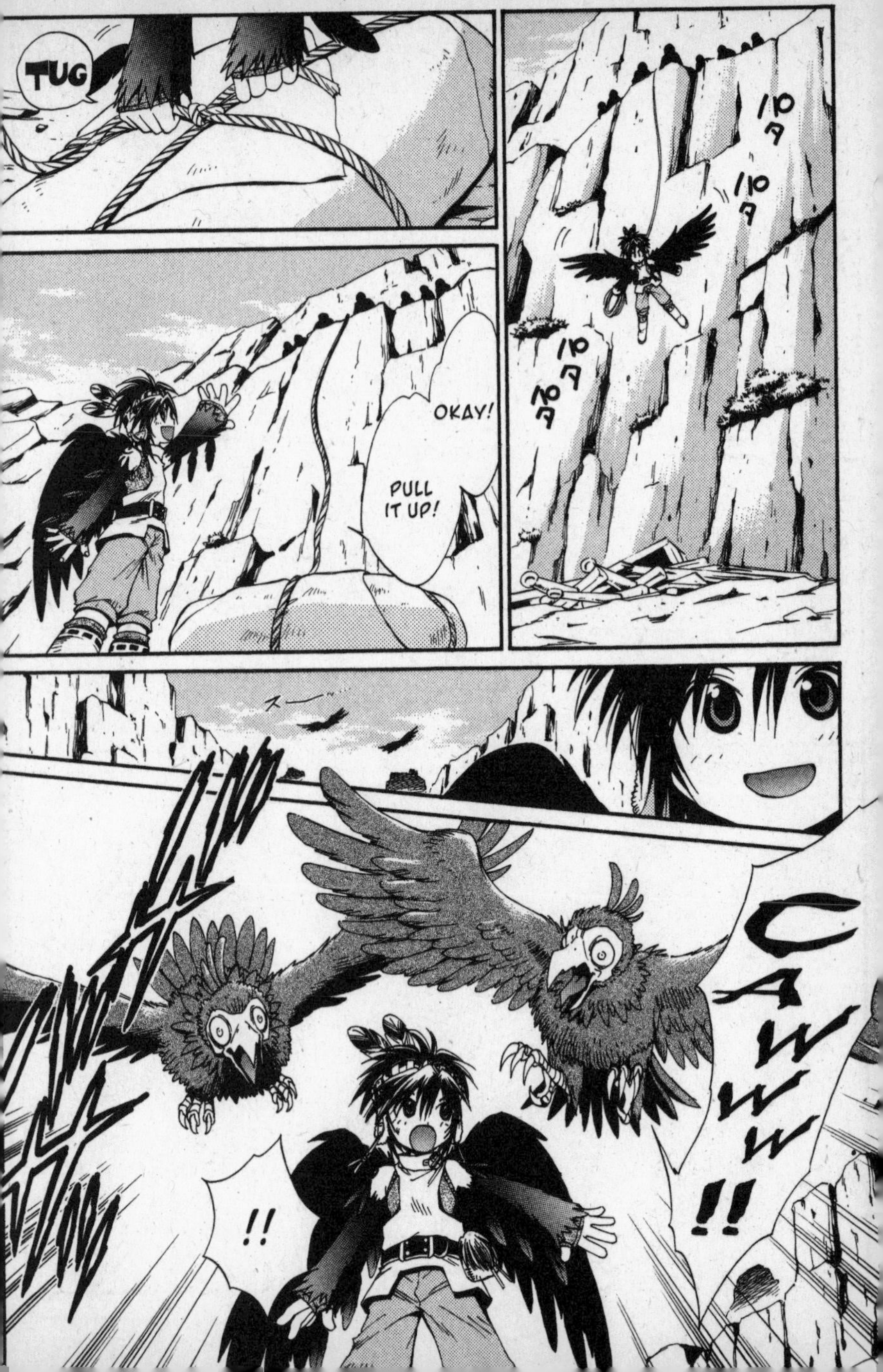
パタ
パタ
パタ
パタ
TUG
OKAY!
PULL IT UP!
スー
CAWWW!!
!!

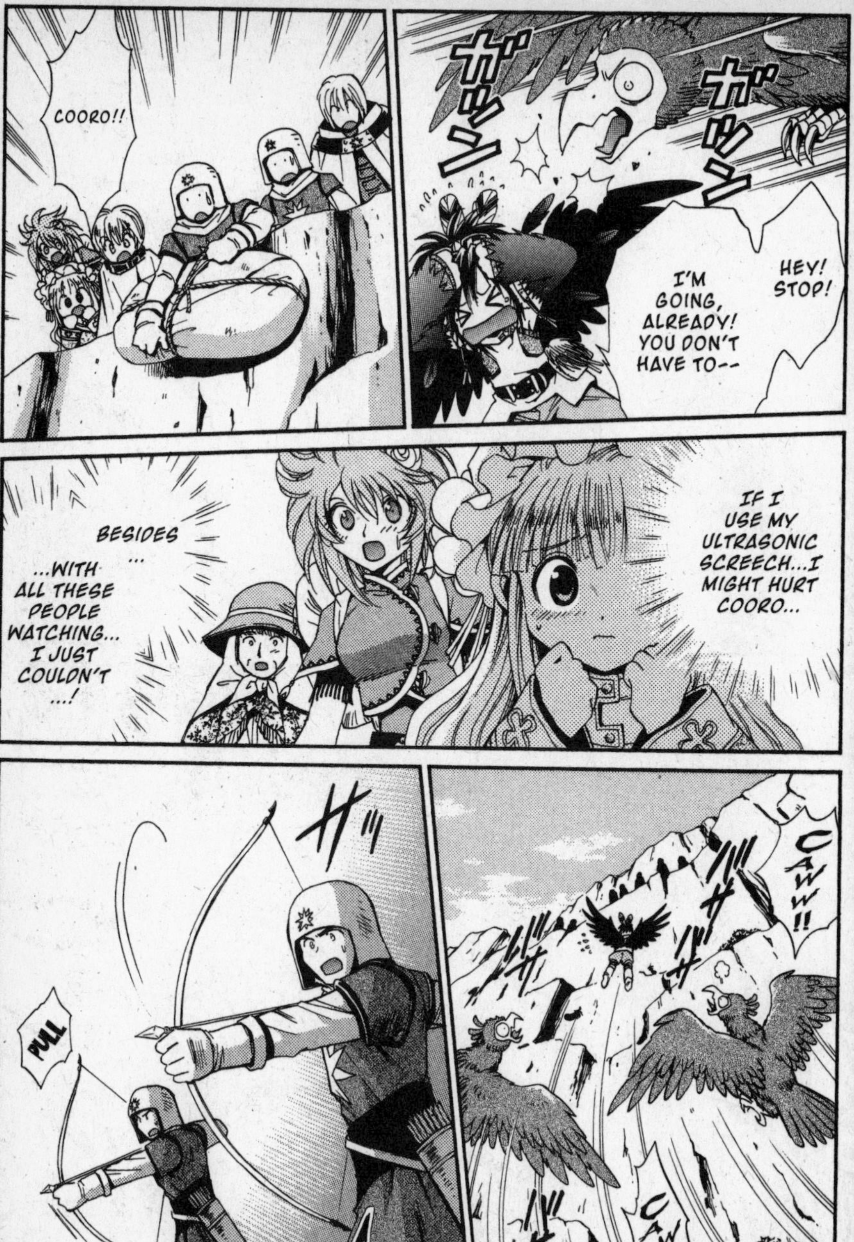

HEY! STOP!
I'M GOING, ALREADY! YOU DON'T HAVE TO--
COORO!!
IF I USE MY ULTRASONIC SCREECH...I MIGHT HURT COORO...
BESIDES ...
...WITH ALL THESE PEOPLE WATCHING... I JUST COULDN'T ...!
CAWW!!
CAWW!!
PULL

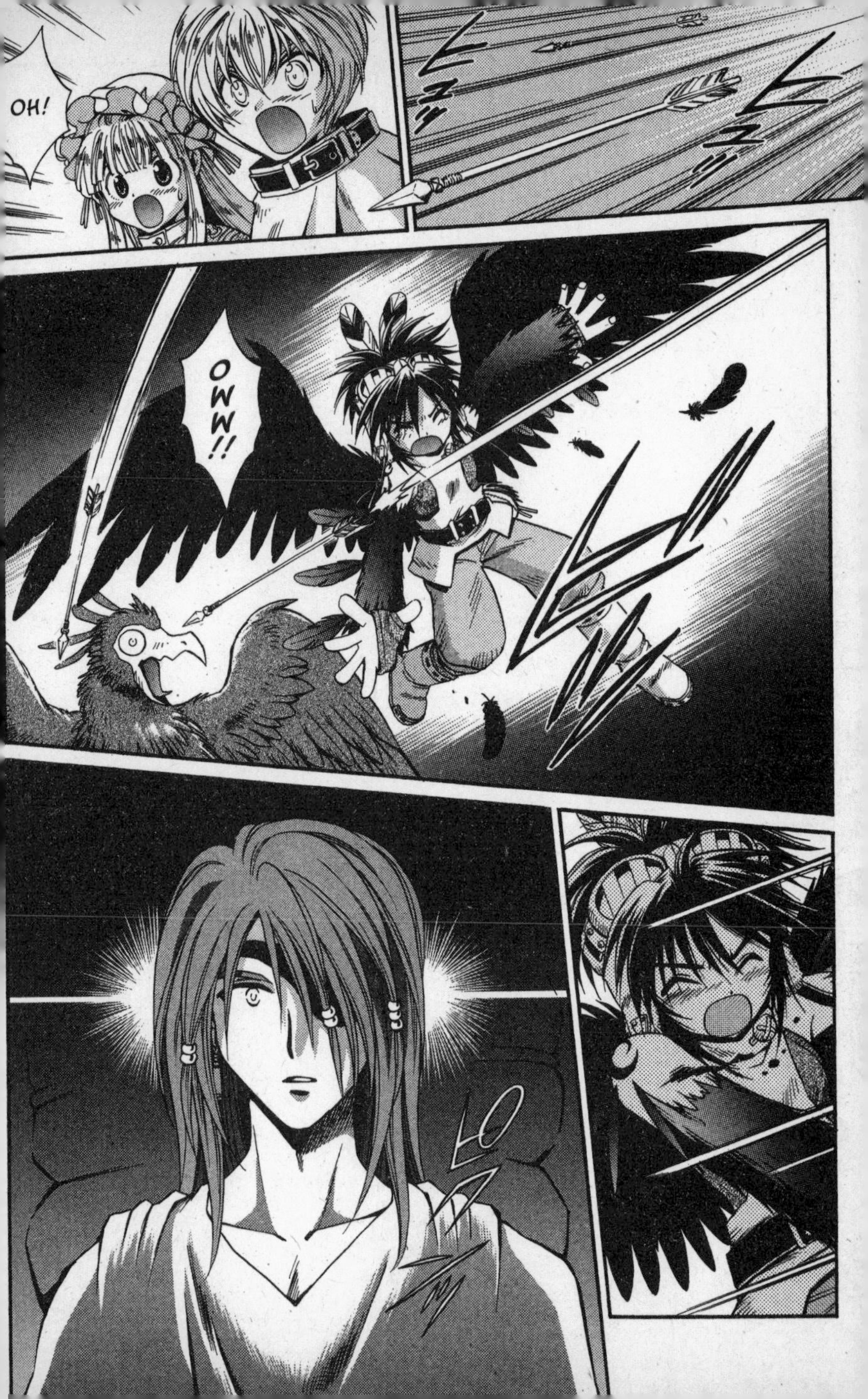
OH!
OWW!!

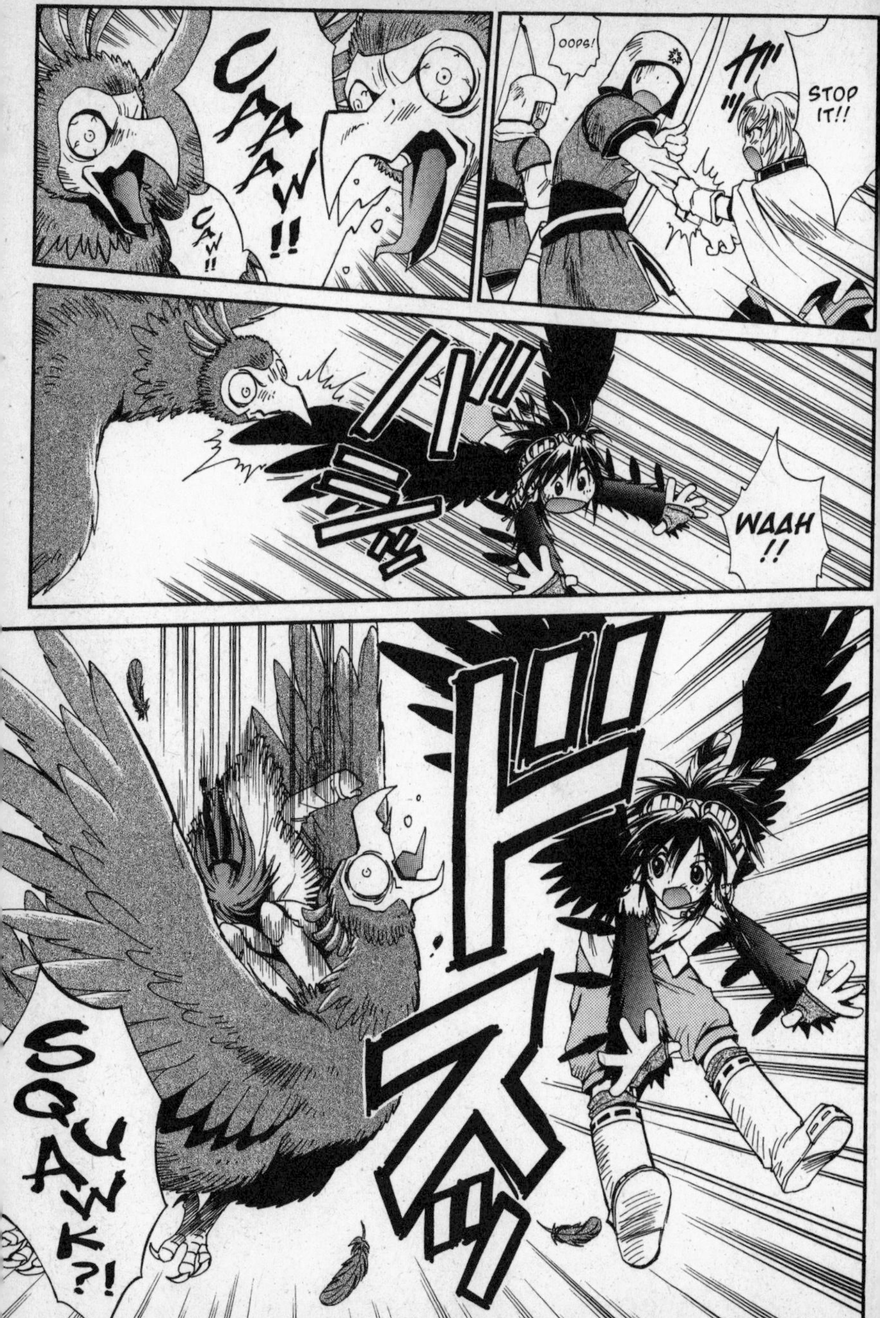
OOPS!
STOP IT!!
CAAAW!!
CAW!!
WAAH!!
SQUAWK?!

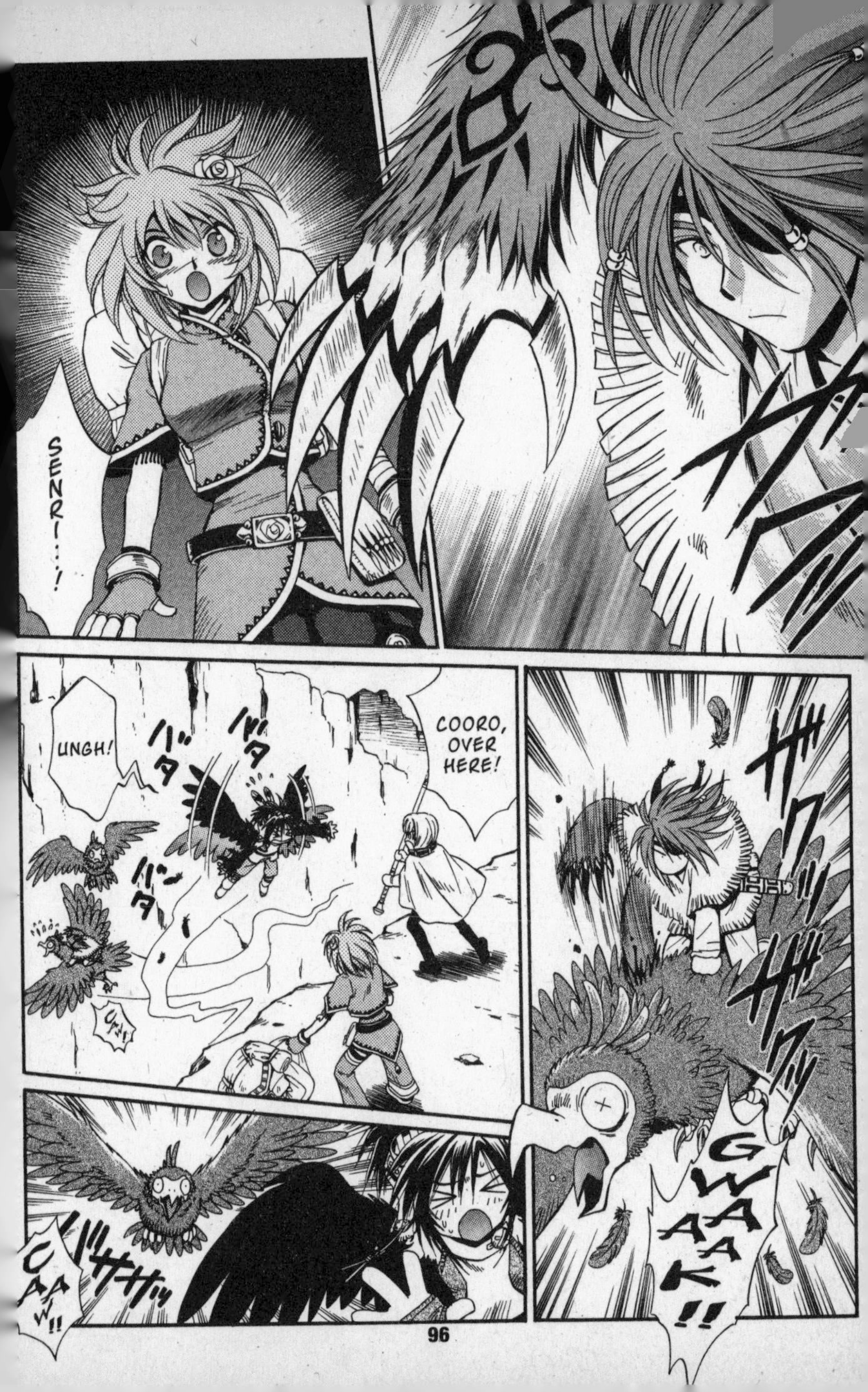
SENRI...!
GWAAAK!!
COORO, OVER HERE!
UNGH!
CAAW!!

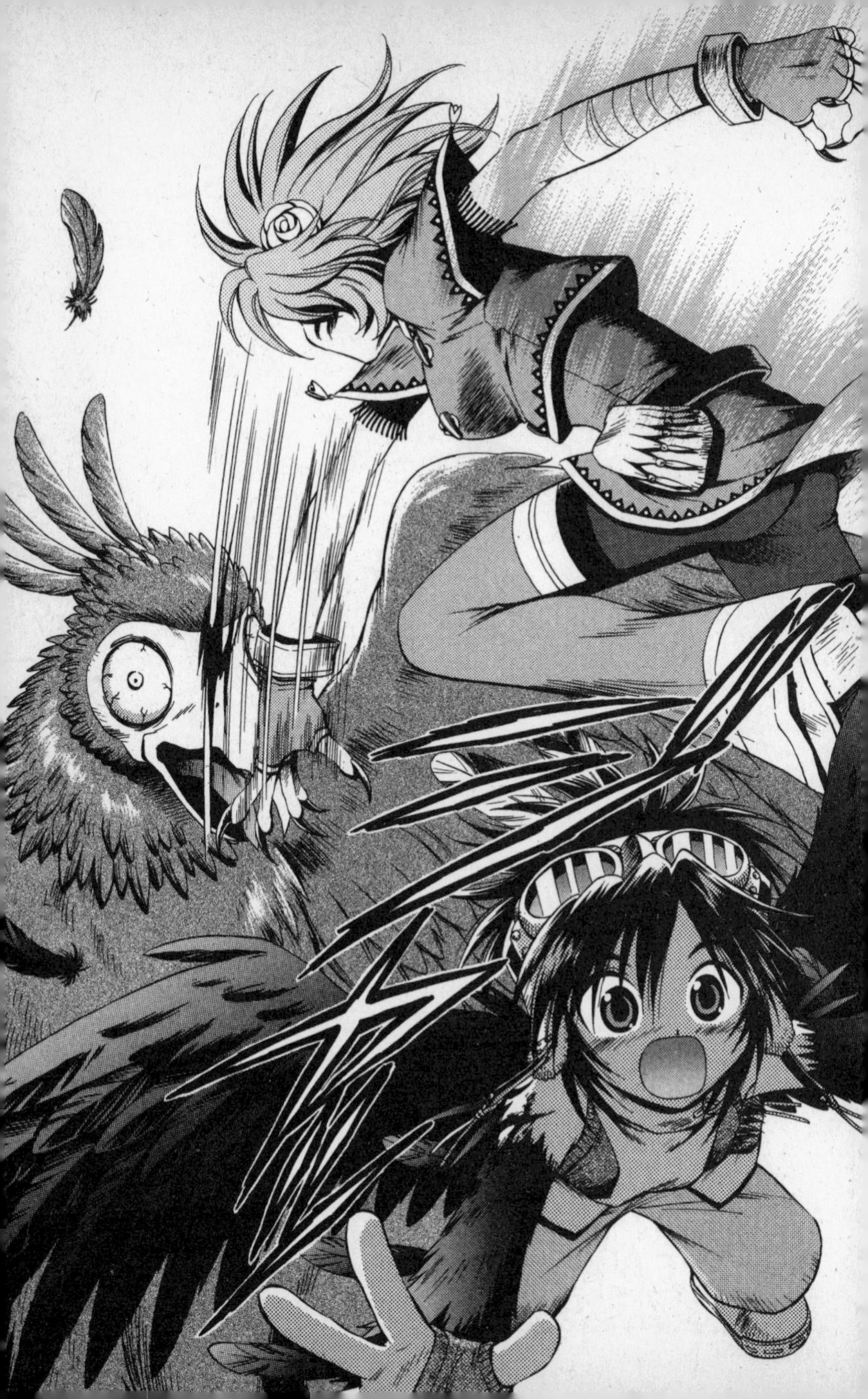

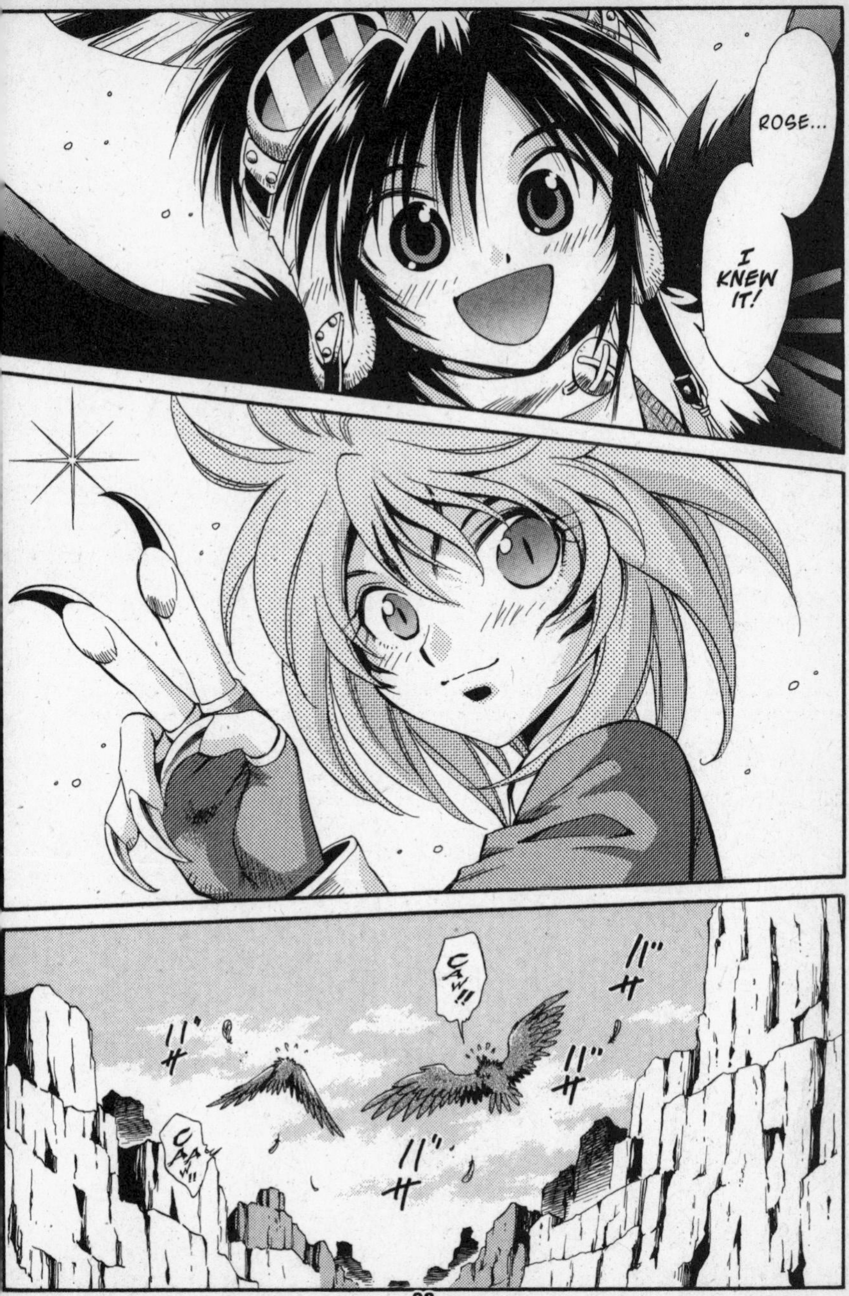
ROSE...
I KNEW IT!
バサ
CAW!!
バサ
バサ
CAAW!!
バサ

OH!

DOWN THERE...

HEY... WHERE'S SENRI?!

HUH?

PAIN IN THE BUTT...

ARE YOU OKAY?

SENRI! THANKS FOR SAVING ME!

COORO! SENRI! YOU'RE BOTH ALWAYS GETTING INTO TROUBLE 'CUZ YOU DON'T THINK AHEAD!

Climbed up the rope.

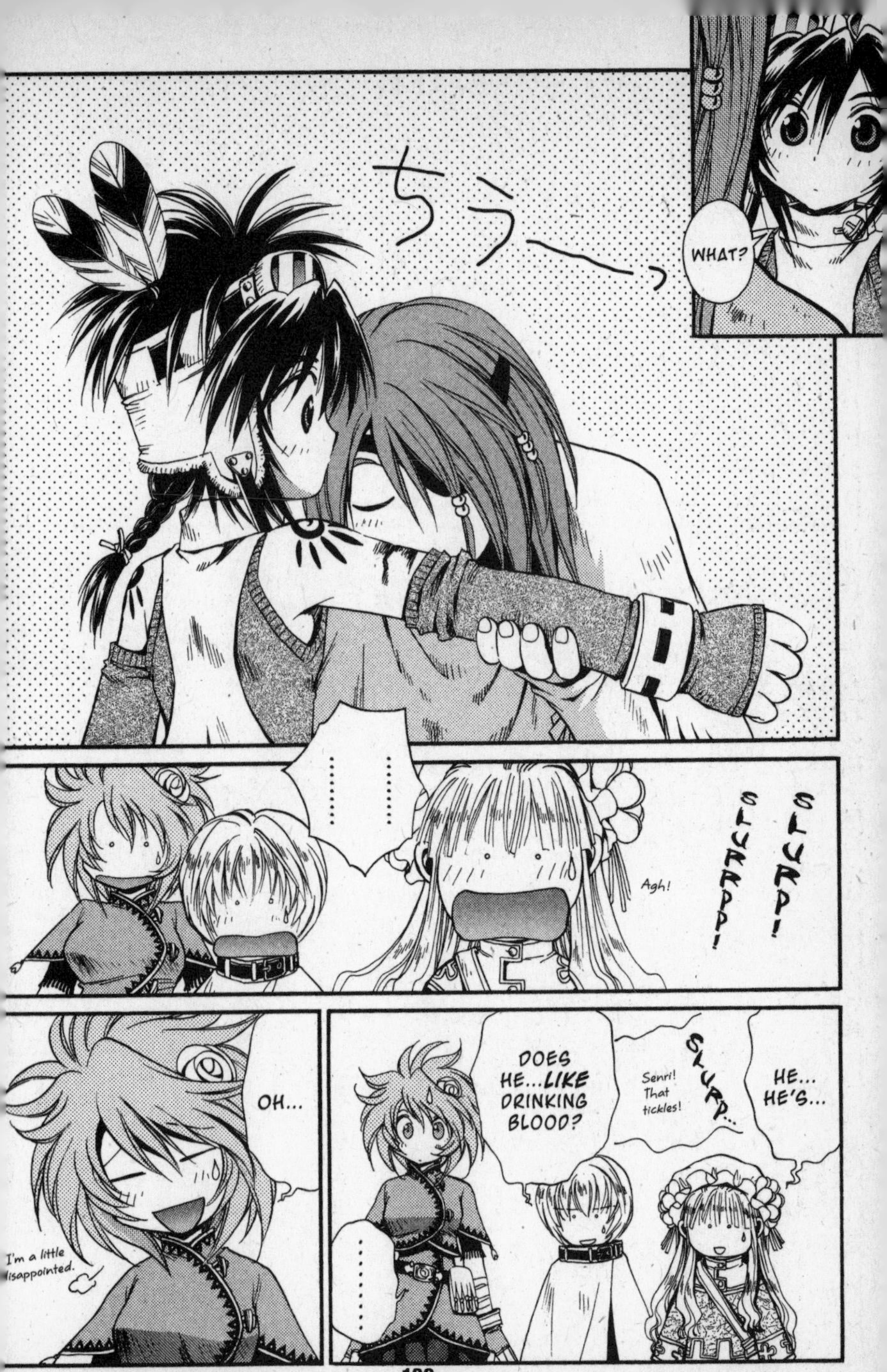
WHAT?
ちうーーっ
SLURP!
SLURRP!
Agh!
......
HE... HE'S...
SLURP...
Senri! That tickles!
DOES HE...LIKE DRINKING BLOOD?
...
OH...
I'm a little isappointed.

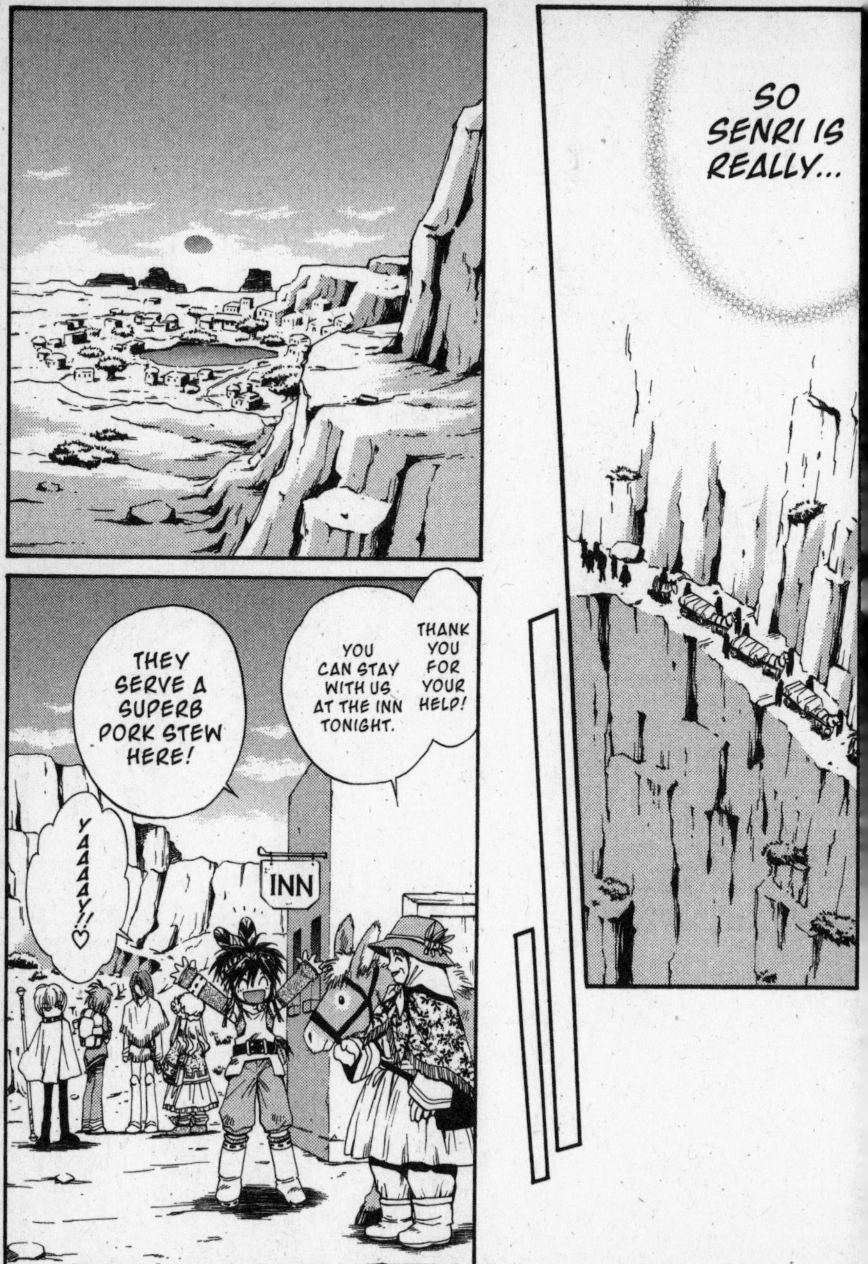
SO SENRI IS REALLY...
THANK YOU FOR YOUR HELP!
YOU CAN STAY WITH US AT THE INN TONIGHT.
THEY SERVE A SUPERB PORK STEW HERE!
INN
YAAAAY!!♡

AFTER THIS STOP, I'LL BE GOING HOME TO SEE HIM FOR THE FIRST TIME IN MONTHS.

SEEING YOU REMINDS ME OF MY LITTLE BROTHER.

SENRI...

HE'S JUST...

...EIGHT YEARS OLD, YOU KNOW?

BUT...

HER LITTLE BROTHER...?!

DO YOU LIKE IT?

I THINK IT WILL LOOK GOOD ON YOU, NANA.

REALLY?

THIS IS FOR YOU!

Y-YES. THANK YOU, ROSE.

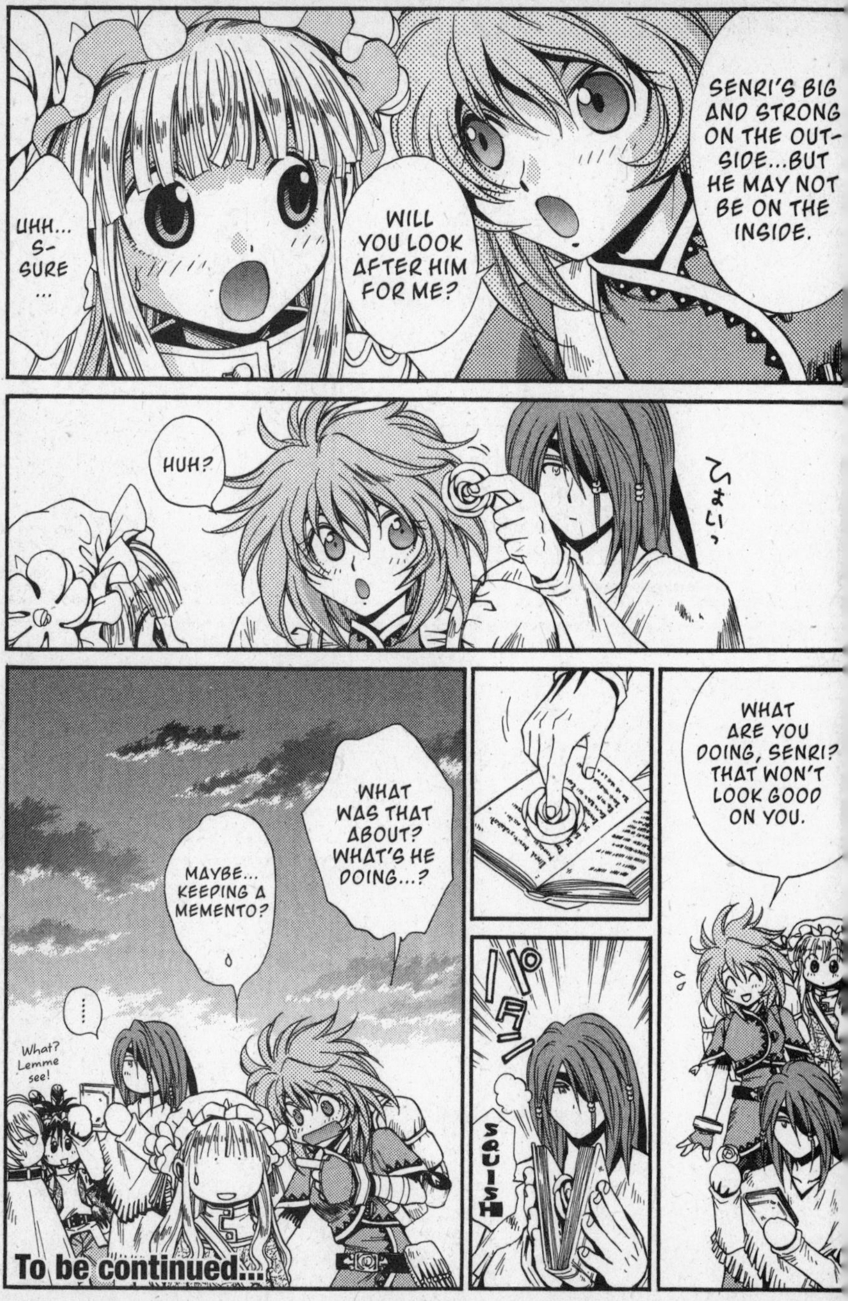
SENRI'S BIG AND STRONG ON THE OUT-SIDE...BUT HE MAY NOT BE ON THE INSIDE.
WILL YOU LOOK AFTER HIM FOR ME?
UHH... S-SURE...
ひょいっ
HUH?
WHAT ARE YOU DOING, SENRI? THAT WON'T LOOK GOOD ON YOU.
パタン
SQUISH
WHAT WAS THAT ABOUT? WHAT'S HE DOING...?
MAYBE... KEEPING A MEMENTO?
......
What? Lemme see!
To be continued...

About Parallel 1–3

The three chapters starting on the next page are special episodes that I drew as a short series before *+Anima* was serialized! There are subtle differences in the character designs of Cooro and the others. I'd love it if you would read (and enjoy) these chapters! Just consider it a parallel world that shows what could have been...

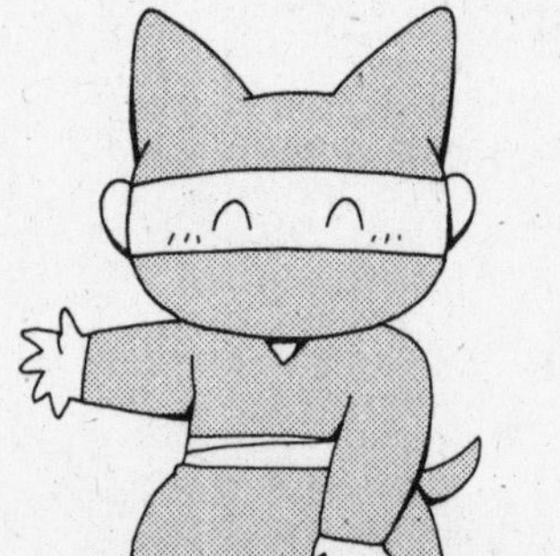

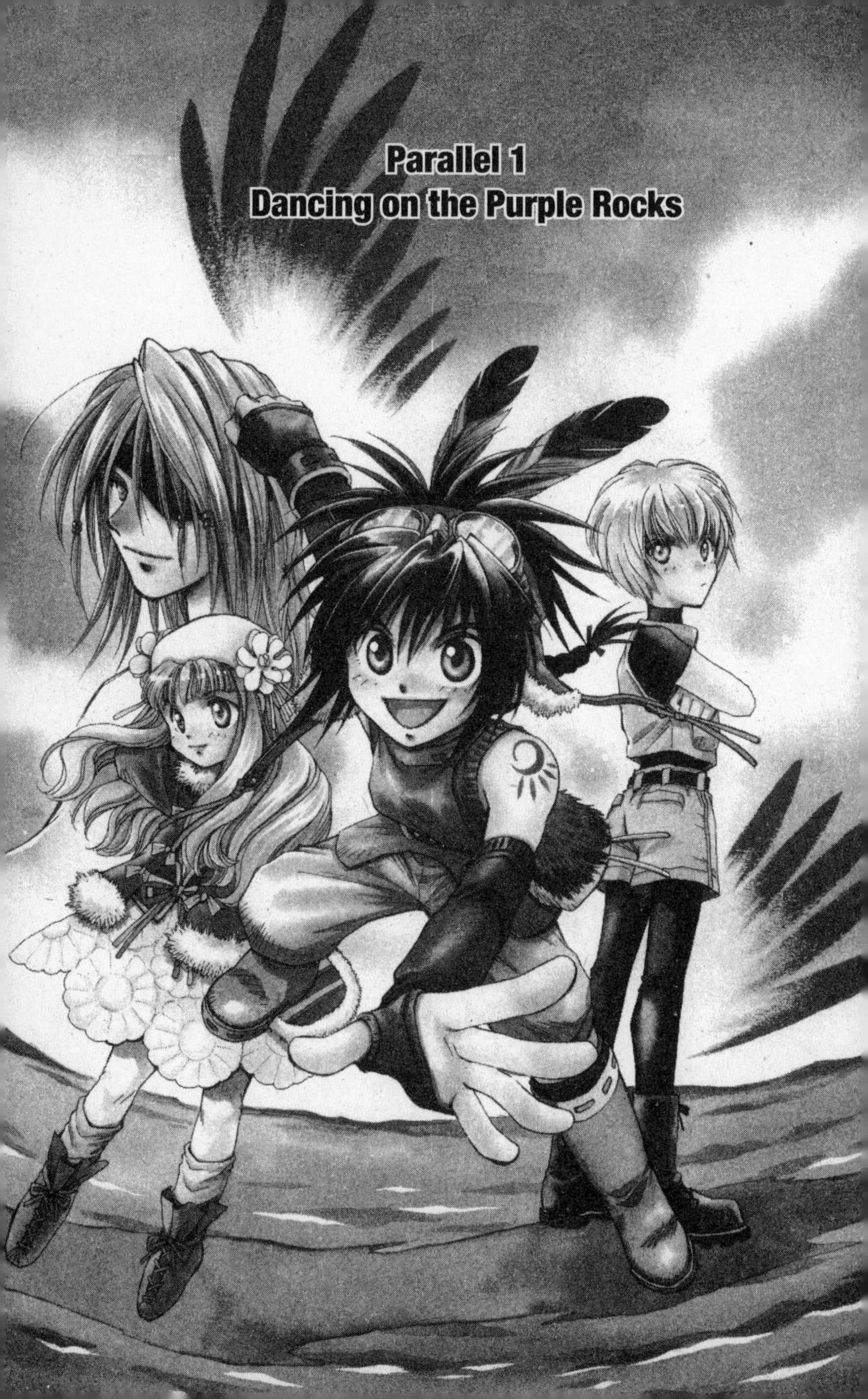
Parallel 1
Dancing on the Purple Rocks

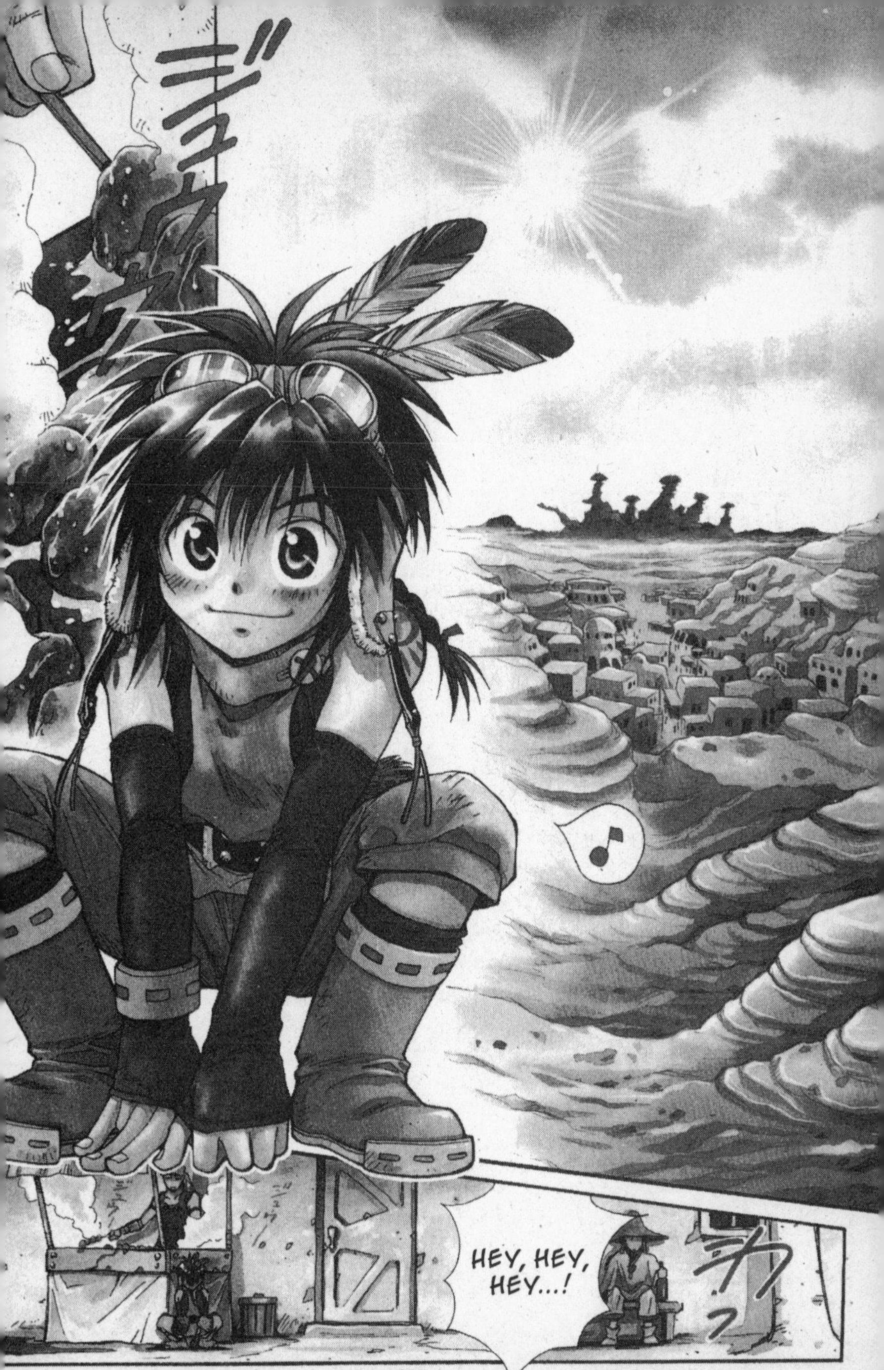
HEY, HEY, HEY...!

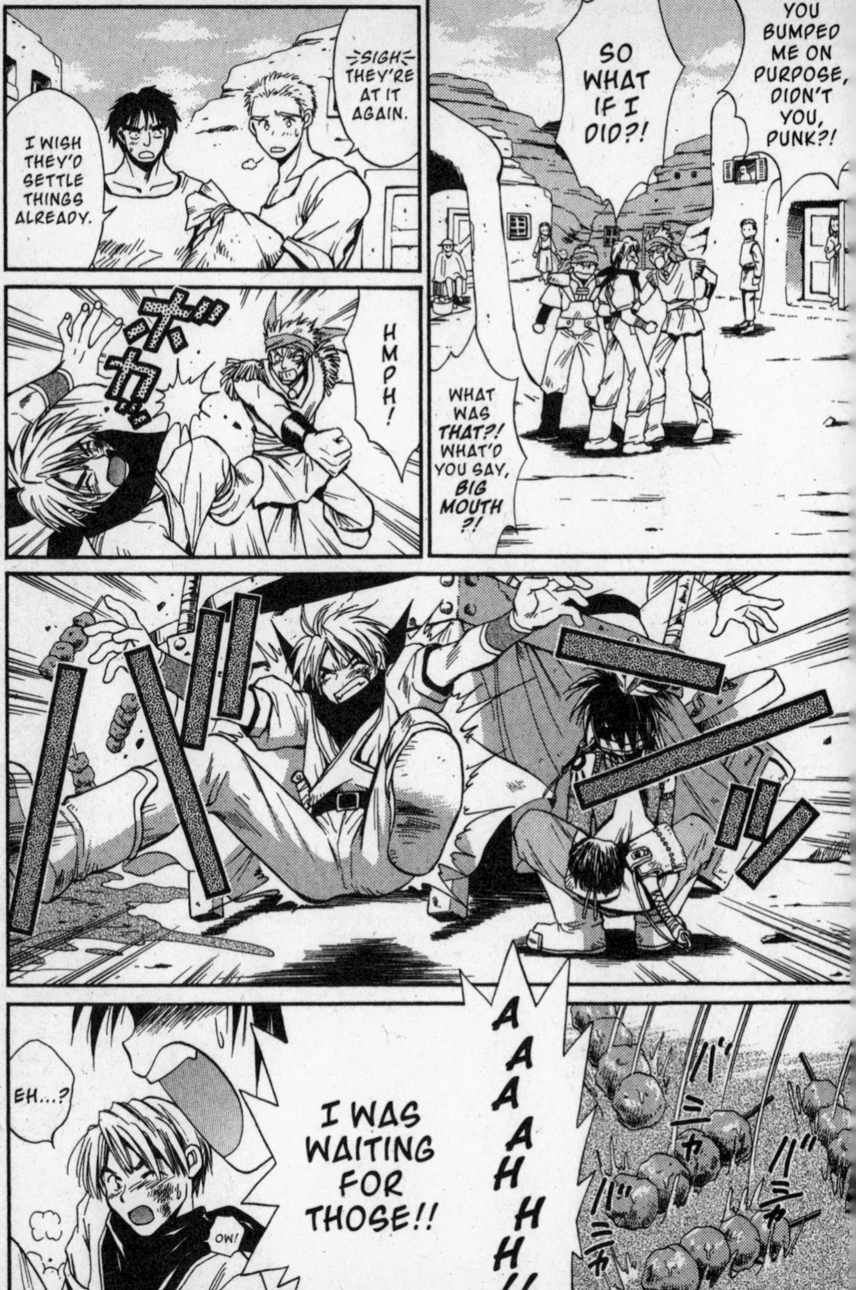
YOU BUMPED ME ON PURPOSE, DIDN'T YOU, PUNK?!
SO WHAT IF I DID?!
WHAT WAS THAT?! WHAT'D YOU SAY, BIG MOUTH?!
-SIGH- THEY'RE AT IT AGAIN.
I WISH THEY'D SETTLE THINGS ALREADY.
HMPH!
ボカッ
AAAAHHHH!!
I WAS WAITING FOR THOSE!!
EH...?
OW!

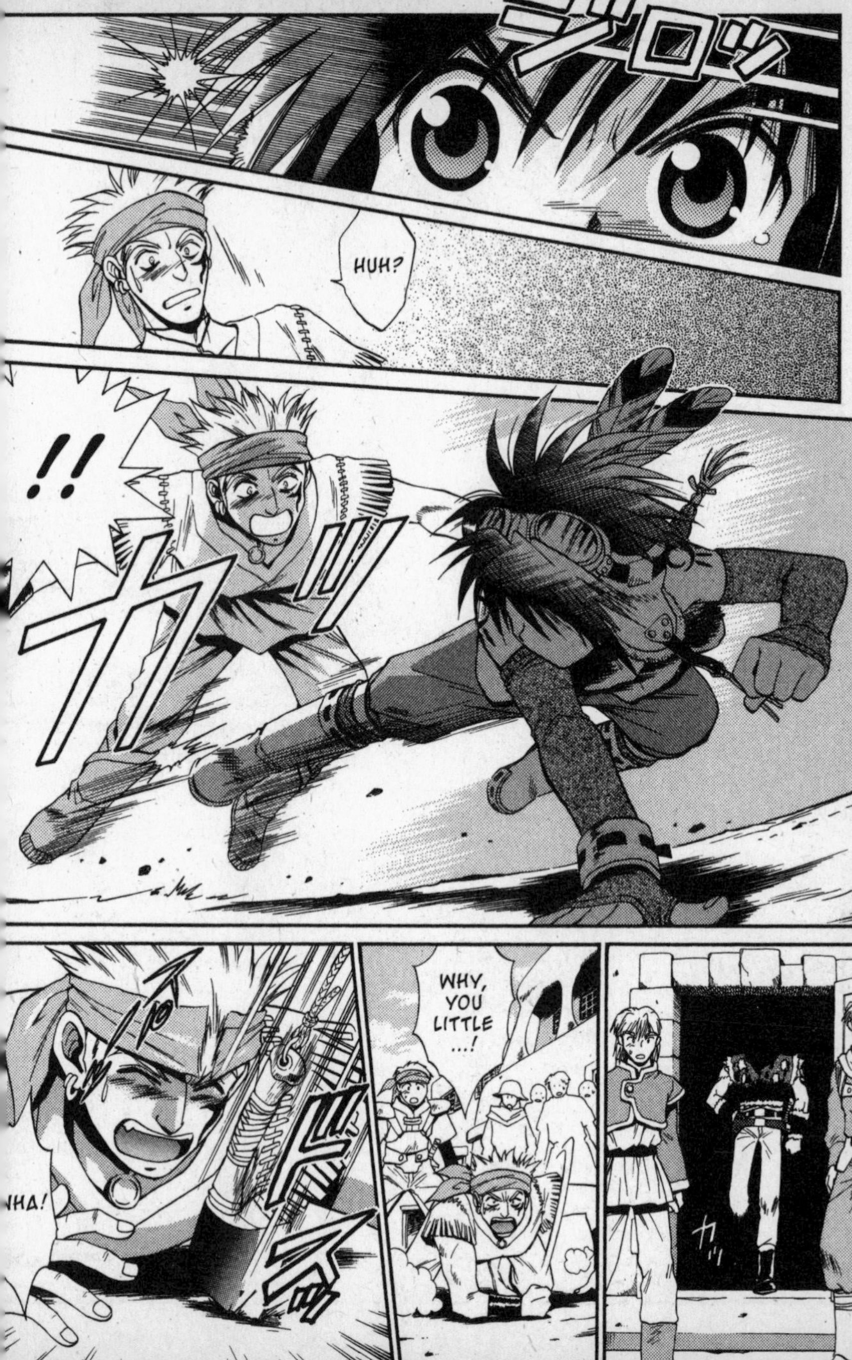

ジロッ
HUH?
!!
WHY, YOU LITTLE ...!
NHA!

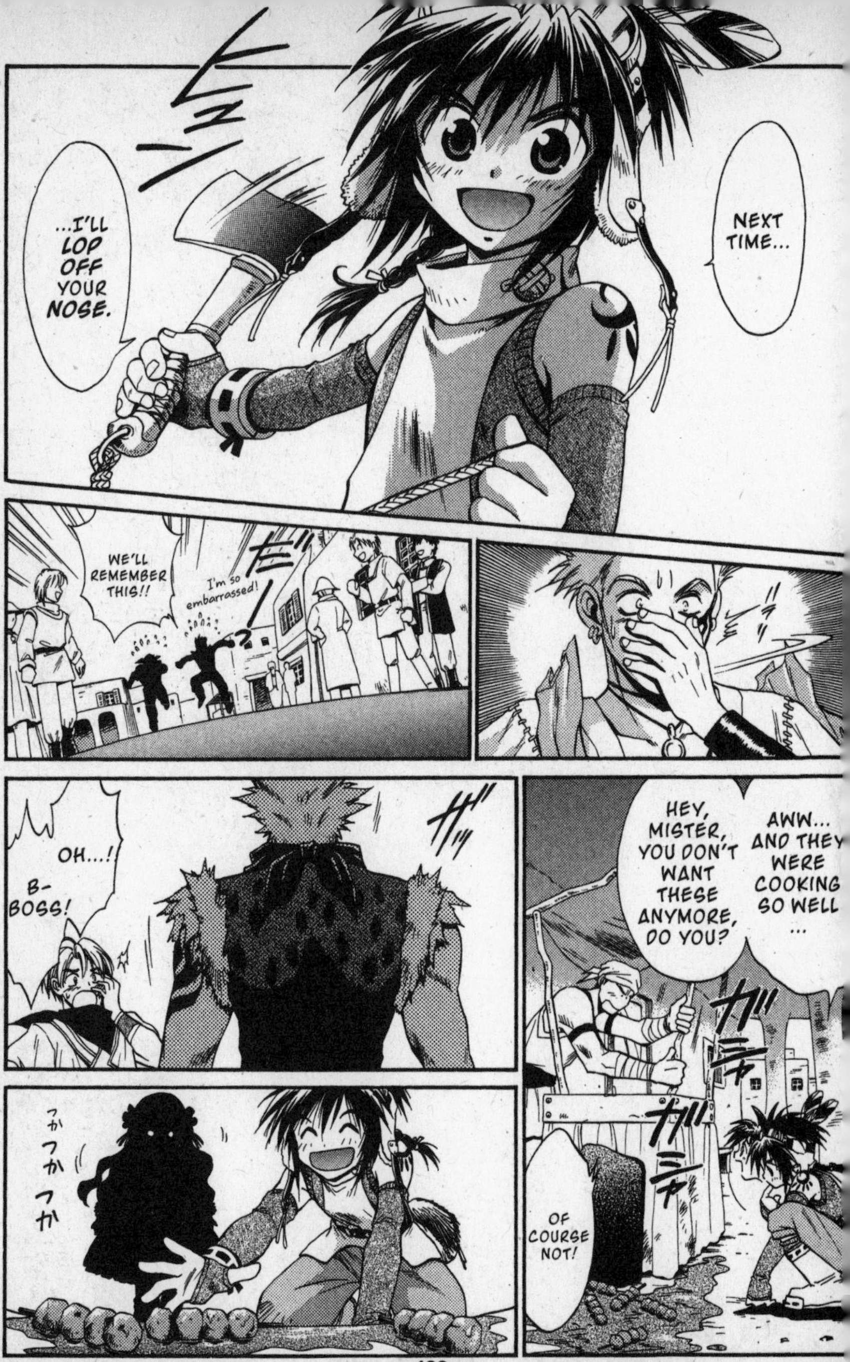
NEXT TIME...
...I'LL LOP OFF YOUR NOSE.
WE'LL REMEMBER THIS!!
I'm so embarrassed!
AWW... AND THEY WERE COOKING SO WELL ...
HEY, MISTER, YOU DON'T WANT THESE ANYMORE, DO YOU?
ガシャ
ガシャ
OF COURSE NOT!
OH...!
B-BOSS!
つかつかつか

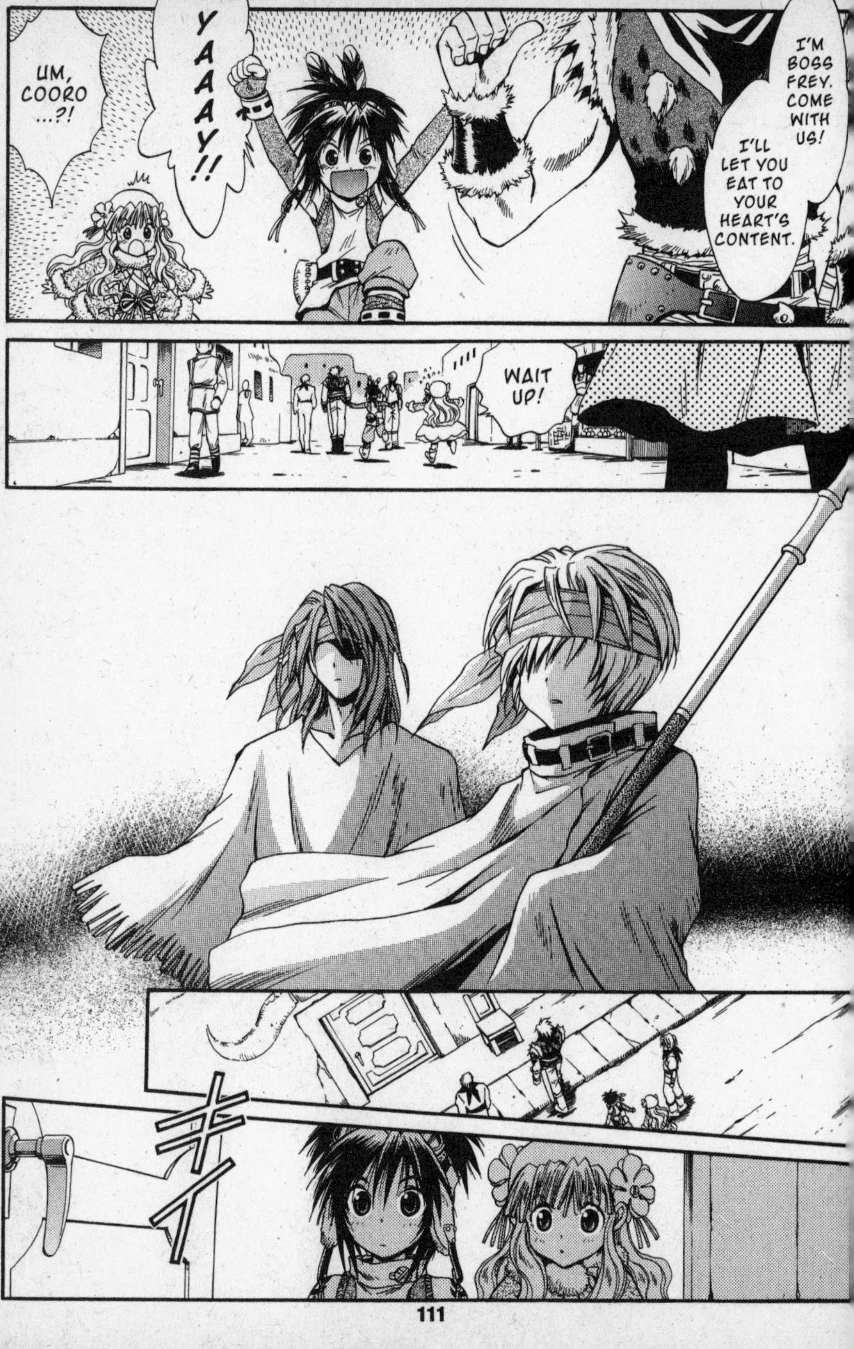
I'M BOSS FREY. COME WITH US!
I'LL LET YOU EAT TO YOUR HEART'S CONTENT.
YAAAAY!!
UM, COORO ...?!
WAIT UP!
キイ

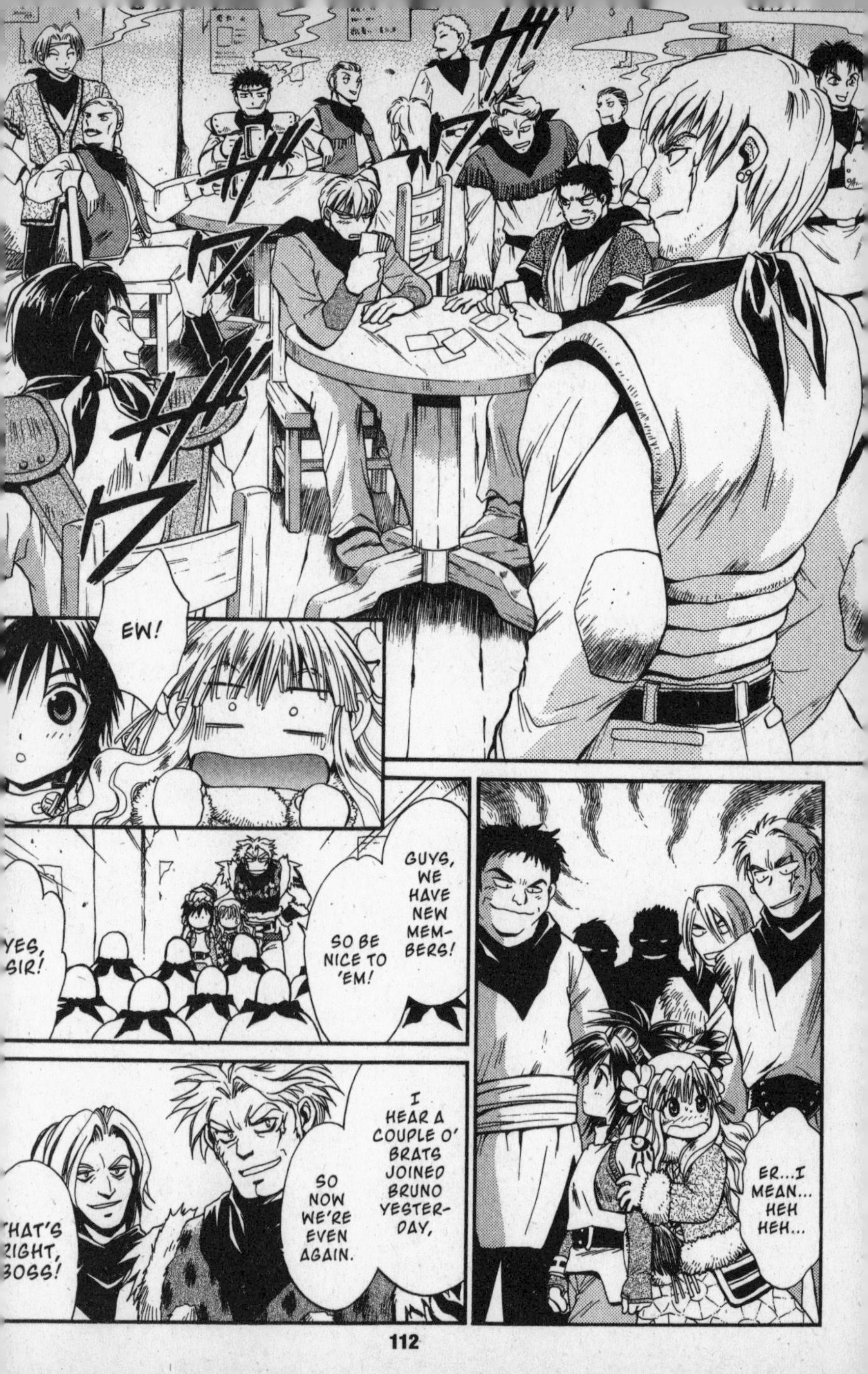
EW!
ER...I MEAN... HEH HEH...
GUYS, WE HAVE NEW MEMBERS!
SO BE NICE TO 'EM!
YES, SIR!
I HEAR A COUPLE O' BRATS JOINED BRUNO YESTERDAY,
SO NOW WE'RE EVEN AGAIN.
THAT'S RIGHT, BOSS!

HERE. EAT!

IF THEY DON'T EAT, THEY CAN'T GET STRONGER!

LET THEM EAT AS MUCH AS THEY WANT!

WOW!!

THE GUYS COORO FOUGHT WITH EARLIER HAD BLUE BANDANAS...

I JUST NOTICED THAT EVERYONE HERE HAS A RED BANDANA.

THE GUYS WITH BLUE ONES AROUND THEIR FOREHEADS ARE FROM BRUNO'S GANG.

THAT'S RIGHT! RED IS THE COLOR OF FREY'S GANG.

FOR GENERATIONS, THAT'S WHERE THIS TOWN'S GANG BOSSES HAVE HIDDEN THEIR TREASURE.

THOSE ARE THE PURPLE ROCKS.

HERE... TAKE A LOOK AT THAT.

AFTER THE HEAD BOSS DIES, THE ONE WHO FINDS THE TREASURE NEXT GETS TO BE THE NEW HEAD BOSS.

IN THE MOUNTAINS, THERE ARE RED ROCK-DRAGONS.

YOU MEAN THE ONES THAT *EAT* PEOPLE?!

NOA... 'VE EVER EN BE RE!!

SO WHY DON'T THEY JUST GO AND GET IT?

THE LAST BOSS DIED A MONTH AGO.

BOSS FREY AND BRUNO, WHO WERE THE LEADERS OF SMALLER GANGS, ARE COMPETING FOR THE TITLE OF NEW HEAD BOSS.

SO WE CAN'T MAKE A MOVE THAT EASILY.

BOTH GANGS HAVE BEEN PREPARING THEIR FIGHTERS AND WEAPONS.

AND OF COURSE, IF WE GO TO THE MOUNTAINS, WE'LL HAVE TO FACE BRUNO'S GANG.

EEP!

COORO! WHAT ARE WE GOING TO DO NOW THAT WE'RE INVOLVED IN THIS MESS?!

AND THAT'S HOW IT IS. YOU GUYS WORK HARD, YOU'LL DO FINE.

UNTIL THEN, E GET O EAT! OT BAD, HUH?

ONCE THEY GET THE TREASURE AND DECIDE ON THE NEW BOSS, THEY WON'T NEED US ANYMORE.

THANKS!

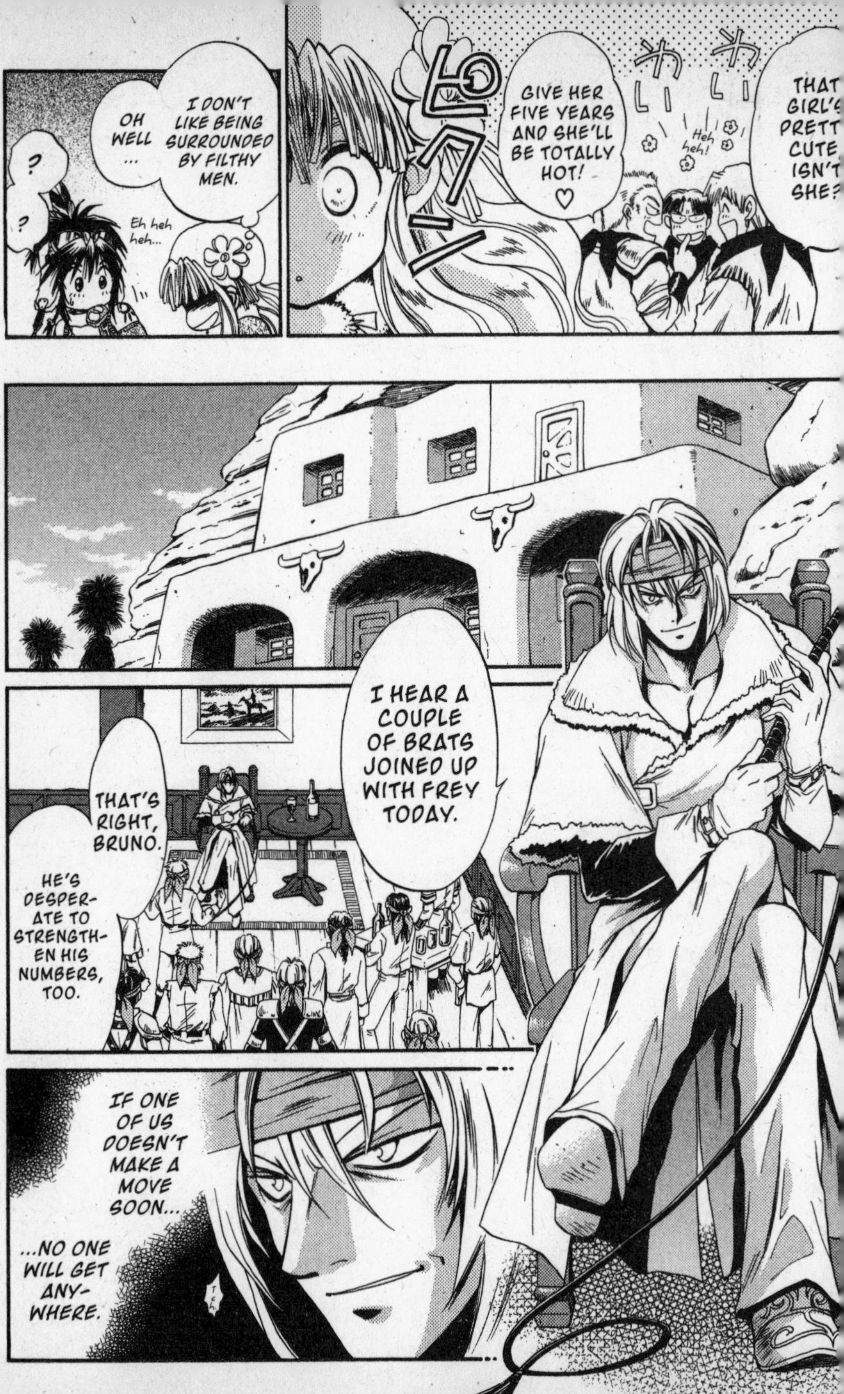
THAT GIRL'S PRETT CUTE ISN'T SHE?
わい わい
Heh heh!
GIVE HER FIVE YEARS AND SHE'LL BE TOTALLY HOT! ♡
I DON'T LIKE BEING SURROUNDED BY FILTHY MEN.
OH WELL ...
Eh heh heh...
?
?
I HEAR A COUPLE OF BRATS JOINED UP WITH FREY TODAY.
THAT'S RIGHT, BRUNO.
HE'S DESPERATE TO STRENGTHEN HIS NUMBERS, TOO.
IF ONE OF US DOESN'T MAKE A MOVE SOON...
...NO ONE WILL GET ANYWHERE.
Tch

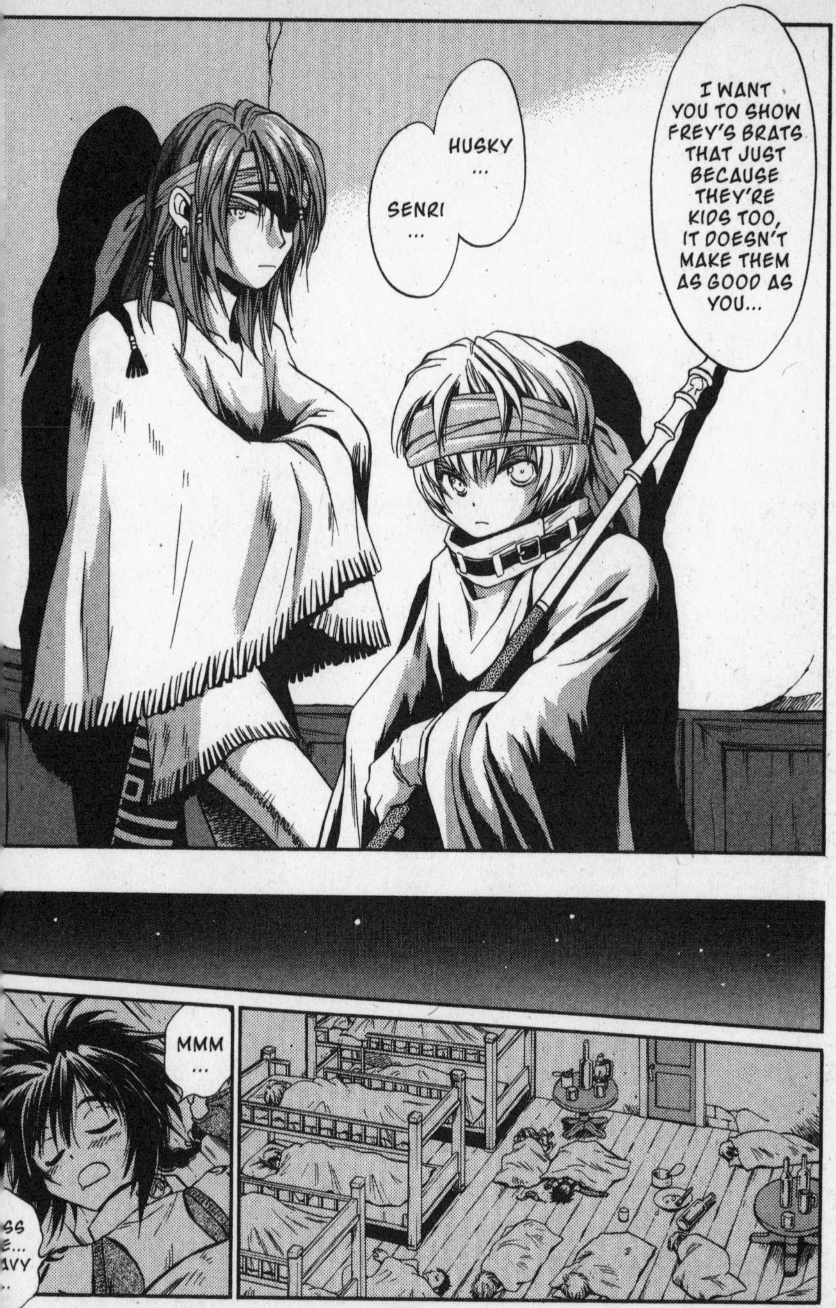
I WANT YOU TO SHOW FREY'S BRATS THAT JUST BECAUSE THEY'RE KIDS TOO, IT DOESN'T MAKE THEM AS GOOD AS YOU...
HUSKY ... SENRI ...
MMM ...

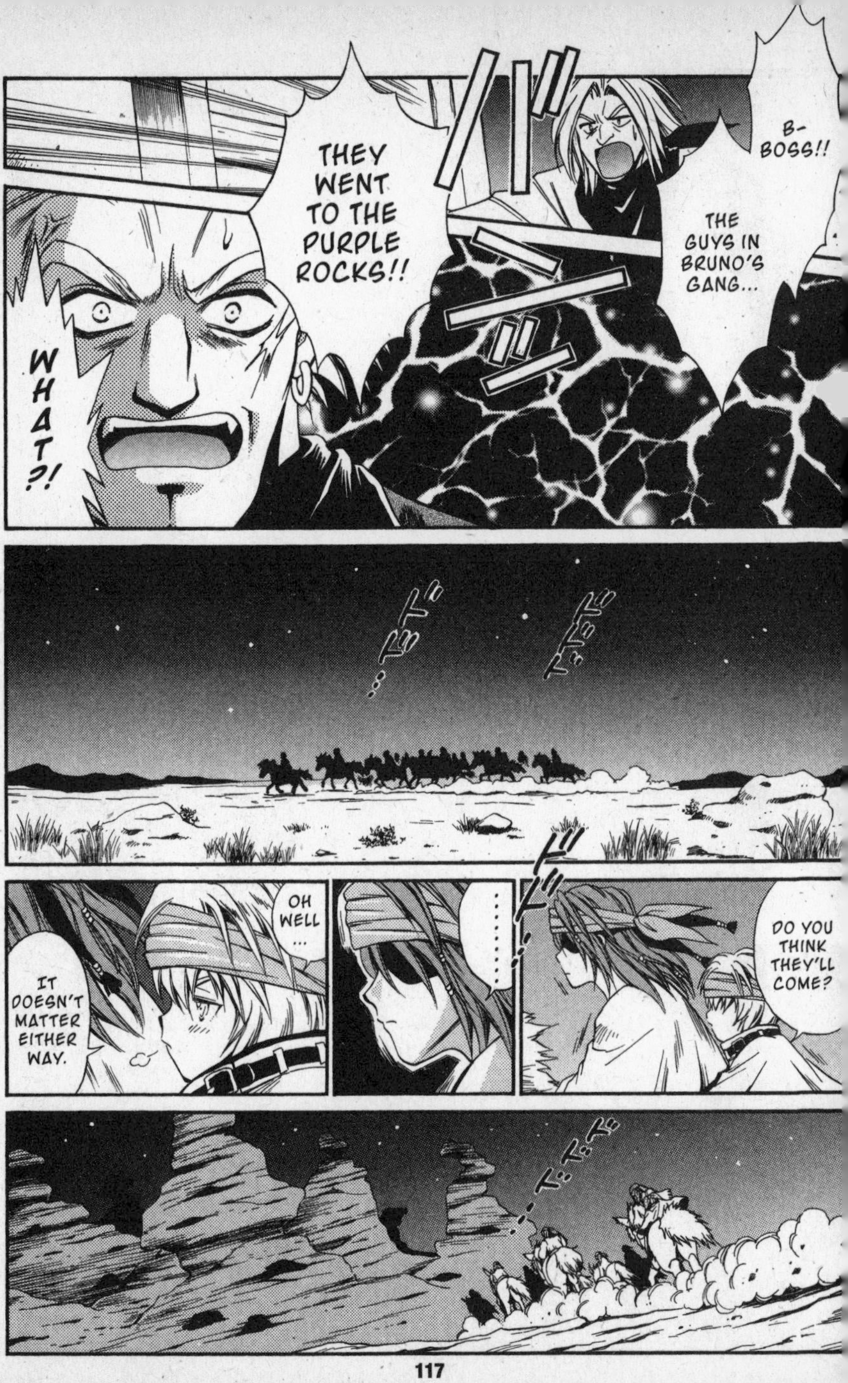
B-BOSS!!
THE GUYS IN BRUNO'S GANG...
THEY WENT TO THE PURPLE ROCKS!!
WHAT?!
DO YOU THINK THEY'LL COME?
......
OH WELL ...
IT DOESN'T MATTER EITHER WAY.

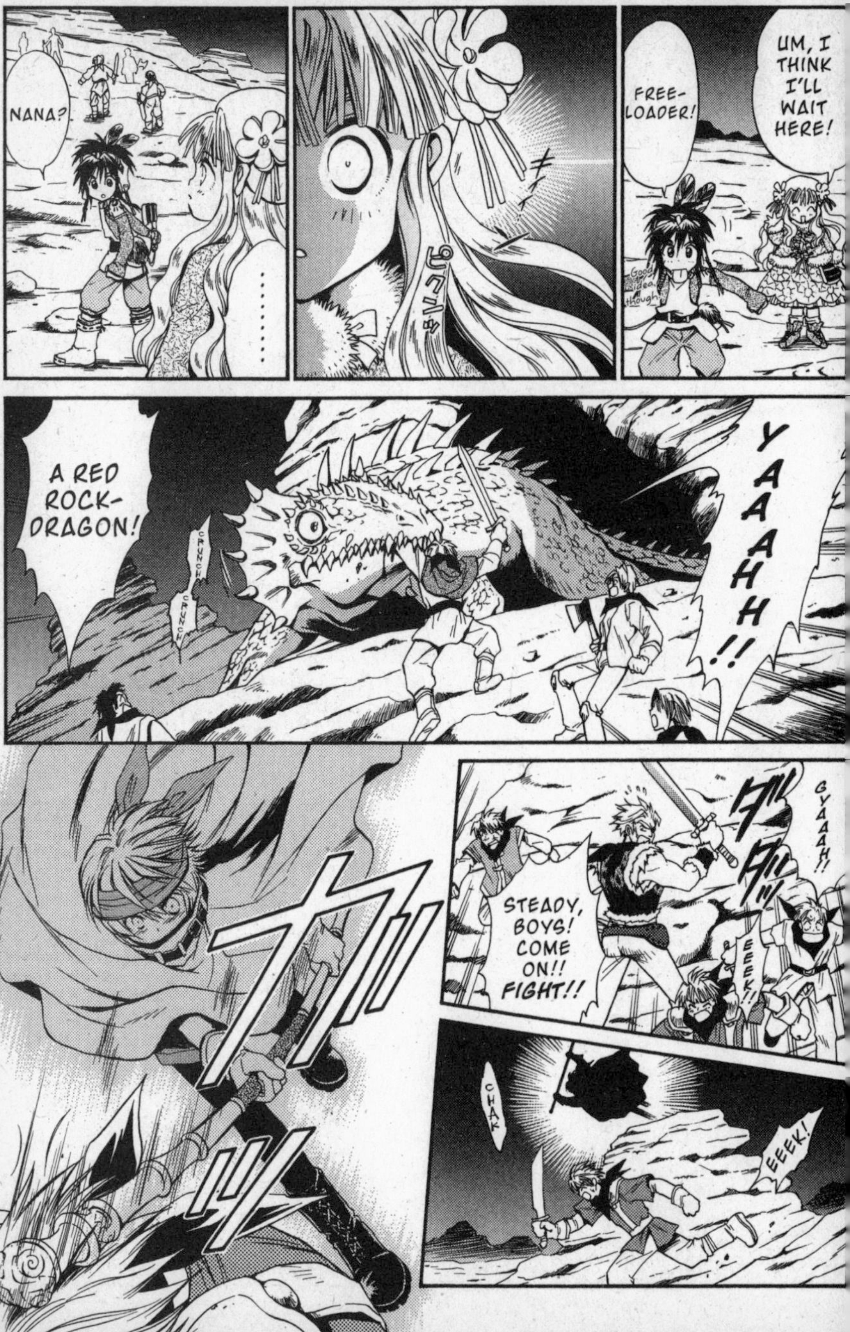
UM, I THINK I'LL WAIT HERE!
FREE-LOADER!
Good idea, though.
NANA?
......
YAAAHH!!
A RED ROCK-DRAGON!
CRUNCH
CRUNCH
GYAAAAH!!
STEADY, BOYS! COME ON!! FIGHT!!
EEEK!!
EEEK!
CHAK

WHAT THE--?!

ドズルル

HUH?!

BRUNO'S GANG?!

WAIT! COORO!!

ジュルルル〜...

BRUNO! I THOUGHT BETTER OF YOU!

THERE'S NOWHERE TO RUN, FREY!!

ONLY A COWARD WOULD STOOP TO AMBUSH IN THIS GAME!!

gasp!

ワリィ

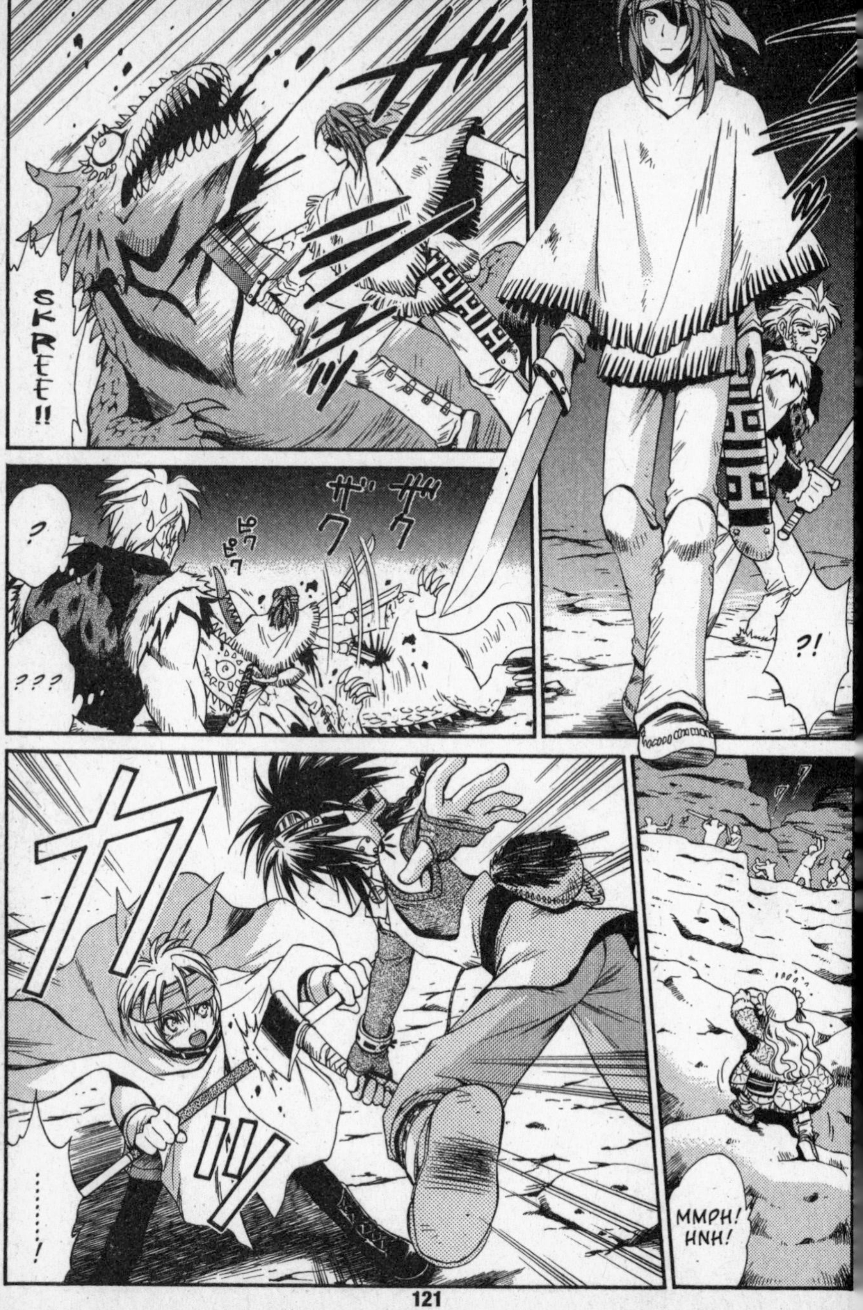
?!
SKREEE!!
?
???
ザク
ザク
ピクピク
MMPH! HNH!
......!

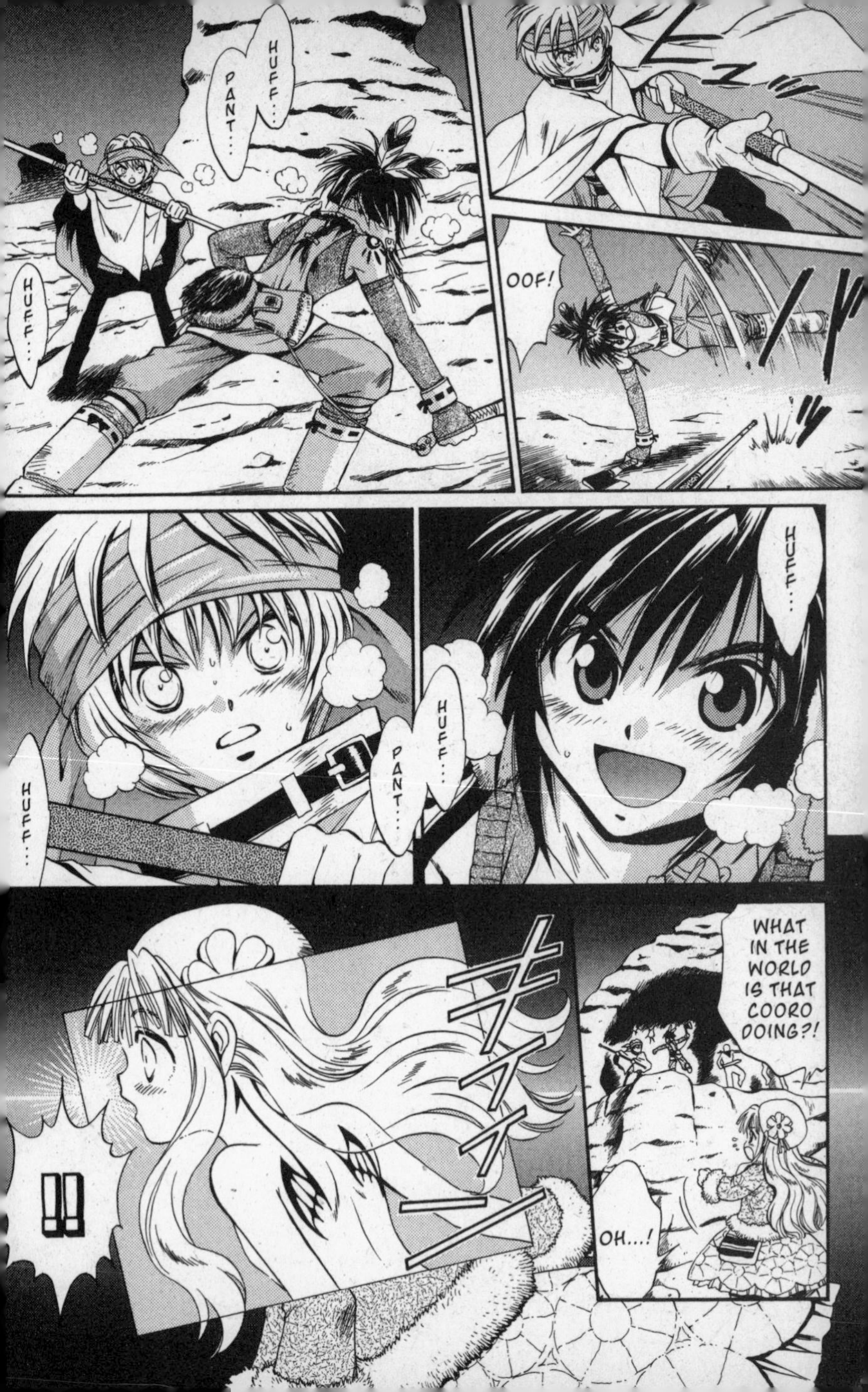
OOF!
HUFF... PANT...
HUFF...
HUFF...
HUFF... PANT...
HUFF...
WHAT IN THE WORLD IS THAT COORO DOING?!
OH...!
!!

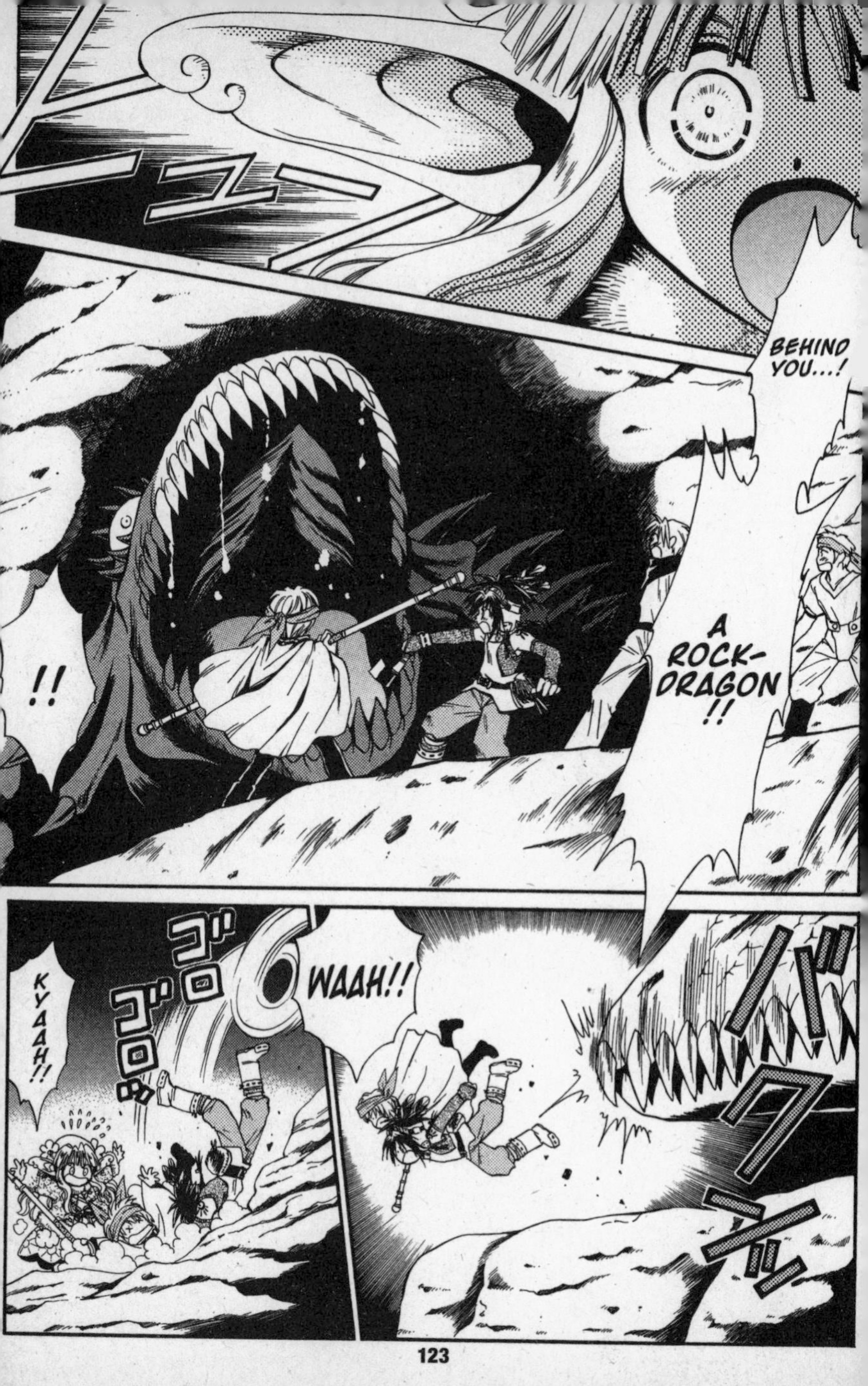
BEHIND YOU...!
A ROCK-DRAGON!!
!!
WAAH!!
ゴロ ゴロ
KYAAH!!

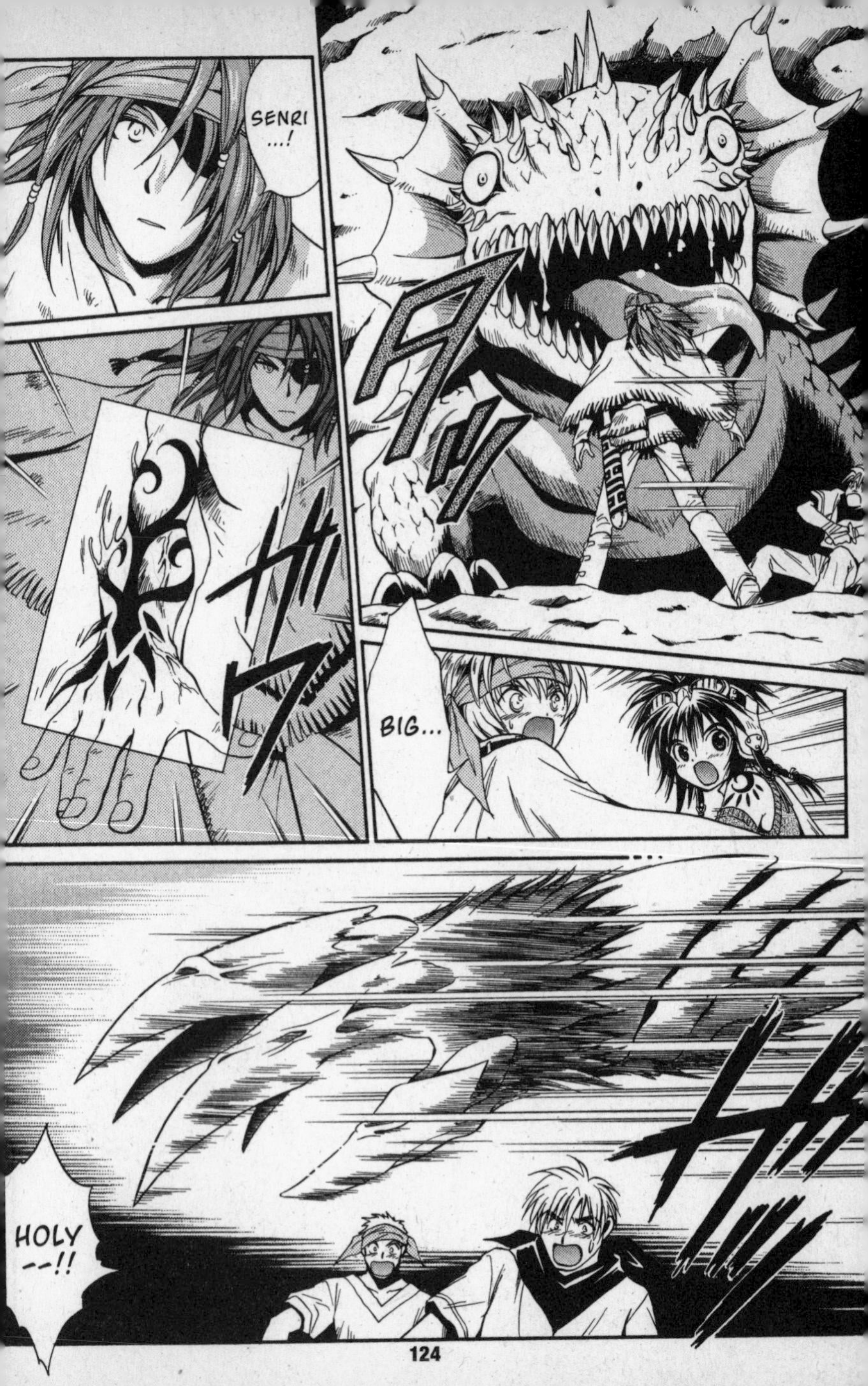

SENRI ...!
BIG...
HOLY --!!

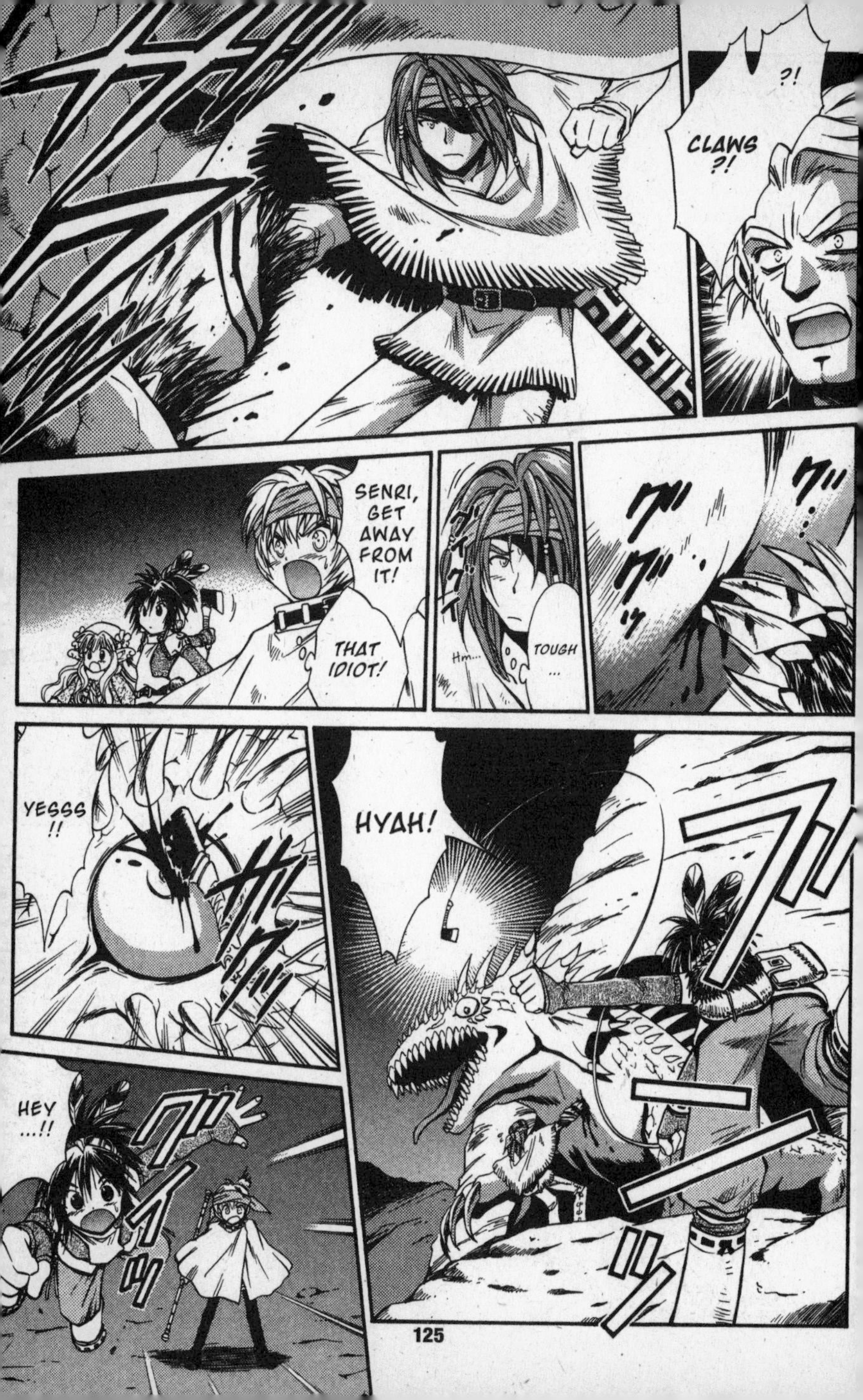
?!
CLAWS ?!
TOUGH ...
Hm...
SENRI, GET AWAY FROM IT!
THAT IDIOT!
HYAH!
YESSS !!
HEY ...!!

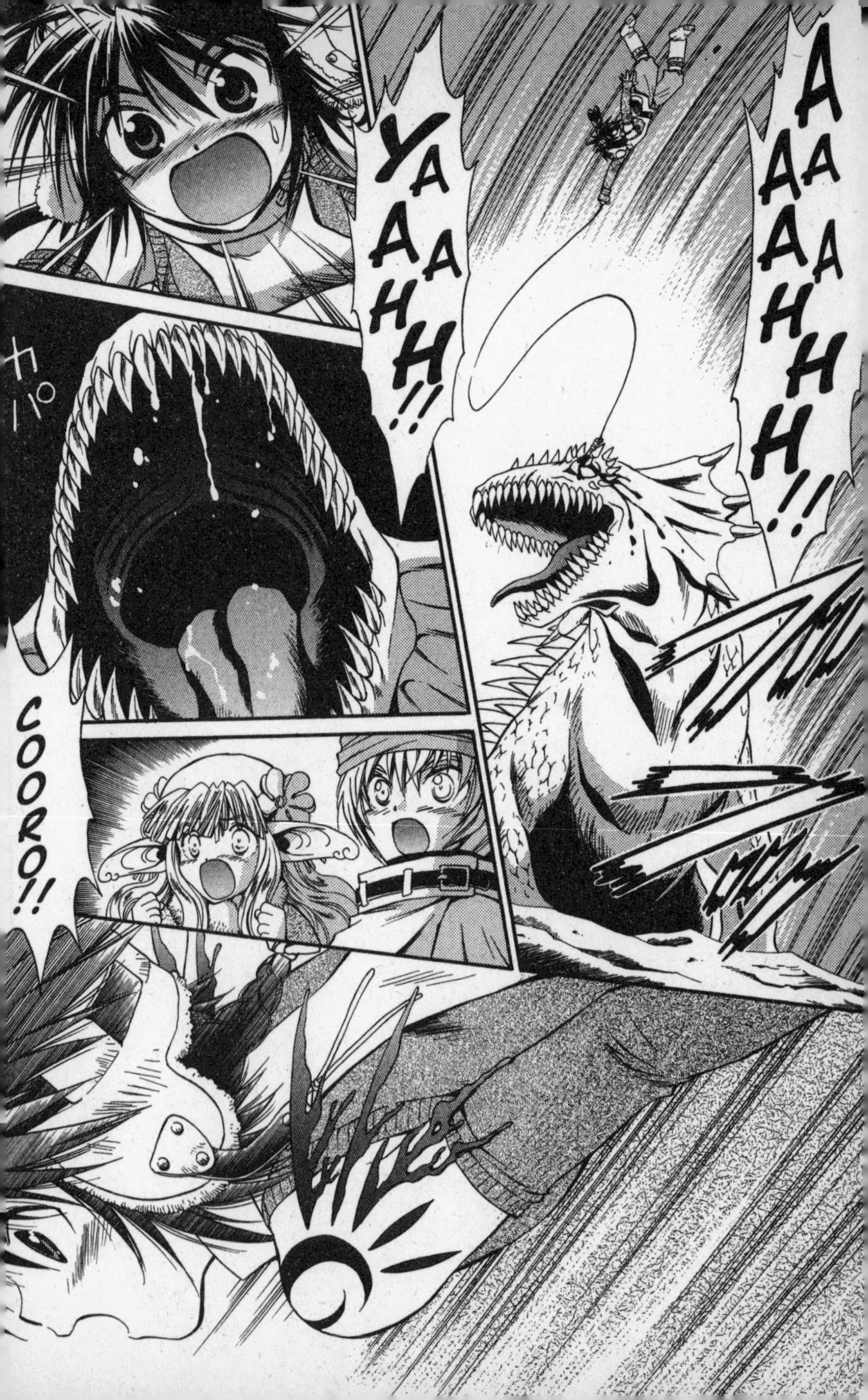
AAAAAHHH!!
YAAAHH!!
カパ
COOORO!!

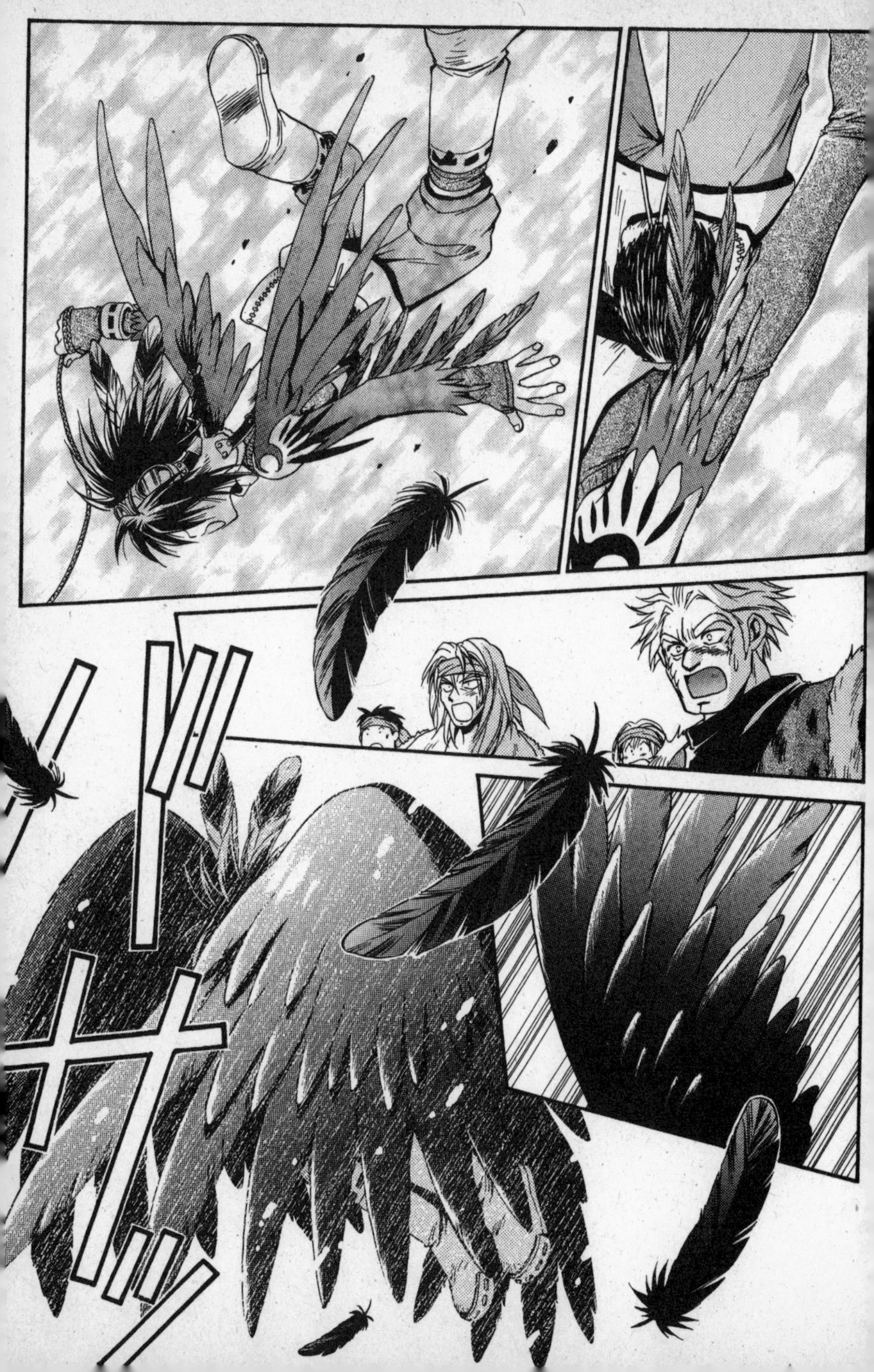

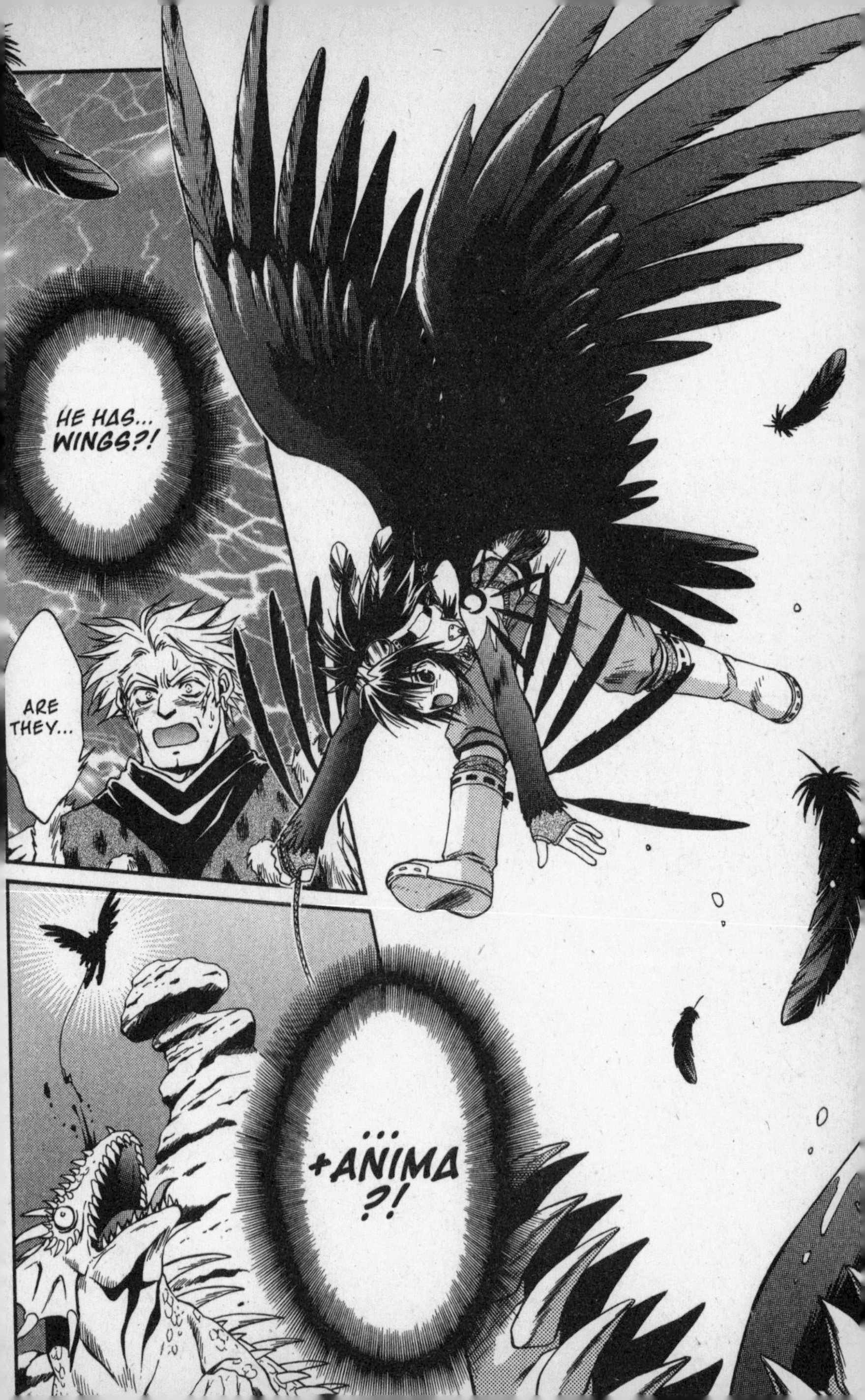
HE HAS... WINGS?!
ARE THEY...
...+ANIMA ?!

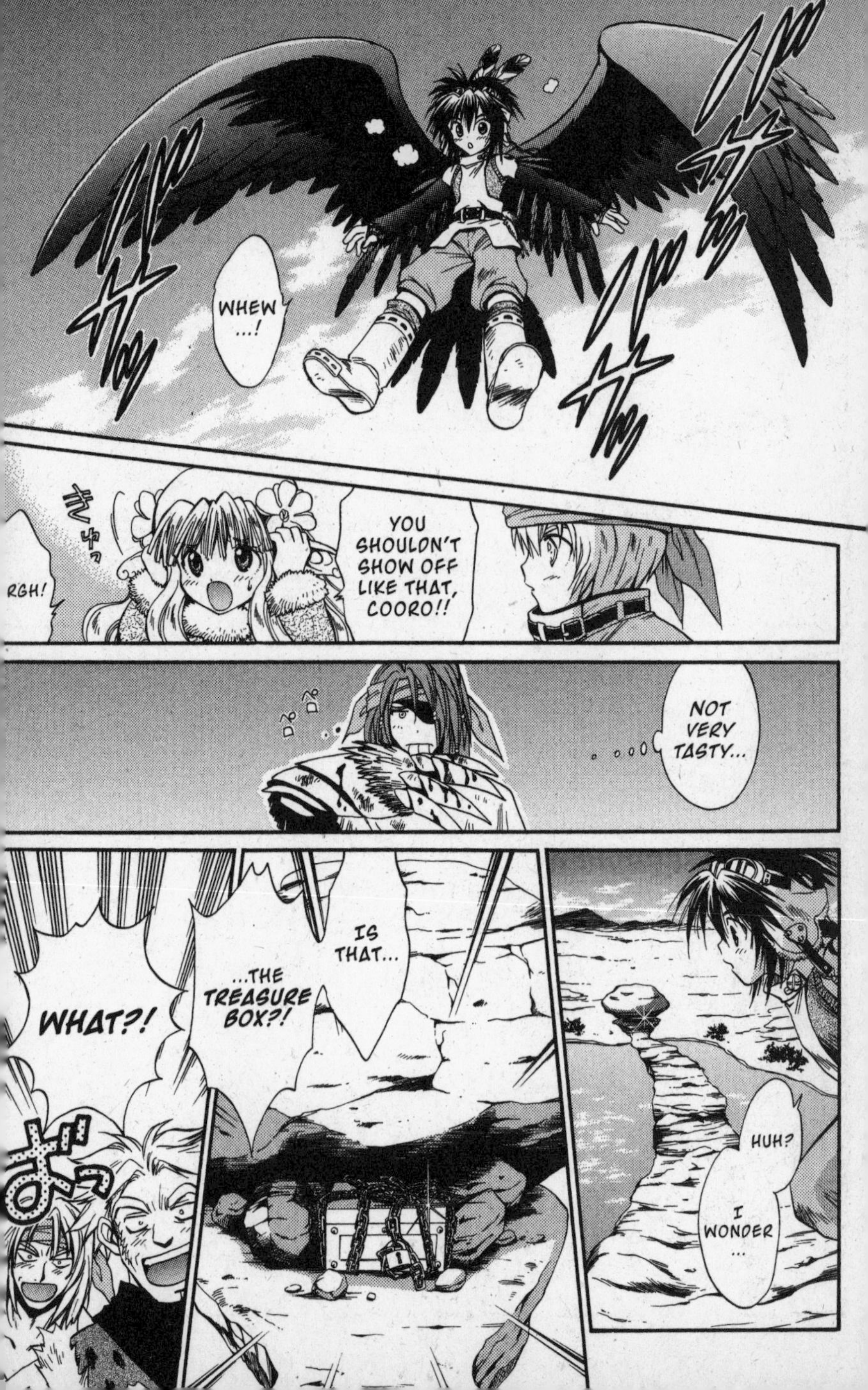
WHEW ...!
YOU SHOULDN'T SHOW OFF LIKE THAT, COORO!!
きゅっ
RGH!
NOT VERY TASTY...
HUH?
I WONDER ...
IS THAT...
...THE TREASURE BOX?!
WHAT?!

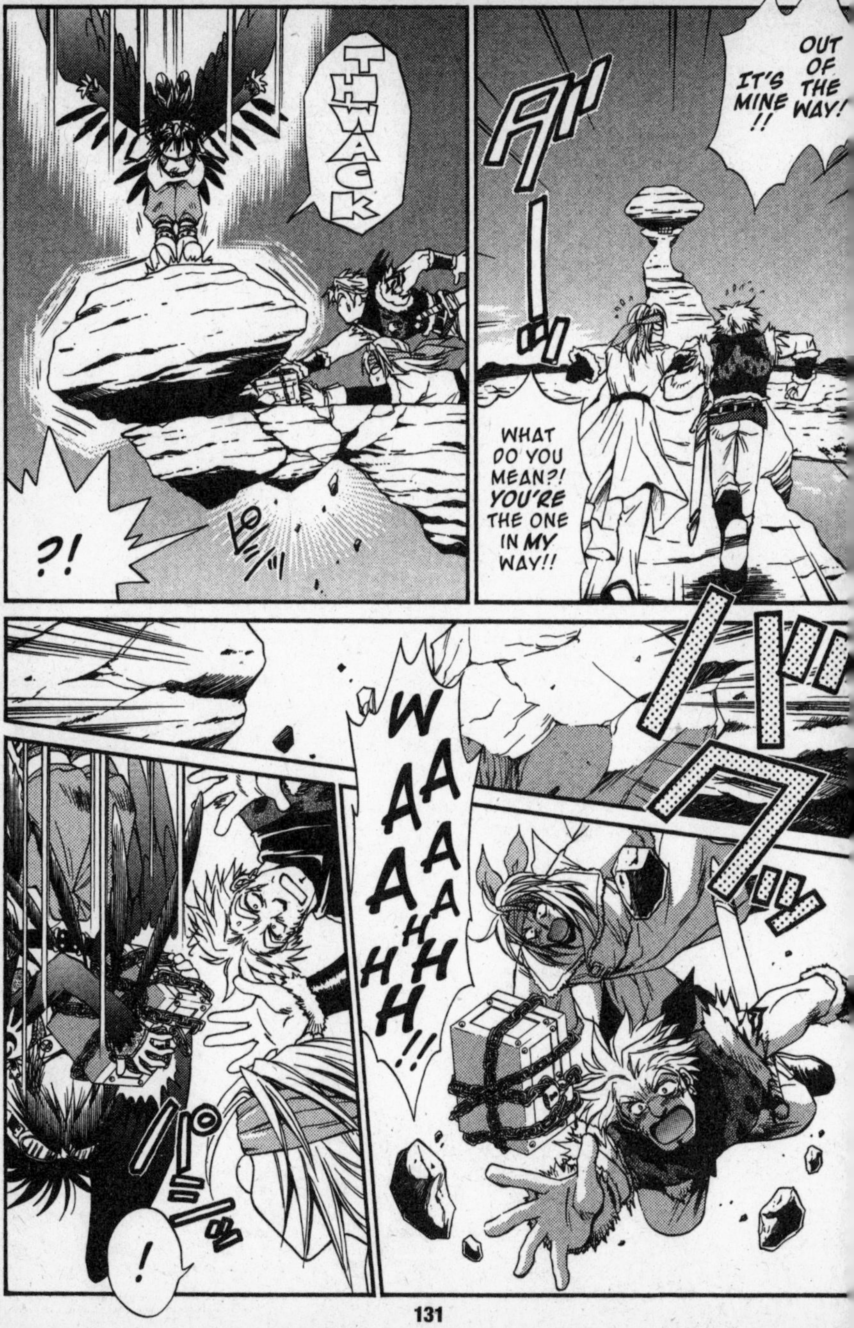
OUT OF THE WAY!
IT'S MINE!!
WHAT DO YOU MEAN?! YOU'RE THE ONE IN MY WAY!!
THWACK
?!
WAAAAAHHHHH!!
!

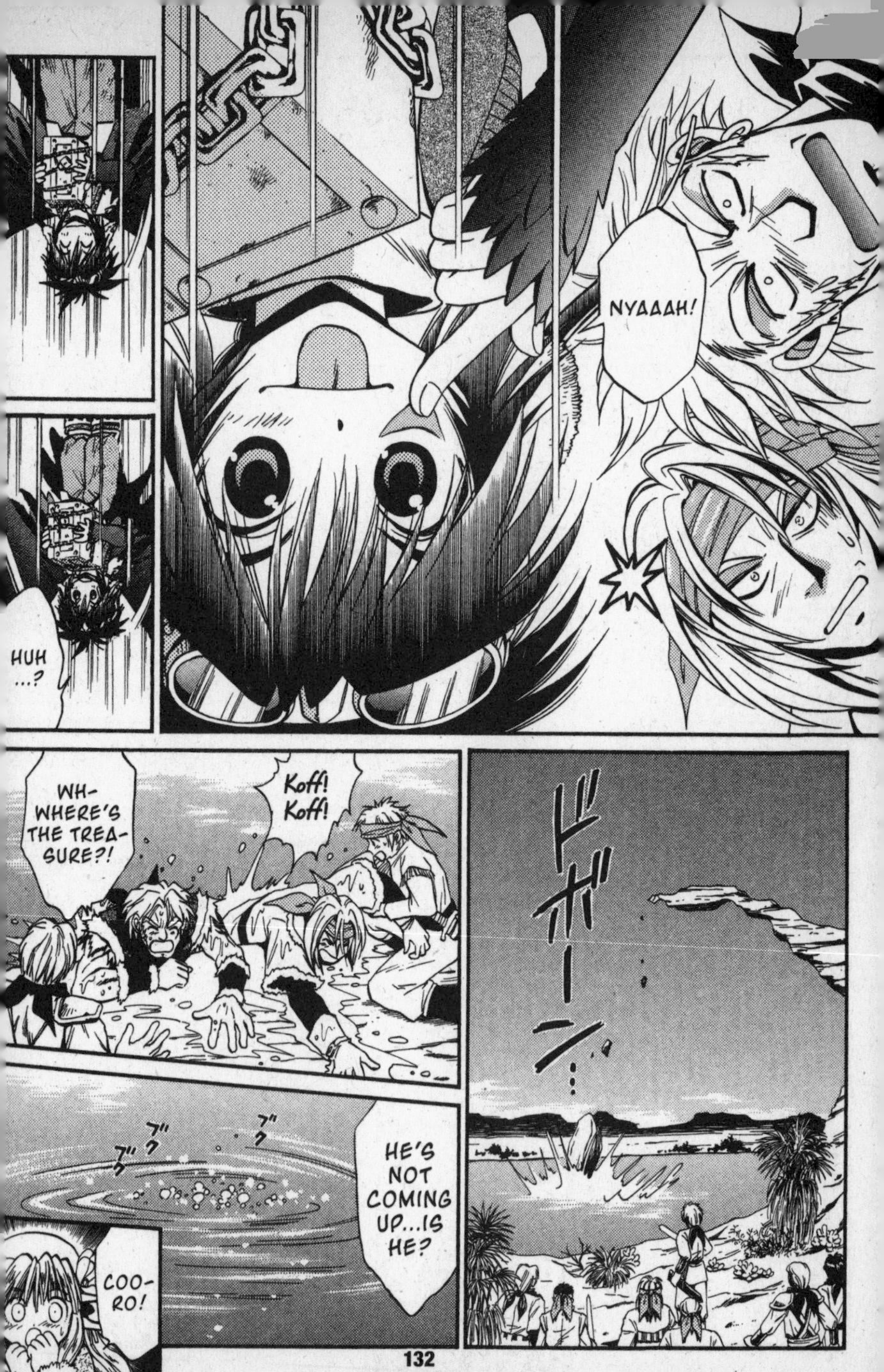
NYAAAH!
HUH ...?
ドボーン…
Koff! Koff!
WH-WHERE'S THE TREASURE?!
ブク ブク ブク
HE'S NOT COMING UP...IS HE?
COO-RO!

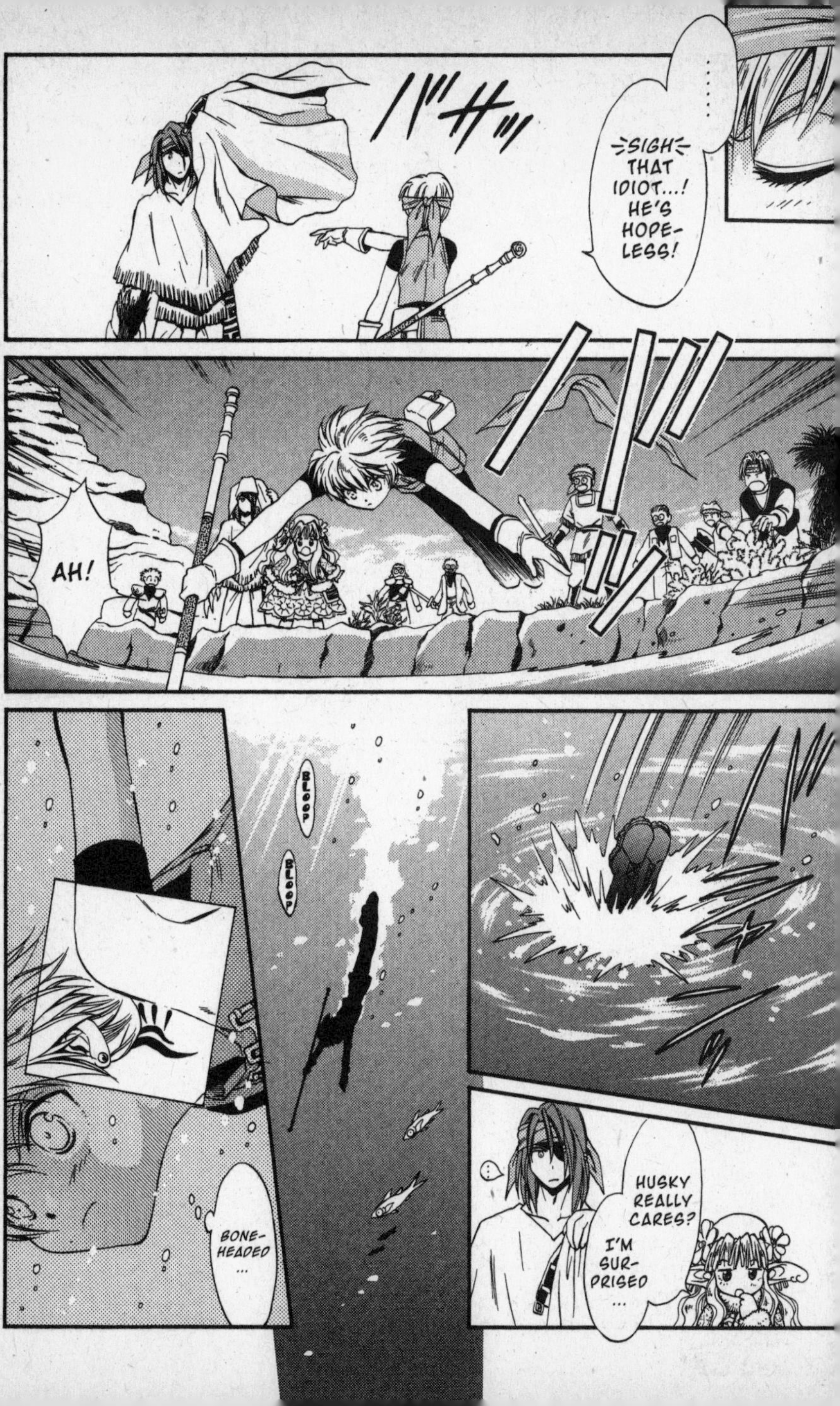

...
SIGH THAT IDIOT...! HE'S HOPELESS!
バサッ
AH!
BLOOP
BLOOP
HUSKY REALLY CARES? I'M SURPRISED ...
...
BONE-HEADED ...

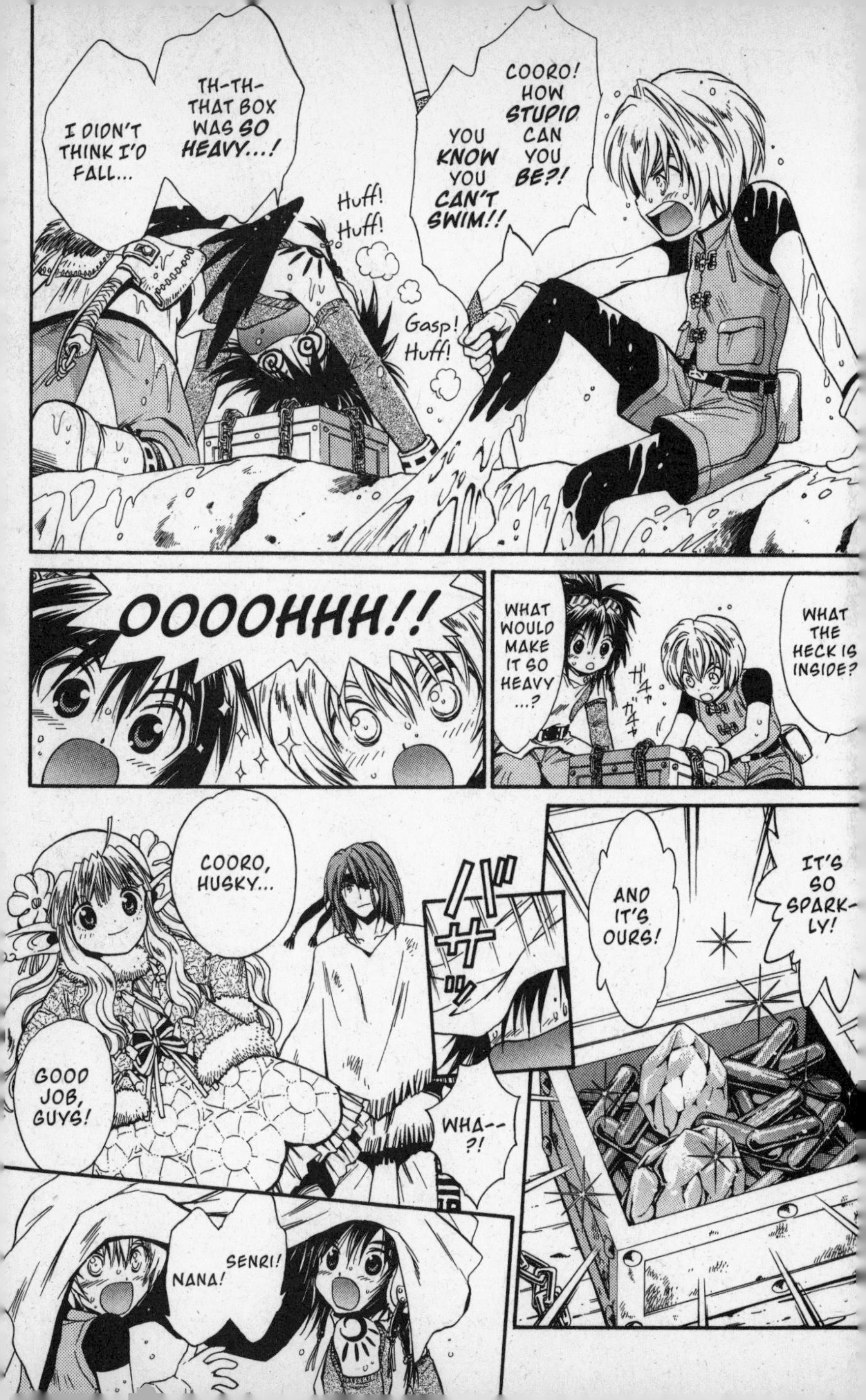
COORO! HOW STUPID CAN YOU BE?! YOU KNOW YOU CAN'T SWIM!!
TH-TH-THAT BOX WAS SO HEAVY...!
I DIDN'T THINK I'D FALL...
Huff! Huff!
Gasp! Huff!
WHAT THE HECK IS INSIDE?
ガチャガチャ
WHAT WOULD MAKE IT SO HEAVY ...?
OOOOHHH!!
IT'S SO SPARK-LY!
AND IT'S OURS!
バサッ
COORO, HUSKY...
WHA--?!
GOOD JOB, GUYS!
SENRI!
NANA!

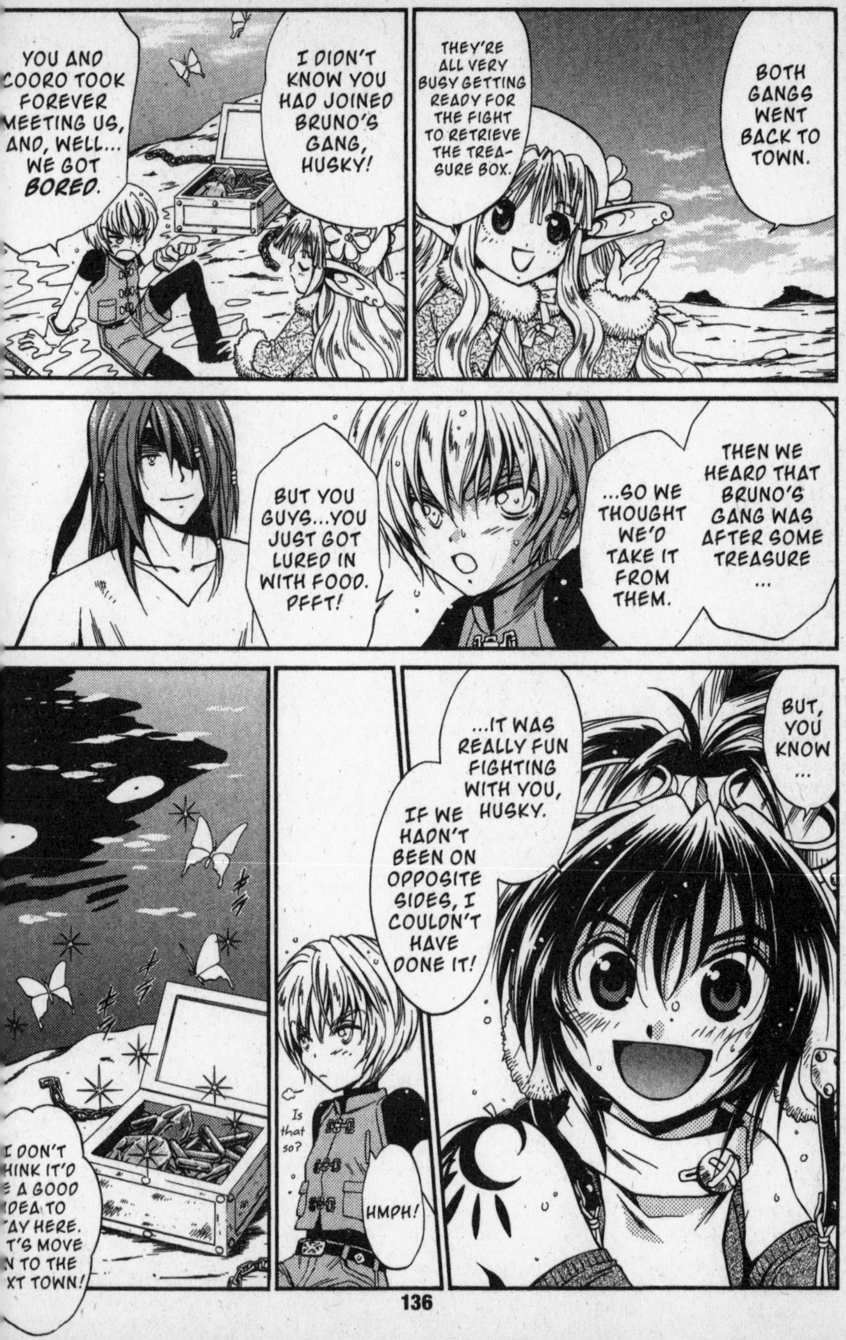
BOTH GANGS WENT BACK TO TOWN.
THEY'RE ALL VERY BUSY GETTING READY FOR THE FIGHT TO RETRIEVE THE TREA-SURE BOX.
I DIDN'T KNOW YOU HAD JOINED BRUNO'S GANG, HUSKY!
YOU AND COORO TOOK FOREVER MEETING US, AND, WELL... WE GOT BORED.
THEN WE HEARD THAT BRUNO'S GANG WAS AFTER SOME TREASURE ...
...SO WE THOUGHT WE'D TAKE IT FROM THEM.
BUT YOU GUYS...YOU JUST GOT LURED IN WITH FOOD. PFFT!
BUT, YOU KNOW ...
...IT WAS REALLY FUN FIGHTING WITH YOU, HUSKY.
IF WE HADN'T BEEN ON OPPOSITE SIDES, I COULDN'T HAVE DONE IT!
Is that so?
HMPH!
I DON'T HINK IT'D E A GOOD IDEA TO TAY HERE. T'S MOVE N TO THE XT TOWN!

Where do you go?

Parallel 2
Dreaming in the Ocean

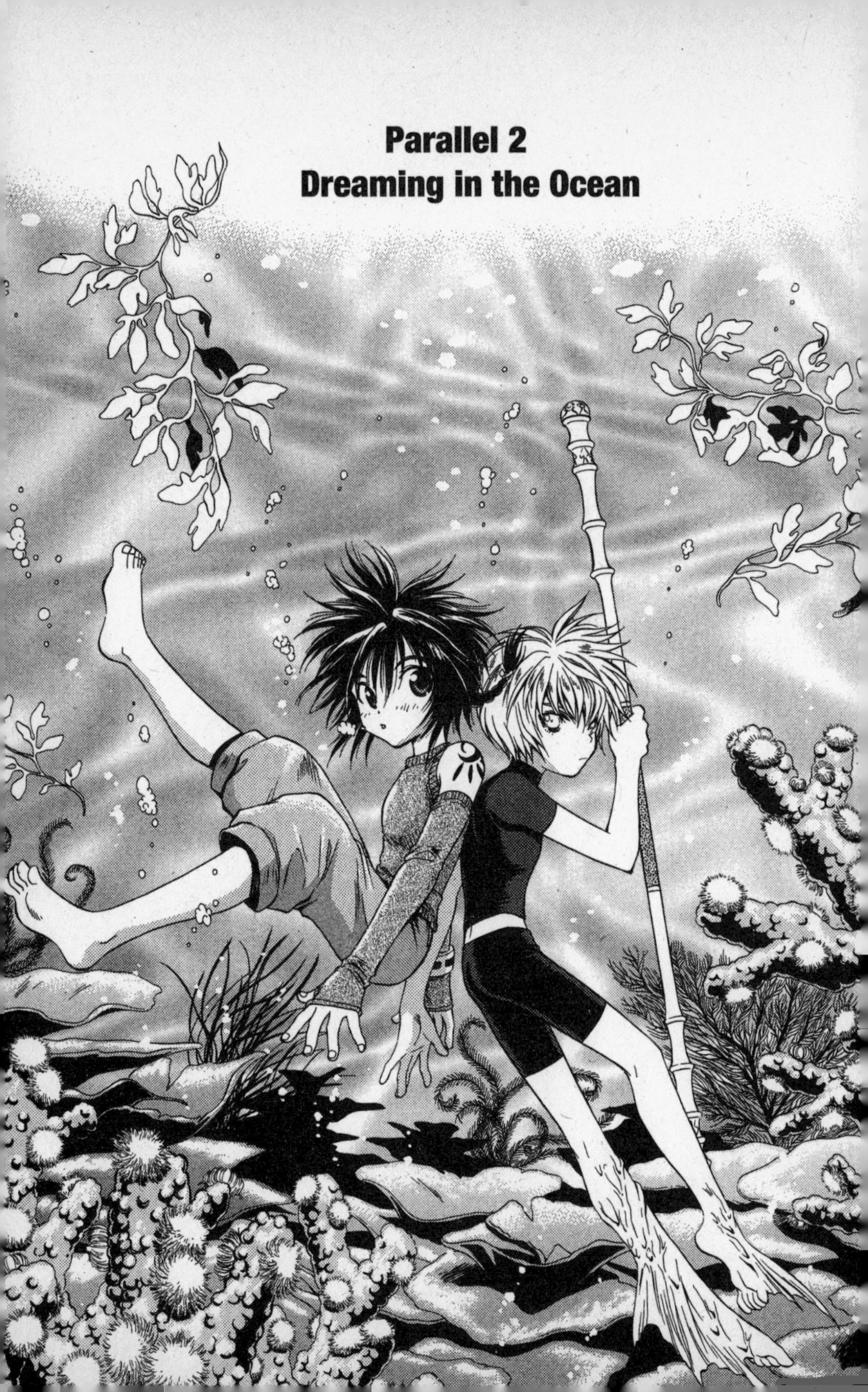

Port City Araku

WHILE OTHERS SAY IT'S A GIANT FISH...

SOME SAY THEY'VE SEEN A PLESIOSAURUS...

THAT'S RIGHT.

WE HAVE A CORAL REEF GOOD FOR FISHING OFF THE COAST OF ARAKU, BUT A MONSTER STARTED APPEARING RECENTLY.

AND THEN THERE ARE THOSE THAT SWEAR IT'S A DEVIL.

NO PROBLEM! SIGN US UP!

SCARY...!

BESIDES, WE CAN'T LET GIRLS ONTO THE BOAT.

Grrr...

WE CAN'T TAKE YOU. EXCEPT FOR HIM, YOU'RE JUST A BUNCH OF KIDS!

KID, WE'RE RECRUITING PEOPLE TO EXTERMINATE SEA MONSTERS.

OH!

Y-YOU'RE NOT? M-MY MISTAKE...!

WHO YOU CALLIN' A GIRL?!

HUH?!

...

WHAT?!

MAKING FOOD.

THE GALLEY...?

TAKE THESE FOUR AND COUNT THEM AS TWO. LET THEM WORK IN THE GALLEY.

HUH? WELL...

JUST THREE.

HEY, HOW MANY PEOPLE DO WE STILL NEED?

Grrrrr!

Now now...

BE GRATEFUL THAT WE GOT HONEST WORK!

DON'T COMPLAIN, COORO!

AW...WE CAN DO MORE THAN THAT...!

YOU TELL HIM, NANA!

WHO'S NOT A WOMAN?!

THAT KID? SURE. IT'S NOT LIKE SHE'S A WOMAN.

CAPTAIN, THEY HAVE A GIRL... IS THAT OKAY?

WAIT FOR ME--!!

HEEEY!!

JUST ONE MORE...

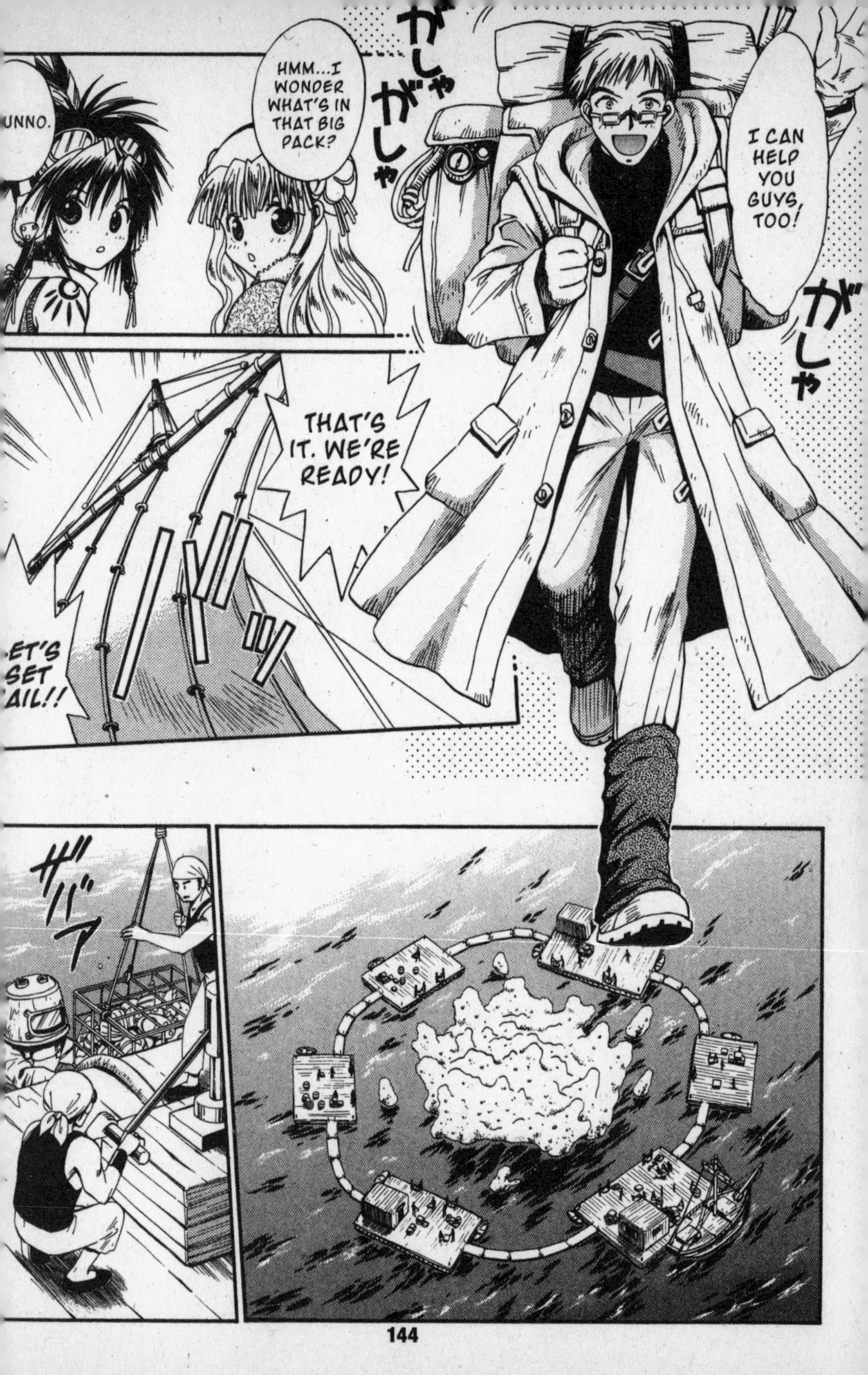
I CAN HELP YOU GUYS, TOO!
がしゃ
がしゃ
がしゃ
HMM...I WONDER WHAT'S IN THAT BIG PACK?
UNNO.
THAT'S IT. WE'RE READY!
ET'S SET AIL!!
ザバア

Y-YES! COMING RIGHT UP!

HEY! IS THAT GRUB READY YET?!

I'M NOT DOING ANY WORK I'M NOT GETTING PAID FOR.

WE'RE IN CHARGE OF FOOD.

THEY SHOULD LET YOU DIVE, HUSKY.

THEY'RE SOLDIERS. IT CAN'T BE HELPED.

OH! THOSE MONSTER HUNTERS! ALL THEY DO IS SIT AROUND ALL DAY BUT AT MEALTIME THEY EAT TWICE AS MUCH AS ANYBODY ELSE!

WHEN THE SEA MONSTER SHOWS UP, THEY'LL BE PLENTY BUSY.

HEY, SENRI... IS THIS DONE?

145

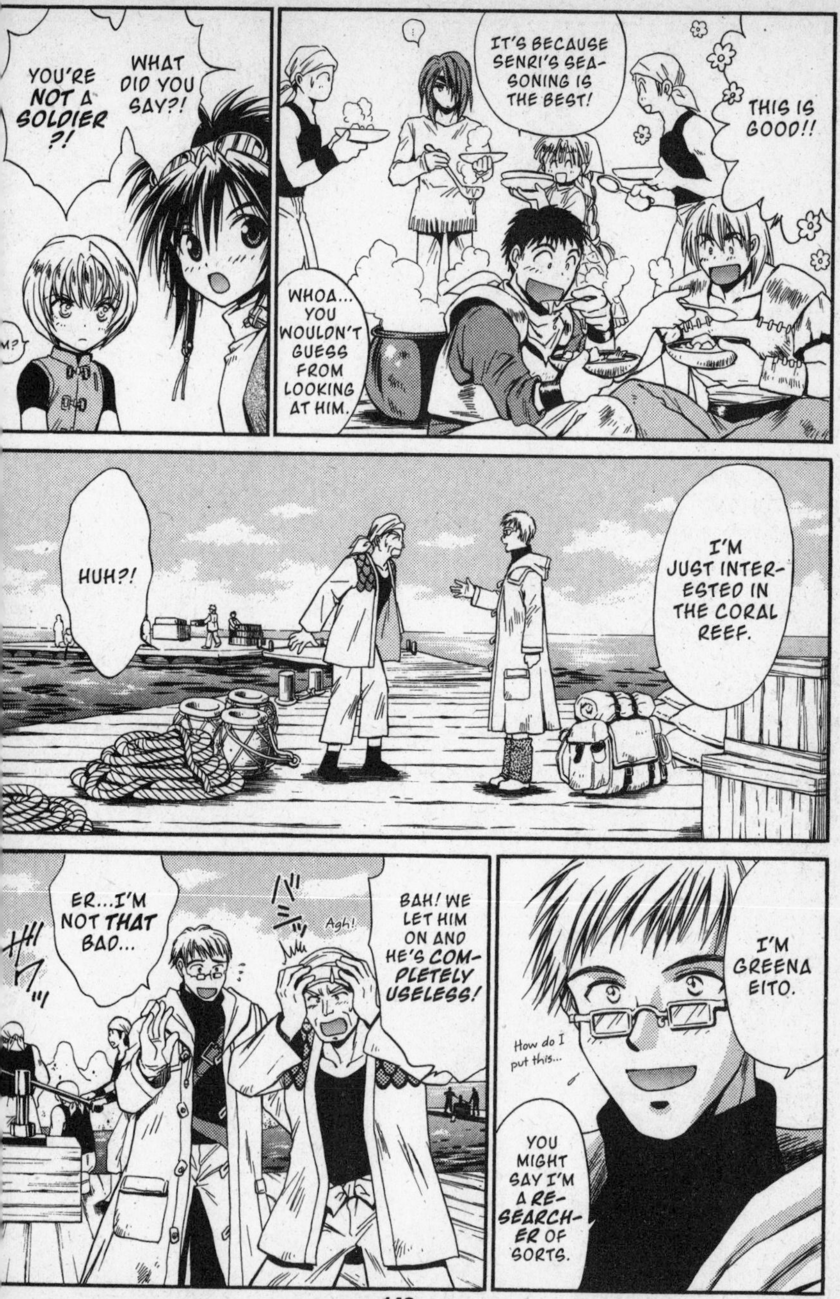
THIS IS GOOD!!
IT'S BECAUSE SENRI'S SEASONING IS THE BEST!
...
WHOA... YOU WOULDN'T GUESS FROM LOOKING AT HIM.
WHAT DID YOU SAY?!
YOU'RE NOT A SOLDIER?!
I'M JUST INTERESTED IN THE CORAL REEF.
HUH?!
I'M GREENA EITO.
How do I put this...
YOU MIGHT SAY I'M A RESEARCHER OF SORTS.
BAH! WE LET HIM ON AND HE'S COMPLETELY USELESS!
Agh!
ER...I'M NOT THAT BAD...

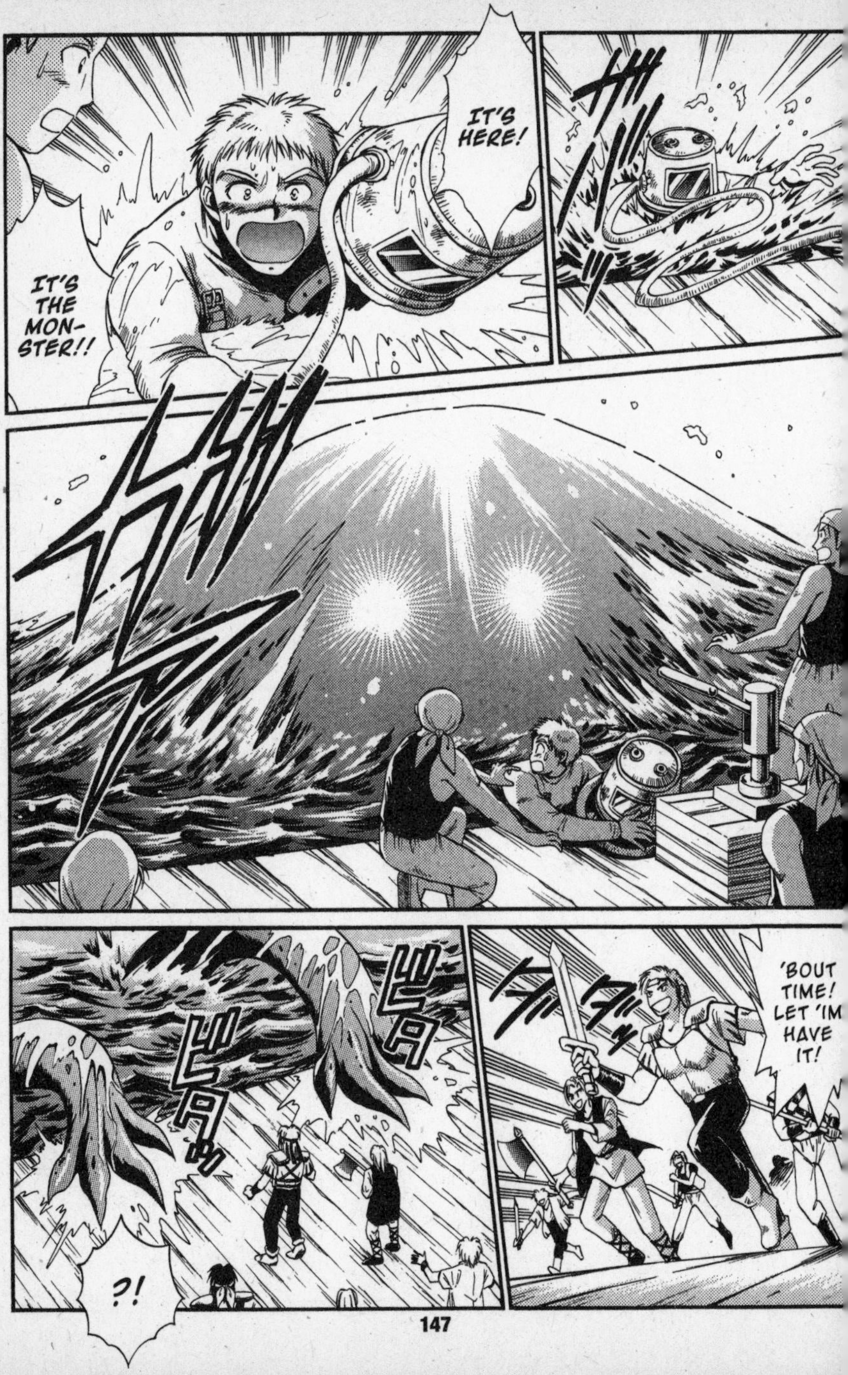
IT'S HERE!
IT'S THE MON-STER!!
'BOUT TIME! LET 'IM HAVE IT!
?!

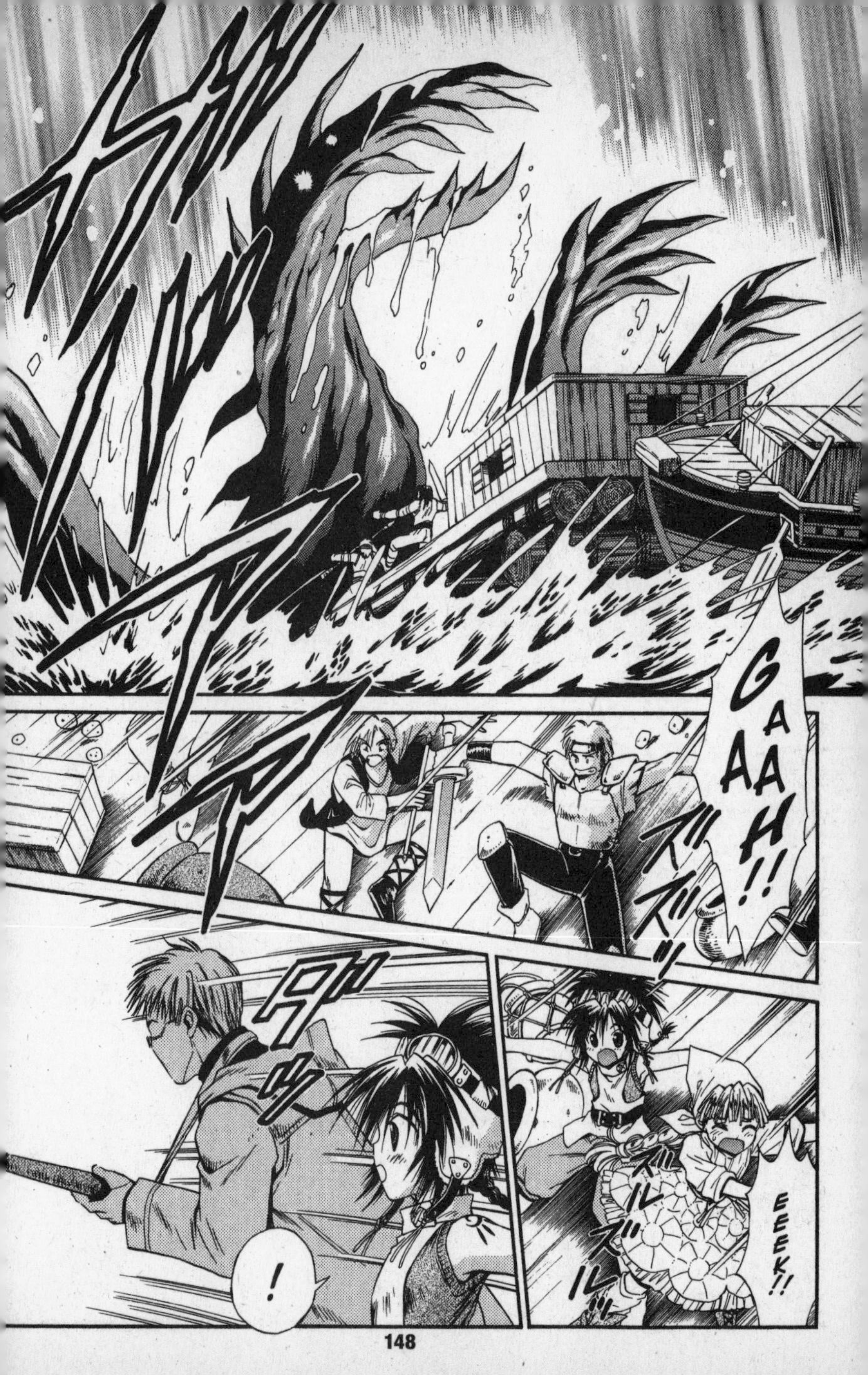
GAAAH!!
EEEEK!!
!

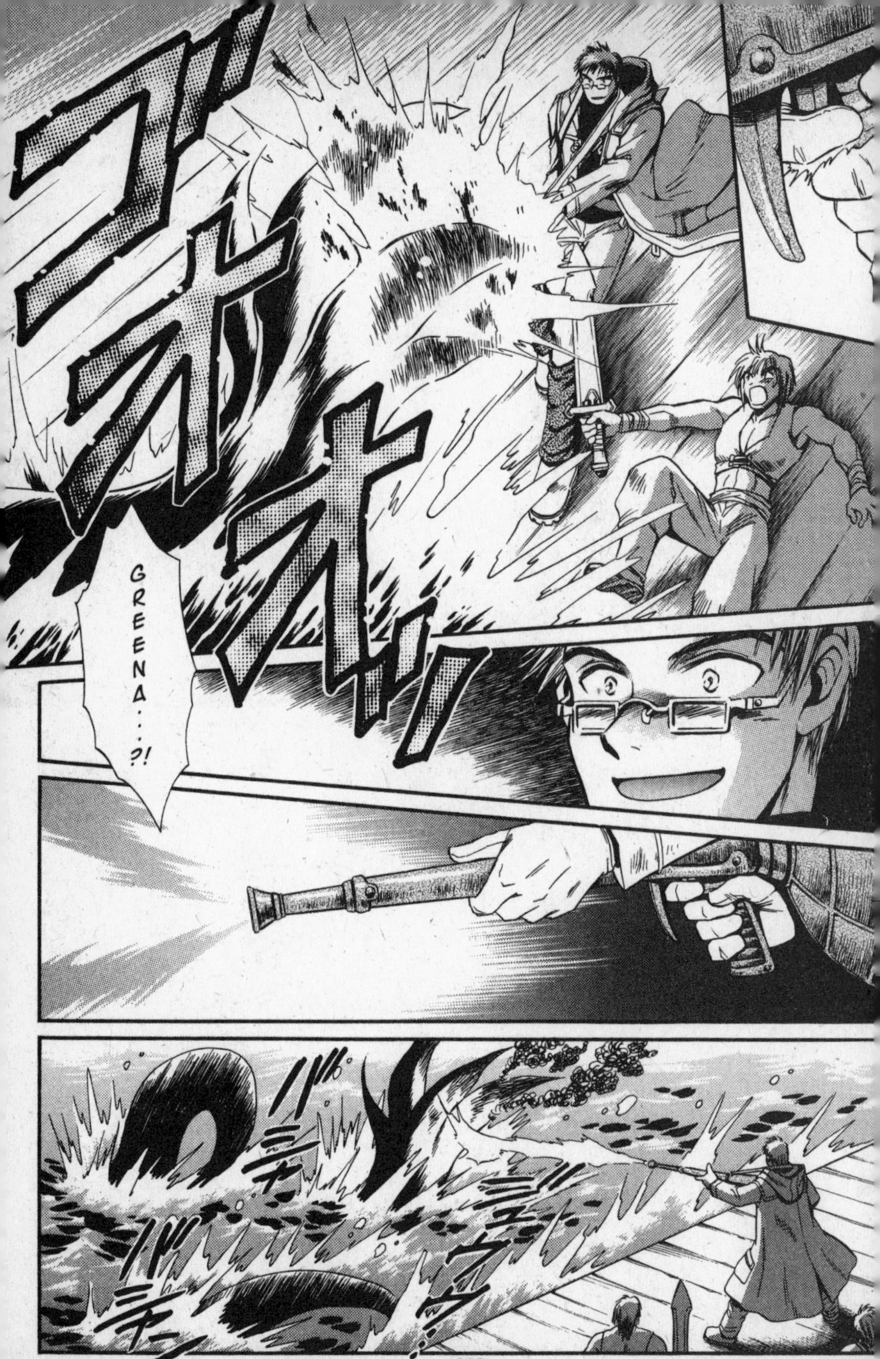
GREENA...?!

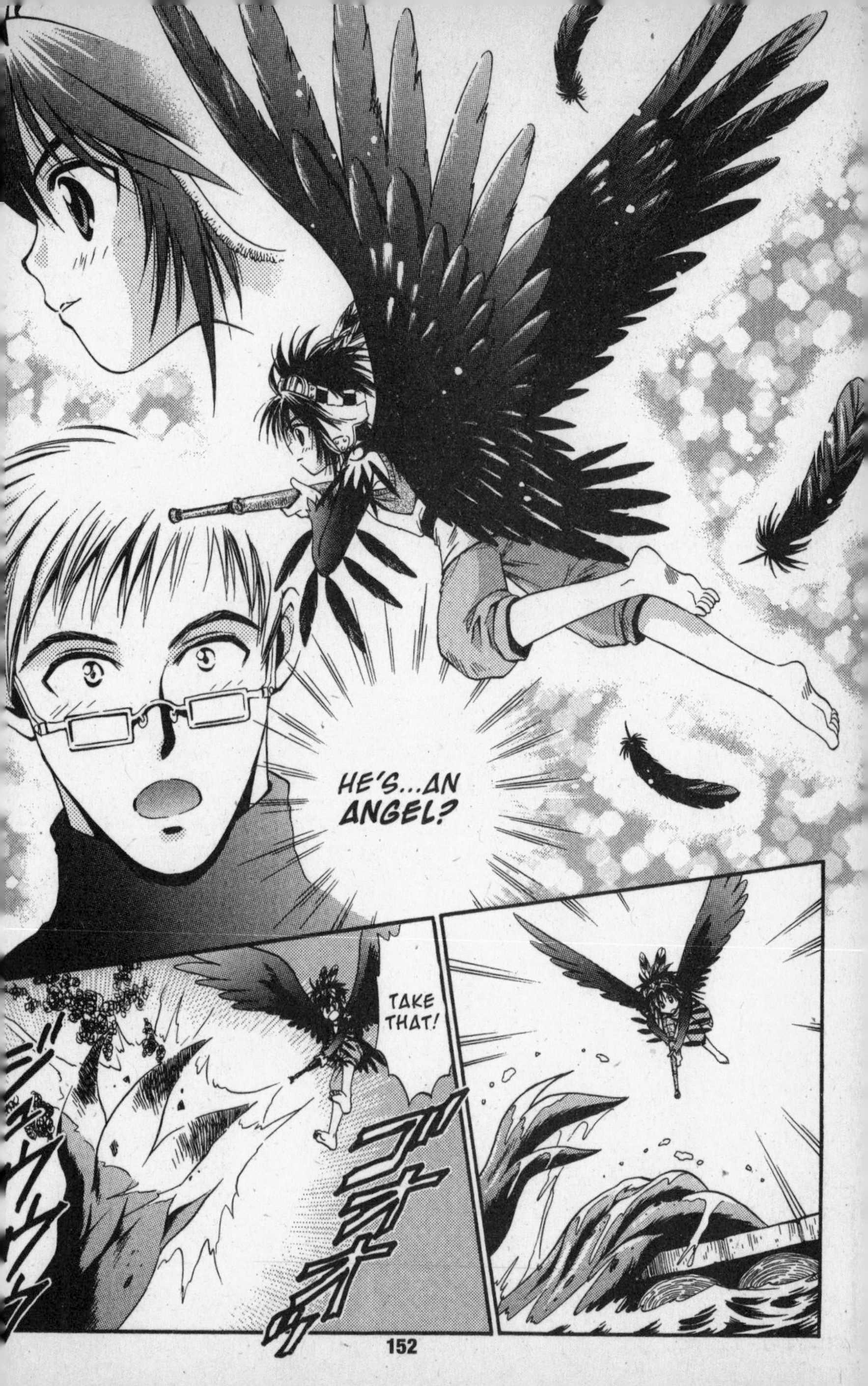
HE'S...AN ANGEL?
TAKE THAT!

Oooohhh!

IT'S RUNNING AWAY!

HE MUST BE A +ANIMA!

BUT THIS IS THE FIRST TIME I'VE SEEN ONE!

I HAD HEARD THAT THERE WERE PEOPLE IN THIS WORLD BORN WITH ANIMAL POWERS...

BIRD WINGS...?

WHAT IS HE...?

...BUT IT'LL COST YA!

I CAN GET THE JOB DONE...

HMM?

PAT

HUSKY...

HE'S GOOD...

153

GOOD LUCK KEEPING WATCH UNDER-WATER, HUSKY!

AND COORO, YOU KEEP WATCH FROM ABOVE!

WHERE IS COORO?

OKAY...!

FISHER-MEN, YOU CAN DIVE SAFELY NOW!

155

AND ARE YOU TRAVELING TOGETHER?

YOU DON'T LOOK LIKE YOU'RE SIBLINGS.

ARE ALL FOUR OF YOU +ANIMA?

BUT ENOUGH ABOUT ME...

IT'S MY JOB TO CONSTRUCT, PLAN, AND... SEARCH FOR VARIOUS THINGS.

...WELL... PURPOSE?

DO YOU HAVE SOME...

PURPOSE? WHAT'S THAT SUPPOSED TO MEAN?

ER...

HE DOESN'T MEAN ANYTHING BY IT.

HE SURE SAYS WEIRD THINGS.

COO-RO!

COME ON, BACK TO WORK!

I didn't mean it like that...

NO... THAT IS...

156

157

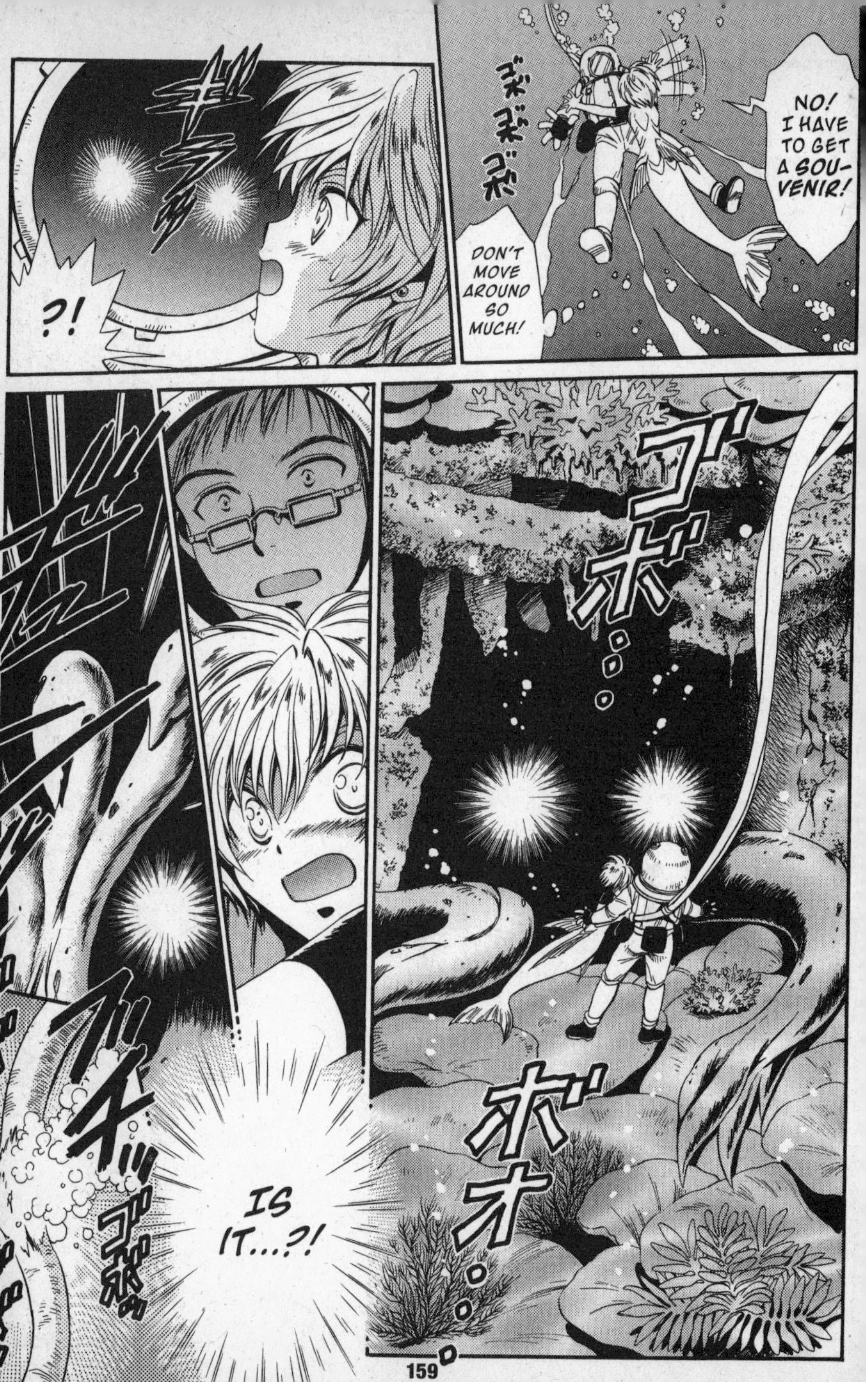
NO! I HAVE TO GET A SOUVENIR!
DON'T MOVE AROUND SO MUCH!
?!
IS IT...?!

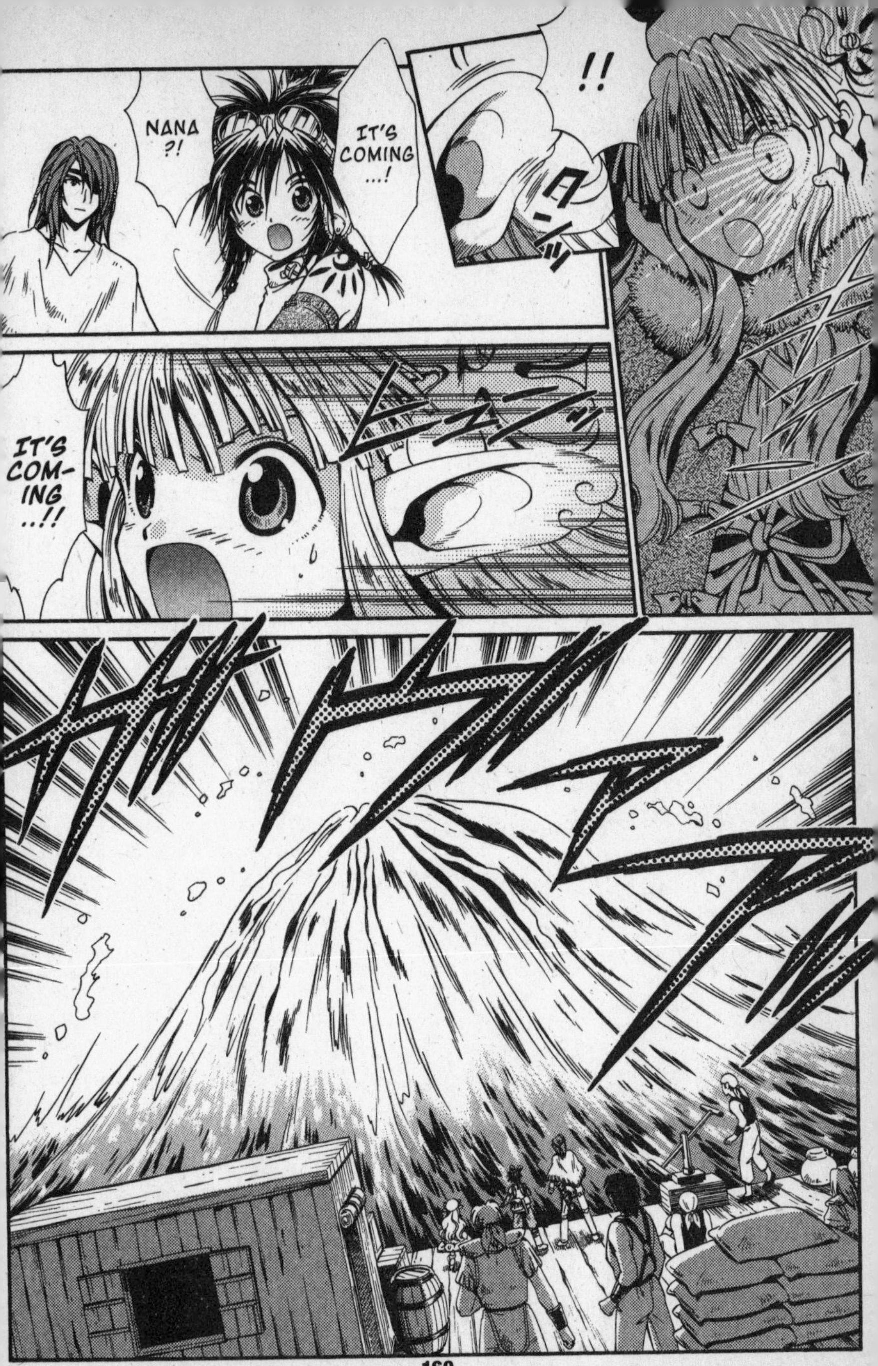
!!
IT'S COMING ...!
NANA ?!
IT'S COMING ..!!

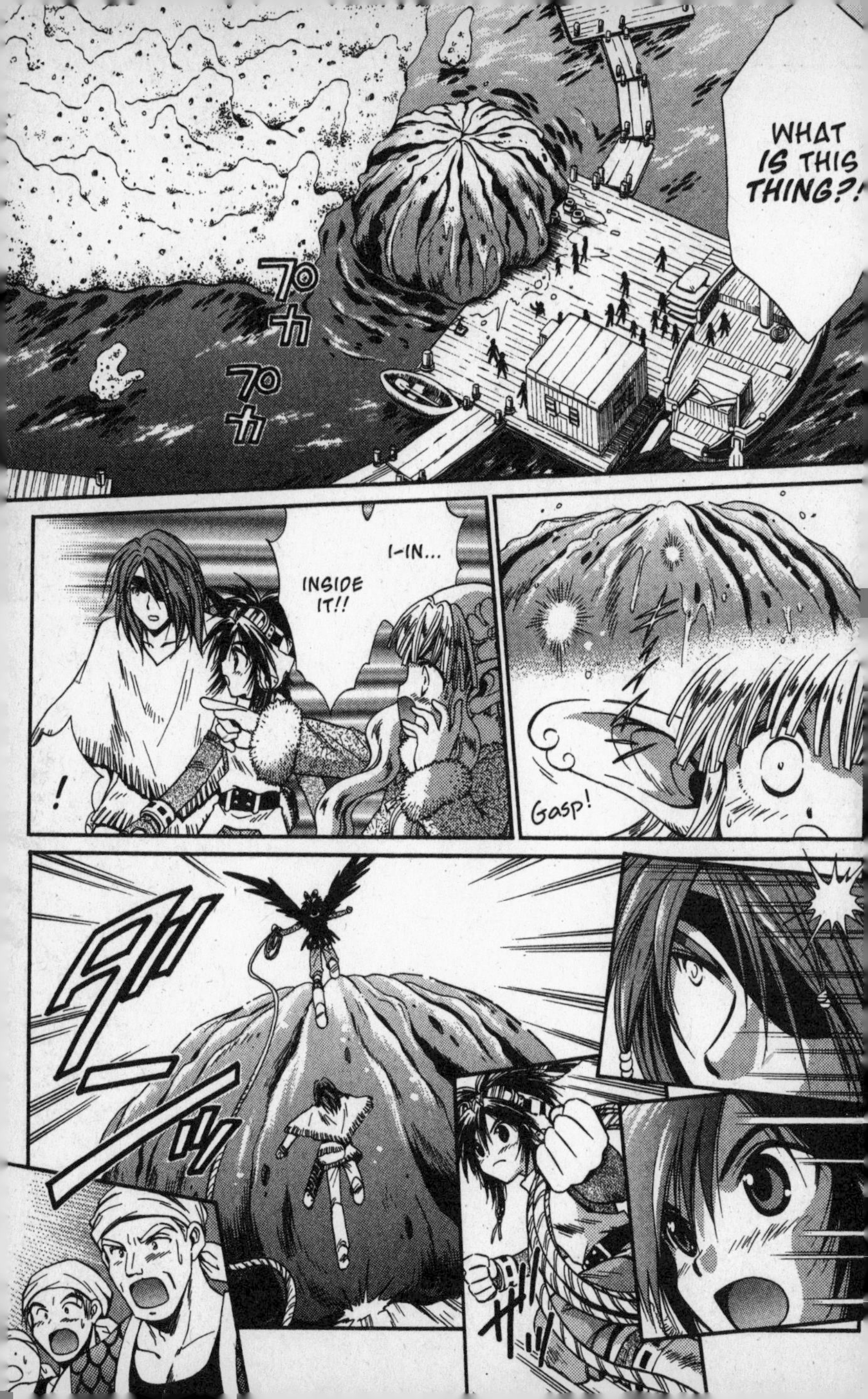
WHAT IS THIS THING?!
プカ
プカ
I-IN...
INSIDE IT!!
Gasp!

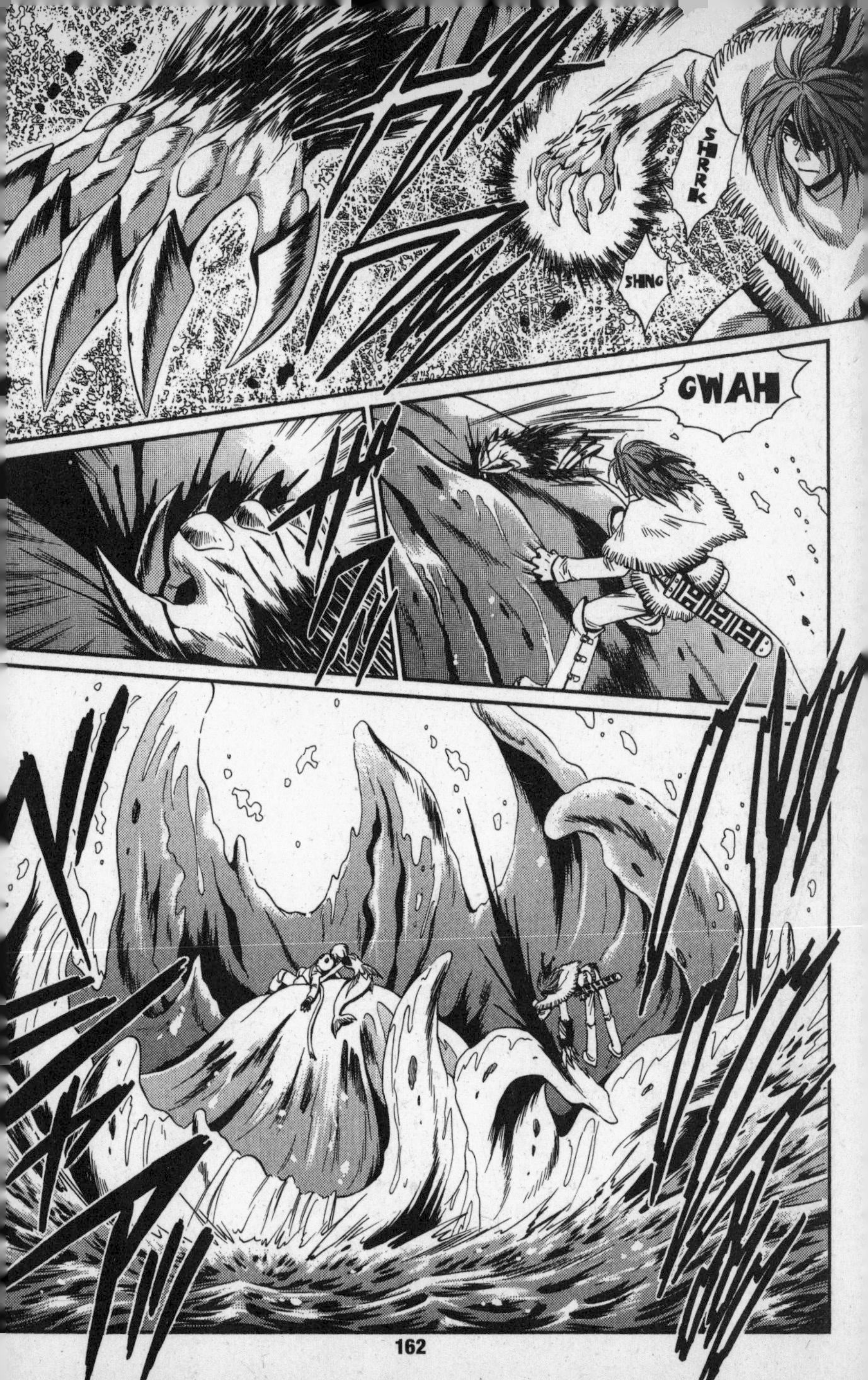
SHRRK
SHING
GWAH

QUICK! IT'LL GET AWAY AGAIN!!

THROW ME THE ROPE!

EH? HEY!

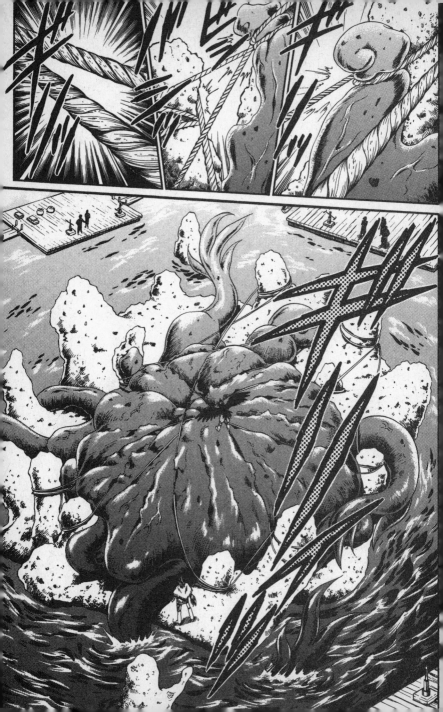

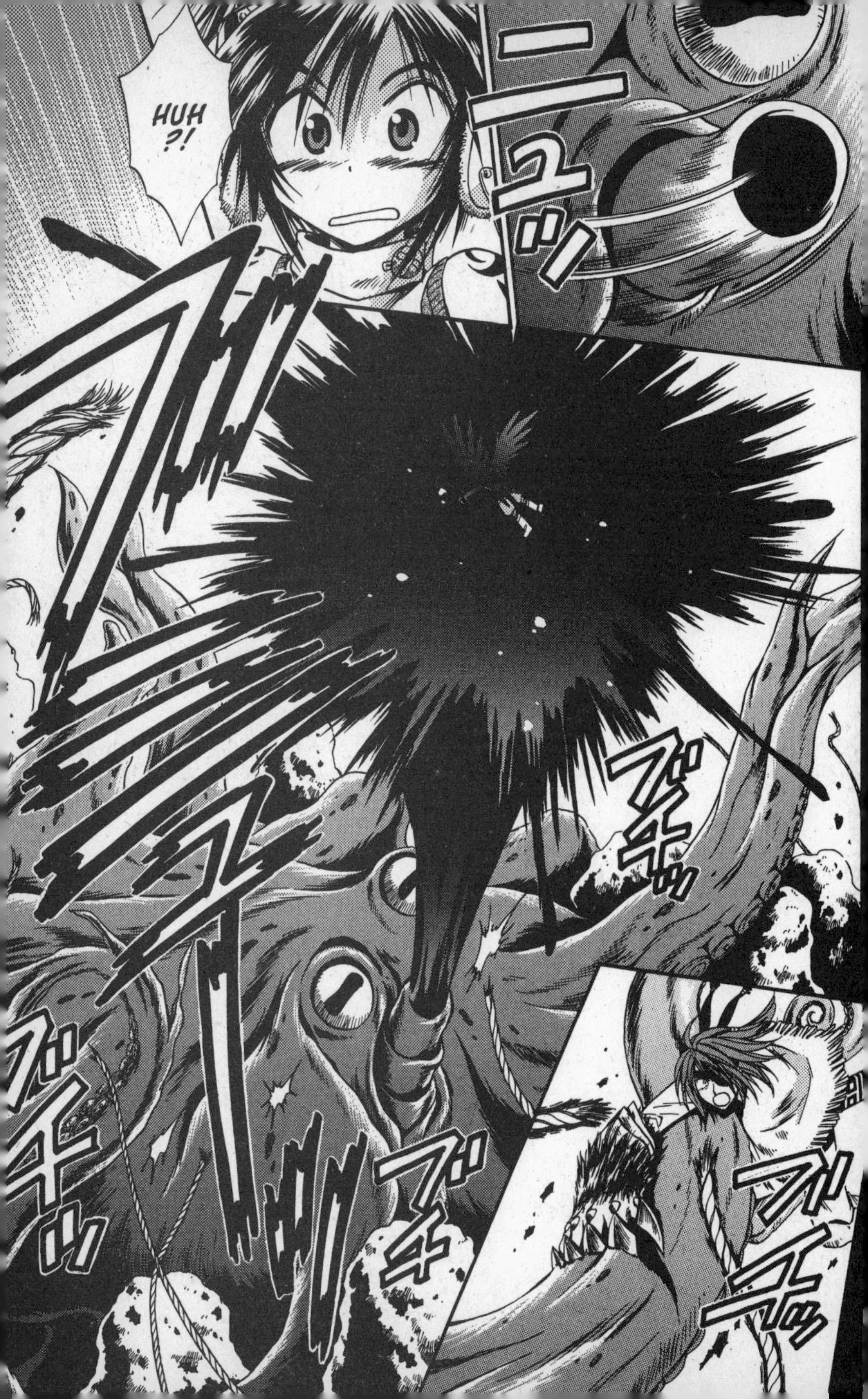
HUH ?!
ニュッ

IT...

IT WAS AN OCTOPUS?!

THAT THING?!

TRUE, IT IS REMARKABLY LARGE...

...BUT IT'S JUST AN OCTOPUS!

OCTOPUSES HAVE THE ABILITY TO CHANGE THE SHAPE AND COLOR OF THEIR BODIES DRAMATICALLY.

ITS DEN MUST HAVE BEEN MADE IN THAT CAVERN...

THE POWER OF ANIMALS... IS FASCINATING.

YAY!

TRULY FASCINATING.

Can you eat that...?

FOR DINNER?!

WHAT?!

The steak of a big octopus!

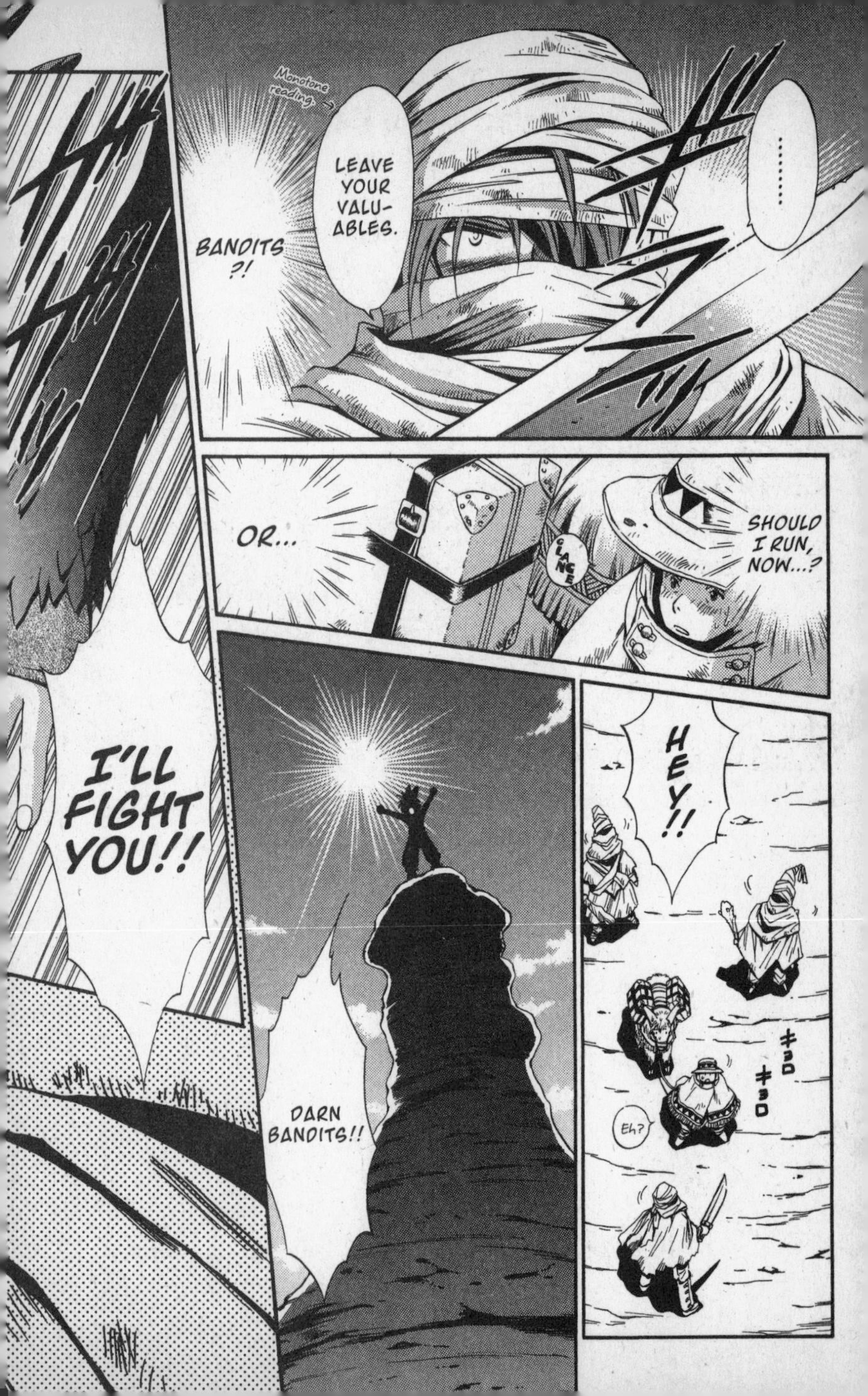
......
Monotone reading.
LEAVE YOUR VALU-ABLES.
BANDITS ?!
SHOULD I RUN, NOW...?
GLANCE
OR...
HEY!!
キョロ キョロ
Eh?
DARN BANDITS!!
I'LL FIGHT YOU!!

Parallel 3
Shining in the Darkness

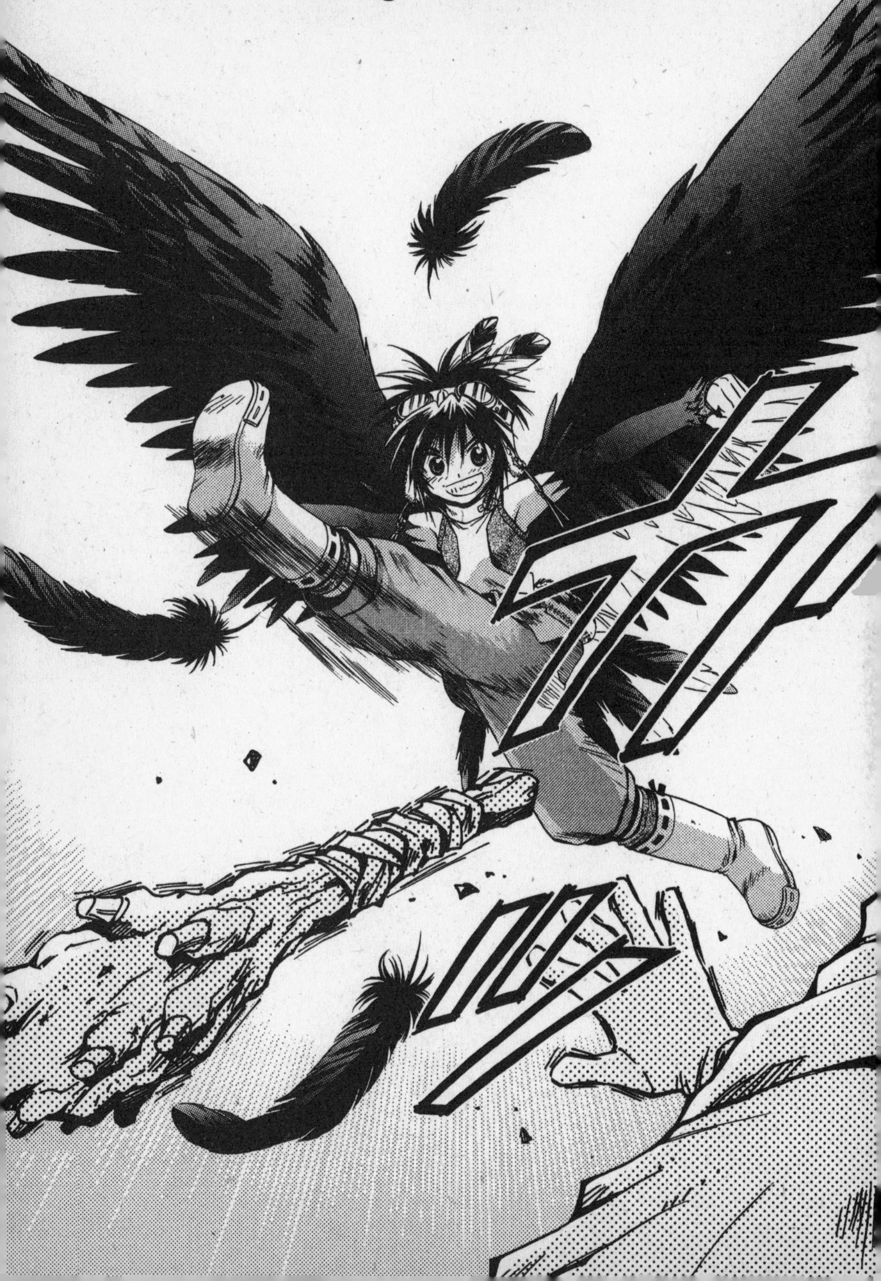

THERE'S A TOWN RIGHT OVER THERE, BUT I DON'T HAVE ANY MONEY.

IT'S JUST... I HAVEN'T EATEN ANYTHING SINCE YESTERDAY.

THEY EVEN CHASED ME OUT OF THE INN...

GRUMBLE

HMM...

CONSIDER IT A THANK YOU FOR CHASING OFF THOSE BANDITS, NOW!

REALLY...?!

USE THIS TO GET SOME FOOD, NOW...

THAT WON'T DO AT ALL, NOW!

GEE... THANKS!

A CROW +ANIMA, NOW?

175

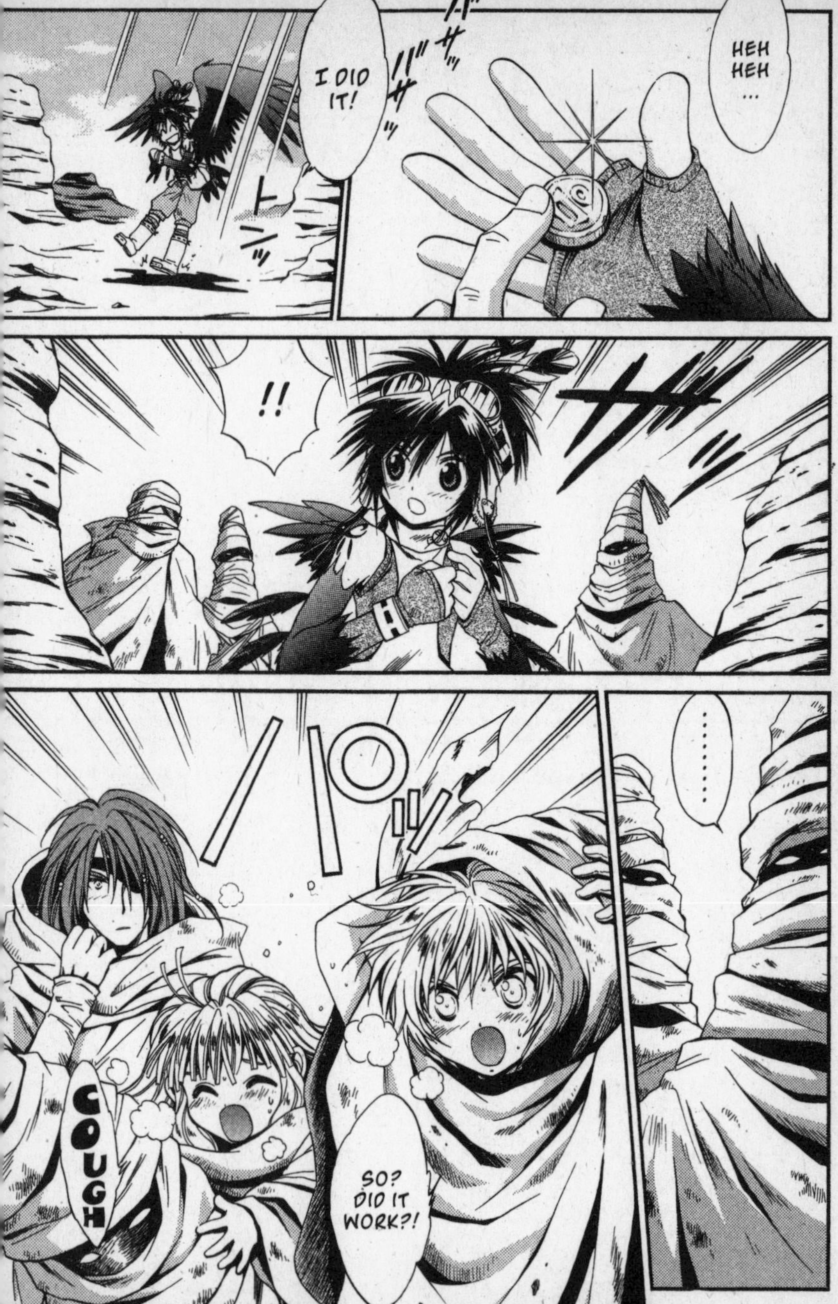
HEH HEH ...
I DID IT!
!!
......
SO? DID IT WORK?!
COUGH

Mountain Town Antsmine

IF YOU WANT TO BUY SOMETHING, EARN YOUR OWN MONEY.

OOOH! THIS CLOTH IS PRETTY! ♡

IT'S SO CUTE! ♡

くるっ

SEE ANYTHING YOU LIKE? I'LL GIVE YOU A DISCOUNT.

. . . .

THERE'S NO WAY . . .

Y'KNOW, IT'S THE FUNNIEST THING...IN THE PAST THREE DAYS...

...BUT THEN A *KID WITH WINGS* SWOOPED IN AT THE LAST MINUTE AND SAVED THEM.

R-REALLY?

...FIVE PEOPLE HAVE TOLD ME THAT THEY WERE ATTACKED BY BANDITS ON THE ROAD...

...IT WAS A +ANIMA.

SWEAT SWEAT SWEAT

YUP. SOUNDS TO ME LIKE...

SWEAT

CUZ THEY KNOW, Y'SEE... THEY KNOW THE KIND OF TROUBLE THEIR LOT CAN GET INTO.

SHOOT... MOST +ANIMAS STAY HID BETTER THAN A TICK ON A HOUND.

THOUGH +ANIMAS AIN'T SOMETHING YOU SEE EVERY DAY.

WELL, MAYBE BECAUSE HE DOESN'T HAVE ANY PROOF.

THEN WHY DIDN'T HE ARREST US?

MAN, I HATE THAT GUY!

AND NOW HE SUSPECTS IT WAS US, DANGIT!

Y'ALL BE CAREFUL OF BANDITS, NOW...

It'll be okay.

180

HELLO, WINGED BOY!

YUM!

HO? ME?

THESE ARE VERY TASTY. WOULD YOU LIKE TO HAVE SOME, NOW?

I'M GATES... NOW.

OH! YOU'RE THAT GUY...

YUP, THAT'S RIGHT.

GAUGING BY THOSE BLACK WINGS OF YOURS... YOU MUST BE A CROW +ANIMA, NOW!

WHAT'S HE DOING OVER THERE?

WHAT'S TAKING COORO SO LONG?

DON'T YOU... FIND IT DIFFICULT, NOW?

!

182

+ANIMA ARE QUITE RARE...

SOME PEOPLE RESPECT THEM, BUT ON THE OTHER HAND, MANY PEOPLE *FEAR* THEM, NOW.

WELL... YOU SEE...

MISTER... YOU SURE KNOW A LOT ABOUT +ANIMA.

I'M...I'M A LITTLE JEALOUS, NOW...

I'M JUST AN ORDINARY HUMAN MYSELF, NOW.

HUH?

...I THINK THAT ANIMA IS A WONDERFUL POWER, NOW!

+ANIMA ARE THE CHOSEN PEOPLE, NOW!!

I WANT TO SPREAD THE WONDERFULNESS OF +ANIMA THROUGHOUT THE WORLD, NOW!

IT WOULD BE AMAZING TO BE ABLE TO USE ANIMAL POWERS. TO HAVE POWERS NOT FOUND IN ORDINARY HUMANS, NOW!

WELL, I WOULDN'T SAY THAT...

183

WAIT, NOW!

AH! OH NO!

COORO!

YEAH... BYE, MISTER GATES!

A FRIEND OF YOURS, NOW?

I... MAY SEEM FRIENDLY, BUT I'M REALLY SHY, NOW...

BY MYSELF?

COME ALONE TO THE ENTRANCE OF TUNNEL NUMBER THREE AT THREE O'CLOCK, NOW.

I JUST GOT TO MEET YOU, NOW. I WANT TO TALK TO YOU MORE, NOW.

WHAT...?

OH, NOTHING.

WHAT WERE YOU TWO WHISPERING ABOUT?

OKAY, SURE. I'LL BE THERE!

IF I TOLD HER, SHE'D PROBABLY FOLLOW ME.

I'VE BEEN WAITING, NOW...

HI, MISTER!

BE-CAUSE YOU'RE A +ANIMA, TOO. HE LIKES TO MEET OTHERS OF HIS KIND, NOW!

YOU KNOW HOW IT IS.

TO ME? HOW COME?

THERE'S ACTUALLY A +ANIMA THAT WANTS TO TALK TO YOU, NOW.

YOU'LL FIND OUT WHEN YOU MEET HIM, NOW.

REALLY?

WHAT ANIMA POWERS DOES HE HAVE?

WE'RE ALMOST THERE, NOW.

HOW FAR ARE WE GOING?

THIS IS A TUNNEL, NOW.

SOMEONE WITH A HORSE ANIMA WOULD HAVE THE LEGS TO RUN FOR MILES...

...AND A WOLF +ANIMA WOULD HAVE HIS OWN SHARP FANGS, NOW.

ANIMA TRULY ARE WONDERFUL, NOW.

HUH?

THAT'S WHY...

I WANT AN ANIMA TOO, NOW.

HUH ...?

IT SURE IS DARK ...

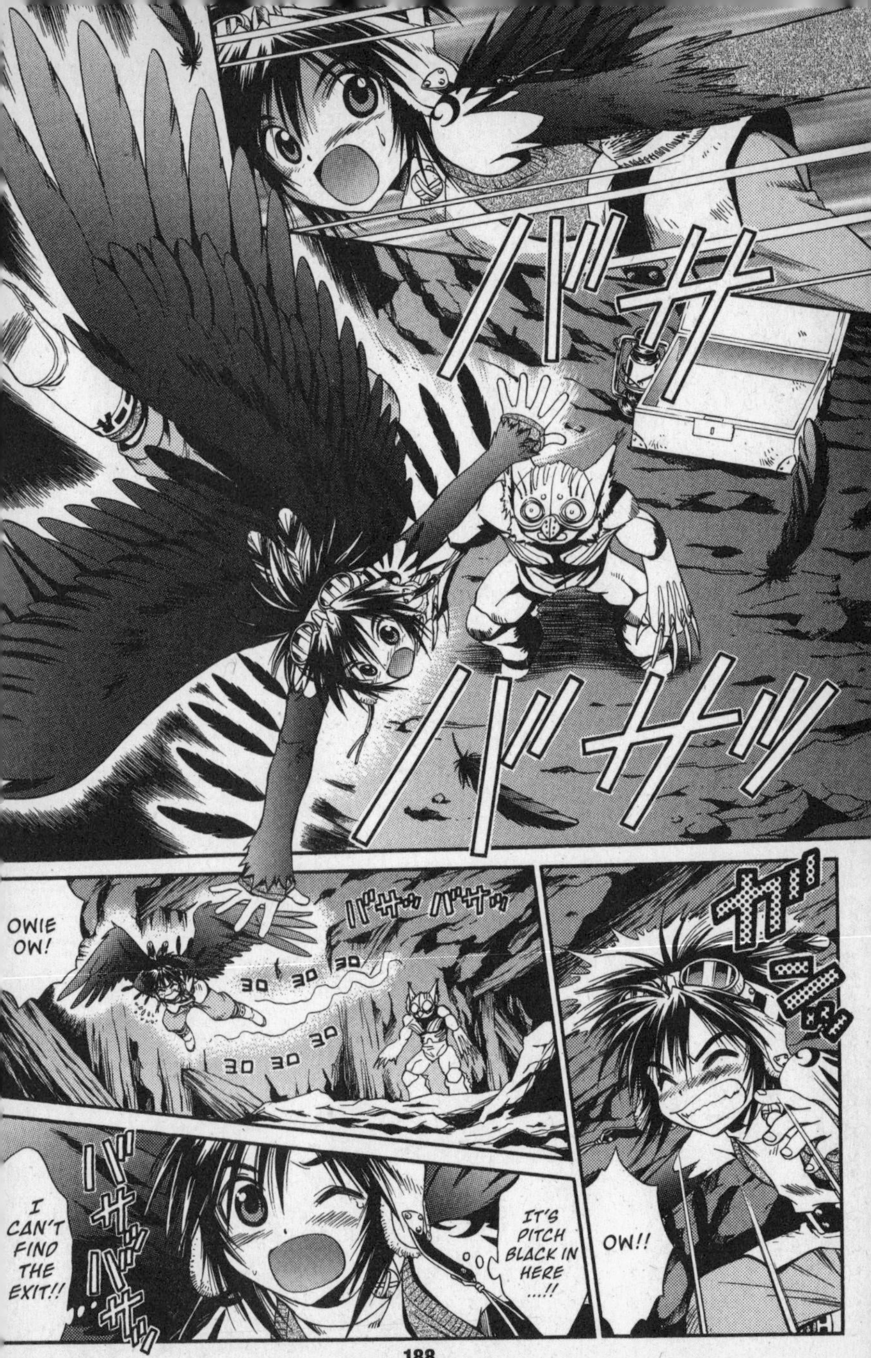
ドサ
ドサッ
ガバッ
OW!!
OWIE OW!
バサッ バサッ
ヨロ ヨロ ヨロ
ヨロ ヨロ ヨロ
IT'S PITCH BLACK IN HERE ...!!
I CAN'T FIND THE EXIT!!
バサッ バサッ

I DON'T ALLOW FIGHTIN' IN MY TOWN!

!

HERIFF HOPPS!

SHERIFF HOPPS!

D-DON'T STARE! IT'S RUDE!

WELL, LOOKY HERE ...

A BAT +ANIMA...

Hmm...

WELL?! ISN'T THAT SUSPI-CIOUS?! MIGHT BE A SLAVE TRADER!

THIS MAN LURED COORO INTO AN ABANDONED MINE!

I WAS BEING ATTACKED BY +ANIMA, NOW!!

I'M JUST AN ORDINARY HUMAN, NOW!

LOOK AT THESE WOUNDS, NOW! HE DID THIS TO ME, NOW!

AND HE'S A BEAR... HUH.

lick
lick
lick

WAH!

HOLD YER TONGUES A BIT.

WHAT *IS* THIS?! ARE YOU SAYING YOU DON'T BELIEVE US JUST BE-CAUSE WE'RE +ANIMA?!

YOU... COME OVER HERE AND TELL ME YER STORY.

Yes sir!

AND DON'T EVEN *THINK* ABOUT RUNNIN' AWAY!

THAT'S RIGHT! HE IS!

SENRI'S HURT TOO, YOU KNOW!

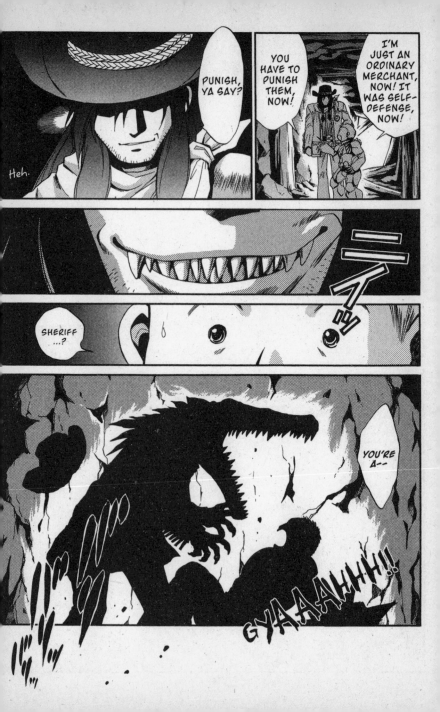

Aw...! Can't you just let us go?

Huh...!

WHAT?!

WELL... THAT'S SETTLED.

TIME FER YOUR PUNISHMENT!

M-MY PS-PSEUDO S-SUIT...!

3p し...!

SNIFF...! SNORT...!

THIS IS THE NORTH GATE.

HERE'S SOME FOOD FER YA.

GET OUT O' MY TOWN.

WHY SHOULD WE?! HE WAS THE BAD GUY AND--

I CAN'T HAVE PEOPLE MAKIN' TROUBLE IN MY TOWN.

IN PAR-TICULAR, KIDS PLAYIN' BANDITS.

SO YOU STOP TAGGING ALONG AFTER SUSPICIOUS PEOPLE!

THAT'S RIGHT!

NANA... YOU DIDN'T WANT TO USE YOUR BAT WINGS BECAUSE YOU'RE EMBARRASSED, BUT...

BUT I THOUGHT THAT YOU WOULDN'T LEARN ANYTHING IF YOU DIDN'T GET HURT, SO I LET YOU GO ALONE!

OF COURSE I DID!

HUH?!

NANA... YOU KNEW?!

HE STILL DOESN'T GET...

OKAY!

slurp slurp

I SAID I'M FINE!

SO SHOULD WE GO SOMEWHERE WITH A LAKE NEXT?

FINE BY ME. SHAPE SHIFTING TIRES ME OUT, ANYWAY.

COME TO THINK OF IT, THERE WASN'T A POND OR AN OCEAN THIS TIME, SO HUSKY DIDN'T GET TO DO ANYTHING!

slurp slurp

It'll never heal at this rate.

HEY...WILL YOU CUT THAT OUT, ALREADY?!

slurp

slurp slurp

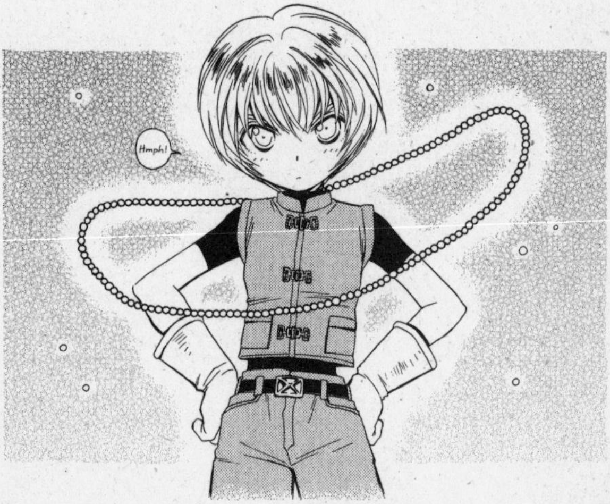
Hmph!

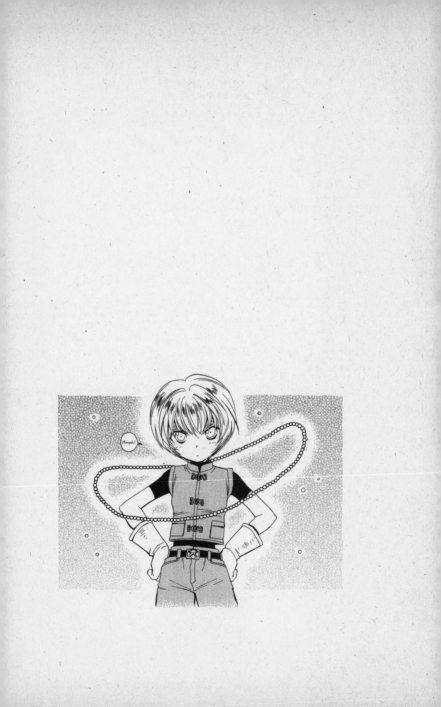

+ANIMA

TOKYOPOP

COORO BEFRIENDS A MAN IN A GLIDER NAMED SHADOW, WHO LONGS TO FLY SO HE CAN TAKE MEDICINE TO HIS FAMILY'S REMOTE FARM. BUT WHEN HE DISCOVERS THAT COORO IS A +ANIMA WITH WINGS, ENVY TEARS A RIFT BETWEEN THEM. CAN COORO SHOW HIS FEATHERLESS FRIEND THE ERROR OF HIS WAYS? LATER, COORO AND COMPANY RUN INTO COMMANDER IGNEOUS AND HIS TROOPS AT A NEARBY TOWN, WHO ORDERS THE LOCAL BLACKSMITH TO STRENGTHEN THEIR WEAPONS. WHEN THE BLACKSMITH REFUSES, IT'S UP TO COORO AND THE OTHERS TO STAND UP TO IGNEOUS. HUSKY'S PAST IS ALSO EXPLORED, AND WE LEARN WHY HE HATES GIRLS SO MUCH.

IT'S ALL IN THE NEXT ACTION-PACKED VOLUME!

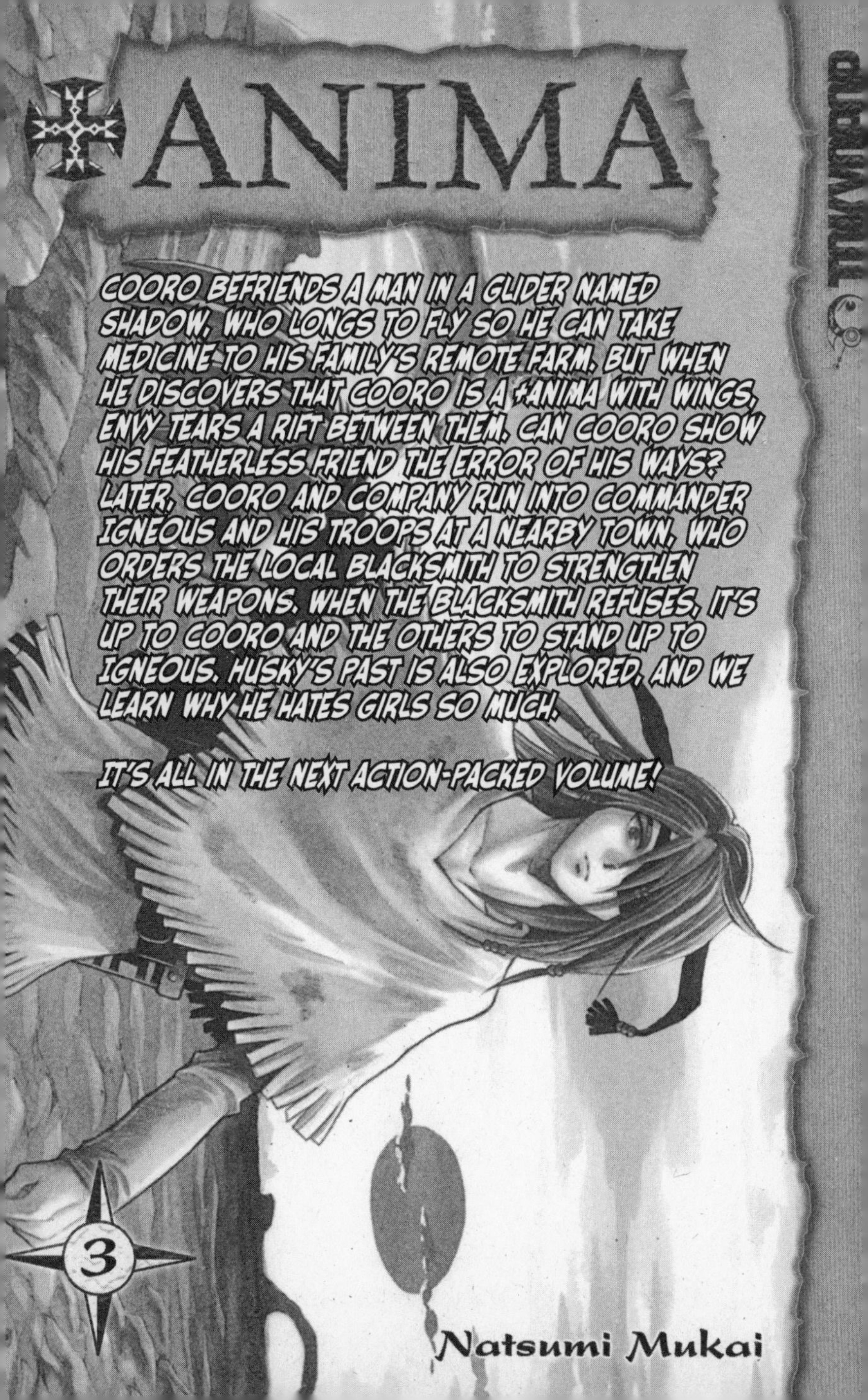

③

Natsumi Mukai

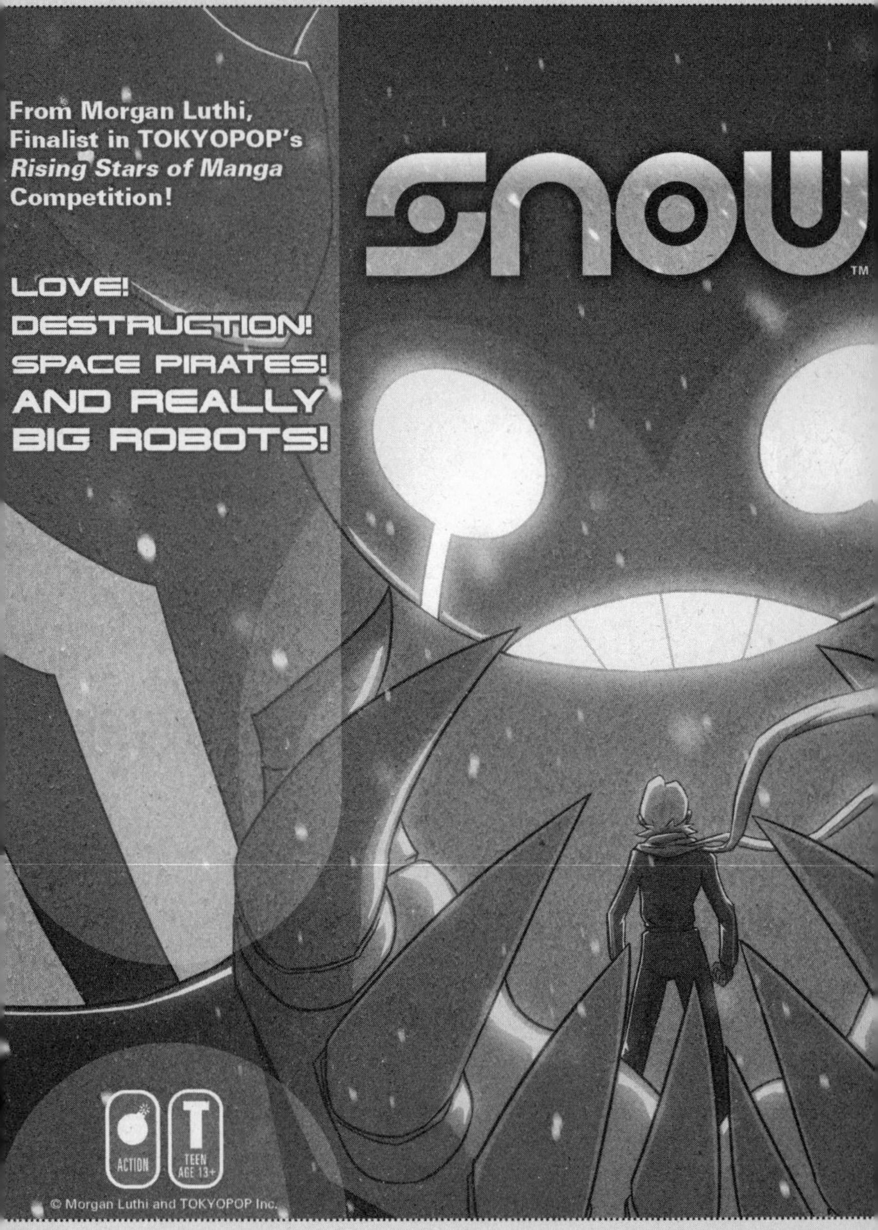
From Morgan Luthi,
Finalist in TOKYOPOP's
Rising Stars of Manga
Competition!
SNOW™
LOVE!
DESTRUCTION!
SPACE PIRATES!
AND REALLY
BIG ROBOTS!
ACTION
T
TEEN
AGE 13+
© Morgan Luthi and TOKYOPOP Inc.

STOP!

This is the back of the book.
You wouldn't want to spoil a great ending!

This book is printed "manga-style," in the authentic Japanese right-to-left format. Since none of the artwork has been flipped or altered, readers get to experience the story just as the creator intended. You've been asking for it, so TOKYOPOP® delivered: authentic, hot-off-the-press, and far more fun!

DIRECTIONS

If this is your first time reading manga-style, here's a quick guide to help you understand how it works.

It's easy... just start in the top right panel and follow the numbers. Have fun, and look for more 100% authentic manga from TOKYOPOP®!